THE OBERON ANTHOLOGY OF

CONTEMPORARY AMERICAN PLAYS

VOLUME ONE

Edited by Mark Subias
General Introduction by André Bishop

KIN by Bathsheba Doran

MIDDLETOWN by Will Eno

COMPLETENESS by Itamar Moses

GOD'S EAR by Jenny Schwartz

OBERON BOOKS
LONDON

WWW.OBERONBOOKS.COM

This collection first published in 2012 by Oberon Books Ltd
521 Caledonian Road, London N7 9RH
Tel: +44 (0) 20 7607 3637 / Fax: +44 (0) 20 7607 3629
e-mail: info@oberonbooks.com
www.oberonbooks.com

CONTENTS

INTRODUCTION

What a pleasure to read the four plays in this volume. Each is fresh, original and distinctive. Each is verbally deft, and delights in language and its power to entertain, disturb, and just plain dazzle. Each is about human connection – the pain and the difficulty of human connection. And each of these four plays is hopeful, and ultimately optimistic.

Kin by Bathsheba Doran is a series of touching and delicately drawn scenes that reveal the tenderness and uncertainty between people: two lovers, a daughter and her father, two best friends. Even the conflict between urban life and rural life comes into play – to comic and serious effect (there is even a bear!). The ending is joyful – a wedding where chaos eventually turns to order as in the best Shakespearian comedies. Ms. Doran writes intelligently and sensitively about the foibles of human relationships and the mysteries of what she calls 'the landscape of the mind.'

Middletown by Will Eno is a verbally dextrous take on *Our Town* – filtered through the bleakly comic absurdities of *The Skin of Our Teeth*. This is a play of language but, like *Our Town*, a play with a heart. People may be looked at as specimens, as examples of life, yet they reach out, lonely and questioning, as we all do. They are involved in the tiny details of their lives and the large issues of humanity. This is a play about men and women in the middle of life separated by birth and death 'a serious mystery, then the middle part, then another mystery.' Mr. Eno is brilliant, warm, adventurous; he has written a lovely play about the beauty and sadness of life.

Completeness by Itamar Moses is another good play about connecting and what it takes to be a human being. Graduate students in computer science attempt to solve problems that run parallel to their personal problems. We see, that for all their academic intelligence, they are ordinary folk who hide behind their articulate scientific jargon rather than confront the problems of love, commitment, and human completeness. Mr. Moses is an intellectual dazzler who nonetheless writes natural and heartfelt characters and puts them in real and true situations.

7

Finally, *God's Ear* by Jenny Schwartz is based on a sad premise: a man and a woman try to come to terms with the near-drowning and eventual death of their son. Their marriage (an absent husband) is in tatters. Again this is a play with an ordinary domestic situation blanketed in astounding verbal riffs; everyday speech turned upside down. Playful, loony rhythmic speeches of lyrical poetry. Sort of Ionesco goes to early Sam Shepard but with an original author's voice. Ms. Schwartz is a linguist and an imagist, and her play is an amazing and daring creation.

So there you have it: four wonderful plays by four writers with bright pasts and bright futures. I saw all four plays in New York and I feel compelled to add that all these plays were well served by impeccable productions. It was thrilling to see them and it is thrilling to read them. The United States is in a golden age of American playwriting – whether we acknowledge it or not – and the four talented writers in this volume strongly attest to that.

André Bishop, Artistic Director,
Lincoln Center Theater, January 2012

KIN

BATHSHEBA DORAN

Bathsheba Doran's critically acclaimed play *Kin* received its world premiere in spring 2011 at Playwrights Horizons, directed by Sam Gold. Her play *Parents' Evening* premiered at The Flea Theater, directed by Jim Simpson; and her play *Ben and the Magic Paintbrush* premiered in spring 2010 at South Coast Repertory Theater. She is currently adapting *The No. 1 Ladies Detective Agency* as a feature for HBO Films; and wrote on Season Two of the acclaimed Martin Scorsese/HBO series *Boardwalk Empire* (for which her episode received a WGA nomination).

Other plays include *Living Room in Africa* (produced Off-Broadway by the award-winning Edge Theater), *Nest* (commissioned and produced by Signature Theater in DC), *Until Morning* (BBC Radio 4) and adaptations of Dickens' *Great Expectations* (starring Kathleen Chalfont at The Lucille Lortel), Maeterlinck's *The Blind* (Classic Stage Company), and *Peer Gynt* (directed by Andrei Serban at the Theater of the Riverside Church).

She is a 2009 recipient of the Helen Merrill Playwriting Award and three Lecomte du Nouy Lincoln Center playwriting awards. She is a Cherry Lane mentor Project Fellow and a Susan Blackburn Award finalist. Ms. Doran's work has been developed by Manhattan Theatre Club, O'Neill Center, Lincoln Center, Sundance Theater Lab, Almeida Theatre (London), and Playwrights Horizons among others.

Ms. Doran's first play *Feminine Wash* was produced at the Edinburgh Fringe festival while she was a student at Cambridge University, from which she holds a BA and an MA. She then went on to Oxford University, where she received an MA before working as a television comedy writer with the BBC. Ms. Doran moved to the United States on a Fulbright Scholarship in 2000, and received her MFA from Columbia University and went on to become a playwriting fellow of The Juilliard School. She is currently under commission from Atlantic Theater and Playwrights Horizons in New York City. Her work is available from Samuel French and Playscripts Inc. She lives in New York City.

INTRODUCTION

I first met Bathsheba (Bash) Doran in the fall of 2003. Marsha Norman and I have been running the Playwriting Program at the Juilliard School since 1994, and we had accepted Bash into the program, one of only four new playwrights joining four returning playwrights. Our program is very small, obviously. We get many applicants, but can only take a small number.

Bash is attractive with short blond hair, and she has one of those British accents that American love. It's kind on the ear.

Marsha and I had loved her submission play, *The Parents' Evening*, which was a funny and elegant two character play in which a married couple discusses their troublesome child before they head off to a teacher-parent meeting. The parents are very articulate, and they blame each other for the child's bad behavior, sometimes politely, sometimes harshly. And as they talk about their off-stage child and the upset teachers, a very funny and messed up parent-and-child situation is conjured up before our eyes. Bash seemed a gifted and comic writer.

Somewhere in her first year, Bash brought in the first half of a play called *A Living Room in Africa*. Marsha and I and her fellow students were stunned by the beauty and emotional complexity of the play.

It was not a comedy, though Bash always has wit; but instead it was the story of a wealthy museum curator who had been sent to a devastated African village to build a museum. It was to somehow help the village, but since most of the people were dying of AIDS, it didn't really seem like 'museum' should be at the top of anyone's list.

There was some humor in this inappropriate, ill-judged endeavor. But it was also the story of the curator and his poet companion, who was delicate and seemed maybe near a breakdown. The play has many more complexities, but in the second act – which we heard a month later when Bash brought it in – she, the companion, finds an inner strength and becomes the moral compass of the play, and decides something should be done, even a small gesture; and she takes in the housekeeper and her children, who are ill and dying. And she becomes their helper and their friend and their witness. Hearing it in class, it was thrilling actually. One forgets how much one wants someone in the world to be a moral compass.

We actually asked Bash to stay a third year with us – something we do with students who are doing especially well, and who we also think will inspire the incoming writers. And Bash left us in 2005.

I had kept up with Bash, but not enough that I always knew what she was up to.

Then I heard that Playwrights Horizons was presenting a new play of Bash's called *Kin*.

I decided to go see an early preview. And I knew nothing of the play or what it was about.

And I was so happy seeing the play. Bash had written another wonderful work, and it was funny, elegant, and once again deeply moving.

Kin begins with a series of scenes that seem perhaps unrelated.

Anna silently listening to a young man explain why they should break up, and how impossible it is for people to know one another anyway.

Helena, an emotionally chaotic young woman, weeping and trying to bury her dog, while the quieter Anna shows up helpfully with a flashlight.

Sean, a physical trainer in America, on the phone with his mother Linda, who is in her house in Ireland; indeed she is always in her house, she never leaves, something bad happened to her, something about a 'man in the mist.'

And later an older man, Adam, is visiting his former mistress Kay, who is dealing with cancer, and is smart and resilient and up to counseling Adam about his failed relationship with his daughter. And his daughter is Anna.

The scenes are interesting and psychologically complex on their own, but we start to figure out that Anna and Sean are the main characters – they are trying to figure out if they are a couple meant to be together, or if they are just passing briefly through each others' lives.

The play is elliptical…and at one point Helena – who is an actress who never works (for pay at least) – explains 'ellipses' to Anna's clueless father: 'They're the little dot dot dot at the end of a sentence. They change everything. For actors.'

The elliptical scenes in this play start to coalesce in an elegant and exciting manner.

The mother Linda and the best friend Helena are part of the walking wounded, a bit like the poet in the early parts of *Living Room in Africa*.

Linda is frozen due to a trauma from the past, and Helena seems to have multiple flashes of craziness and weeping. Sean does his best to comfort his mother Linda, but he also did move to another continent to separate from her as well. And Anna does her best to help Helena, but in a significant scene realizes she can never share moments of happiness with Helena, because Helena then goes into a funk that *she* isn't happy.

I want to add that Helena is a hilarious creation of Bash's – we all know these unstoppably troubled people, we've befriended them and sometimes run away from them. Helena's demons are real and moving, and yet Bash has a sly comic ability in her writing, and on the page – and in the performance of Laura Heisler that I saw off-Broadway – Helena is maybe a pain in life, but a joy onstage.

And two-thirds through the play there is a surprising phone call scene, when usually calm Anna is overcome with a panic she has kept under wraps; and suddenly needy Helena rises to the occasion, and lovingly talks her friend how to get through a panic attack.

And Linda is probably my other favorite character. In some ways she reminds me of Miss Havisham, who famously stops her life cold when she is jilted at her wedding. Linda's freezing of her life is due to something violent and unexpected, and the fear she's gotten stuck in is, well, understandable, if not healthy.

There is a scene of connection between the agoraphobic Linda and Anna's emotionally inaccessible father Adam that is so unexpectedly moving that while I watched it be performed, I thought to myself, this kind of moving presentation of humans is why I first loved theatre. Linda was played off-Broadway by the great Suzanne Bertish, who gave another superb performance. And Adam by the fine actor Cotter Smith.

Anna and Sean are 'healthier' than her friend and his mother – yet, like them and like all human beings, they are confused and saddened by life and disappointments and expectations, and yet they do move forward. All the characters move forward.

I am so glad this play is included in this anthology. Bash was exceptional when I first met her at Juilliard, and she is even more exceptional now. And *Kin* is a brilliant and haunting play.

Christopher Durang
January 27, 2012

FOR KATIE

Playwrights Horizons, New York City, produced the World Premiere of *Kin* Off-Broadway in 2011.

Kin by Bathsheba Doran. Artistic Director, Tim Sanford; Managing Director Leslie Marcus; General Manager; Carol Fishman. Director: Sam Gold. Scenic Design: Paul Steinberg. Costume Design: David Zinn. Lighting Design: Jane Cox. Sound Design: Matt Tierney. Dialect Coach: Stephen Gabis. Casting: Alaine Alldaffer, CSA. Director of New Play Development: Adam Greenfield. Press Representative: The Publicity Office. Production Manager: Christopher Boll. Production Stage Manager: Alaina Taylor.

LINDA	*Suzanne Bertish*
MAX	*Bill Buell*
ANNA	*Kristen Bush*
SEAN	*Patch Darragh*
KAY	*Kit Flanagan*
HELENA	*Laura Heisler*
SIMON / GIDEON	*Matthew Rauch*
ADAM	*Cotter Smith*
RACHEL	*Molly Ward*

CHARACTERS

ANNA	(30s)
ADAM	Anna's father (60s)
HELENA	(30s)
SEAN	(30s)
LINDA	Sean's mother (55-65)
MAX	Linda's brother (55-65)
RACHEL	(30s)
KAY	(60s)
GIDEON	(34)
SIMON	(40s)

(GIDEON and SIMON should be played by the same actor. This should not be emphasized, but an unrecognizable transformation is not required)

TIME AND PLACE

The action of the play takes place over the last seven years in various locations in America and Ireland.

A NOTE ON DESIGN

When I began writing I thought of this play as taking place in what I found myself referring to as 'the landscape of the mind.' Many of my characters were based in what I only thought of as 'the city'. It could have been any major Western Capital – New York, Paris, London, or an imaginary city entirely. Other characters were simply placed 'far away.' I was attempting to conjure the globe. Eventually I found it helped the story to be specific so now there is a literal geography, but I hope that the director and design team will help recapture my early sense that this play was taking place above all in a non-literal landscape.

A NOTE ON STAGING

This is a play made from largely two-person scenes that is nonetheless about an ensemble. To underline this my original idea was to have the entire cast on stage for every scene except the first and last. Sam Gold refined this suggestion into something more delicate, complex and idiosyncratic. I now think it suffices to say that I hope future directors will find their own way to maintain a sense of ensemble so that we feel all characters throughout, hidden sometimes, in shadows maybe, but present.

'What can I say? God help me, what can I say? Silence will stifle me...'

Sophocles, *Electra*

'I saw a crow running about with a stork. I marveled long and investigated their case in order that I might find the clue as to what it was that they had in common. When amazed and bewildered I approached them then indeed I saw that both of them were lame.'

Rumi, *Spiritual Couplets*

'A man who calls his kinsman to a feast does not do so to save them from starving. They all have food in their own homes. When we gather together in the moonlit village ground it is not because of the moon. Every man can see it in his own compound. We come together because it is good for kinsman to do so.'

Chinua Achebe, *Things Fall Apart*

SCENE 1: AN OFFICE AT COLUMBIA UNIVERSITY

ANNA sits. SIMON stands. Everything awkward, uncomfortable.

SIMON: I thought it was best not to leave you dangling, you know? But at this stage of life…I mean…I know what I'm looking for, you know what you're looking for, we know what we're looking for, or maybe we don't, maybe that's the thing, maybe I don't know what I'm looking for but I know it's not you. That sounds terrible, doesn't it? But no, fuck it, I'm trying to be truthful here, let's have truth in human relations for once, how about that? Let's be truthful with one another. I mean did you think this was going anywhere? Really?

ANNA shakes her head.

Thank you. Thank you. Now I feel less like an ass. And I mean – I'm so much older than you, that's probably why you picked me, right? A father figure? You lost your dad when you were very young, right? So that was probably part of the attraction, don't you think? But that's not healthy, that's not sustainable, or maybe it is, I don't know.

ANNA: My father's still alive.

SIMON: Oh. Then I'm confusing you with someone else. Sorry. Of course he is. The point is – and this is where I'm the real asshole – I don't know what I want. Not really. I mean, sometimes I think I want something long term, but I've *been* married, you know? And it was no fun. Now maybe that was her, maybe that was me, maybe it was the combination but…but…I just want someone I can talk to, you know? And fuck. And we *had* that. I'm not denying it. We had that. But now…it's over, isn't it? I mean the conversation is over. Can't you just feel it? There's something dead here. The light's gone out. And if the light's gone out then put out the light. Or maybe not. I don't know…we could try to ignite it. But love shouldn't be so much effort. Or maybe it should. It's such a fucking construct, you know? Literature is such a fucking *trap*. Unrealistic expectations. I don't know. I'm just so fucking lonely. And I know you are too, maybe that's what brought us together, right? Loneliness. A love of Keats. Your mind, you have a fucking brilliant mind, you know that? Your thesis is fucking brilliant. You're going to have an incredible career, and you'll forget all about me! I'll just be some old professor of yours that you inveigled into bed with your skinny arms and your brilliant mind. Because let's be real. We admire each other but…this is even a little sordid. The rest of the faculty knows, I think. Clancy made a veiled comment…and it's not against the rules, exactly, you are an adjunct and this *is* the English department, we are all poets here, and poets fuck, but Clancy's comment…I think fundamentally…it made me feel cheap. And it made you…cheap by association… So I think… You haven't said anything… Are you going to make this hard on me? Don't. Please don't. This is just human relationships. I wrote a poem once. When I was in my thirties and I still wrote poetry. And I compared a woman's vagina to a revolving door. People come in. They go out. That's life. And you know what my simile for the penis was? A staple gun. In an office. Punch, punch, punch. Revolve, revolve, revolve. That is life. That is the fucking monotony of searching for your soul mate. Okay? I still stand by that. So just… Did we even love each other?

ANNA: No.

> *SIMON stares at ANNA, hoping for a better cue to exit. He doesn't get one. So he sighs and leaves.*

SCENE 2: CENTRAL PARK

Midnight.

HELENA on the grass, cradling a dead dog. Paroxysms of grief.

HELENA: Zoë! Don't be dead, don't be dead, don't be dead. I love you, I will always love you. Oh my dog! My life partner !My love! How could you die? How could you die and leave me here! I don't even know what to do with your body! They say it's illegal to bury you in the park! You loved the park! They say, they say if I don't have any money I should put you in a bag, in a big black bag, and I should write on the bag "dead dog" and leave you out with the garbage as if you weren't a *soul*! As if you weren't *my* soul!

> *Her cell phone rings.*

(Into the phone:) Anna? Where are you? Where the fuck are you? I need you, Anna, I need you to get here. I'm freaking out, I'm too upset, I can't even see. Tears are literally blinding me. Plus it's dark. Totally. You're right. I'm overreacting. Well, you kind of sound like you think I'm overreacting.

> *And now we see ANNA on her cell phone. HELENA does not see her. ANNA does not see HELENA. ANNA has a flashlight.*
>
> *She turns and the beam from her flashlight hits the sorry sight of HELENA and her dead dog.*

HELENA: There you are.

ANNA: Here I am.

HELENA: *(Eternally grateful.)* You brought a flashlight. So practical.

ANNA: Can I see Zoë? *(She looks at the dog.)* She looks peaceful.

HELENA: You think?

ANNA: Absolutely.

HELENA: I brought a…

> *HELENA produces an inadequate gardening tool.*

ANNA: Do you want me to dig?

HELENA: I'll dig the grave. She was my dog.

ANNA: Of course.

HELENA: Keep watch. Fucking city regulations, I mean what the fuck, it's sick, it's Greek, it's…what happened to universal space? Isn't it my fucking planet? Wasn't it Zoë's fucking earth? I mean, why does everybody seem to own a piece of the universe but me. Well fuck that, my earth, my dirt, my tax dollars.

> *HELENA digs. Eventually…*

ANNA: The last open grave I saw was my Mom's.

HELENA: You know what I'm feeling…because your Mom…I mean it's probably not the same. Your mom. My dog. That's really offensive.

> *Beat.*

ANNA: I know what you're feeling.

HELENA: I can't imagine what you felt…I mean…your Mom. And you were just a kid…and your Dad crying, didn't you say you'd never seen him cry before?

ANNA: Never before, never since. I just kept looking at him at the graveside, this strong man, you know, this strong, army man, the Colonel, displays of emotion antithetical to his being. And he was broken, completely broken. My Dad was so crippled with grief at the graveside and all I could think was that the way he was crying made me want to fall in love.

SCENE 3: SEAN'S APARTMENT, NYC

SEAN on the telephone to his mother, LINDA. If we see LINDA she's far, far away and we should feel this.

LINDA: Describe the sky for me, Seany.

SEAN: The sky's black, Mum.

LINDA: Just black?

SEAN: A little grey, a little green even.

LINDA: Any clouds?

SEAN: It's too late at night for clouds.

LINDA: Is it? I get confused. Did I wake you up?

SEAN: No.

LINDA: Silly isn't it. After all these years I can't remember what time it is there, what time it is here. It's yesterday there, isn't it? My yesterday.

SEAN: That's right. It's Saturday. Saturday night.

LINDA: It's Sunday here. Worst day of the week, Sunday. They just drag on and on and

SEAN: I've been thinking…

LINDA: *(A joke.)* Don't do that, you'll hurt your head.

SEAN: You could start going to church again. The priest you saw, he's dead now. *(Beat.)* Mum?

SEAN: Claire told me. Two of us were thinking–

LINDA: You and your sister deciding what's best for me. Bit early for that don't you think? Senility hasn't hit yet. I don't piss and shit myself –

SEAN: Mum.

LINDA: Yet.

SEAN: There's a new priest now. You might like him. Or Claire could take you. *(Beat.)* Mum? *(Beat.)* Don't go quiet, Mum…

LINDA: Banished, Seany. I was banished.

SEAN: No…

LINDA: Yes, if you don't repent, you're banished. So I'm banished. That's that. Linda's not welcome in the house of God and Linda doesn't care because I know what I saw through the mist. God isn't good, Seany.

SEAN: The church is changing. It's in the papers all the time. The whole world is.

Remember I told you about that woman I'm training? The fat, fat woman? Not fat any more. Lost eighty-five pounds. She cried! She didn't think it was possible. But change she did. We all have the potential for change.

LINDA: Says who? Where are you getting this stuff?

SEAN: I'm reading a book about it.

LINDA: What kind of book?

SEAN: It's about happiness.

LINDA: *(Sarcastic.)* You'll have to send me a copy.

SEAN: I will. It's a self-help book.

LINDA: A *what*? You've been living in America too long… You certainly are undergoing a process of change if you're reading a self-help book. *(Beat – then slightly anxious.)* What are you reading that for? *(Beat.)* Seany? *(Beat.)* Don't *you* go quiet… What are you reading a book about happiness for? Are you sad? Seany?

SEAN: I'm worried about you. Claire says you don't leave the house at all now.

LINDA: Let's not have a conversation with Claire in it, let's have a conversation that's just you and me, all by ourselves.

SEAN: Mum, you can't stay locked up in that house for the rest of your life!

LINDA: *(Beat.)* At night sometimes… I go to the window, and I open it a tiny little crack, and I listen.

SEAN: What do you hear?

LINDA: *Little* life. Insects and things. I think I'm a night creature. You were always a night creature. You used to be out on Saturday nights.

SEAN: *(Closing off, shutting down.)* I work on Saturdays now. I'm tired.

LINDA: What's the point of living in the big city if you don't go out on the town, Sean? That's what New York's *for*. Painting red. *(Beat.)* Are you lonely, Sean? *(Beat.)* I can hear you being lonely down the telephone. *(Beat.)* Is it that girl?

SEAN: *(Surprised.)* What girl?

LINDA: Rachel. You brought her home for a Christmas. She was Saturday nights. You'd come back sometimes and call me up, drunk and so happy, you were so full of love. You'd say "I love you, Mum. I love you so much…" and I could hear her laughing in the background and you sounded so happy, Sean.

SEAN: You know we broke up.

LINDA: Did she hurt you? Did she break your heart?

SEAN: I broke hers.

LINDA: *(Reassured.)* Oh well then…Looking for someone else, then, are you?

SEAN: Sure.

LINDA: What kind of person are you looking for?

SEAN: Someone who doesn't freebase.

LINDA: What?

SEAN: Nothing.

LINDA: You're not looking very hard if you're staying indoors on a Saturday night.

> *Pause.*

SEAN: I'm just taking a break, Mum. I'll get back out there.

LINDA: *(Emphatically.)* You should do. You're too good to waste.

> *Beat.*

SEAN: I have to put on my pajamas and go to bed. I have to be back at the gym at six thirty.

LINDA: If we stay on the phone just a little longer we'll be talking on the same day of the week. Shall we do that, Seany? Shall I describe the sky to you? Imagine a bucket of off-white paint. Do you see it?

SEAN: I do.

LINDA: Now stir in some black paint. Just a little bit. Stir it and stir it and stir it and stir it until it's nearly mixed through but not quite…that's what the sky looks like. Like dirty seagulls or dirty doves.

SEAN: I see it.

LINDA: I see yours. Black, green, like witches.

SEAN: Had a few drinks, have you?

LINDA: *(Distant.)* Oh who cares what I do with my time? It passes.

SCENE 4: COLUMBIA UNIVERSITY CAMPUS

> *ANNA and HELENA on a bench. Sandwiches. Spring. HELENA crying.*

ANNA: I'm so sorry.

HELENA: That's what she said to me. "Maybe it's time for you to get another dog." In this like…bored tone. Like my grief is boring to her. Maybe it is. Maybe it's boring to you.

ANNA: It's not –

HELENA: It's boring to me actually. Feelings are boring. but they're *life*, what can you do? And my mother, my fucking mother, she thinks I should just buy another dog and magically… And I get it. I mean it's been a year. It's just that she was all I had.

ANNA: That's not true.

HELENA: She's who I slept with every night. I mean she knew everything about me. Everything. She knew when I ate, when I cried, when I took a crap. And I loved her. It doesn't stop being real love just because it's a *dog*. I mean, if it had been another human being that I had lived with for fifteen years that suddenly died, if I had walked home and found a human being dead on the floor, lying in their own shit and piss with a look of pain, of twisted pain on their face, then a year later nobody would be surprised if I was still *upset*. Or would they? Who the fuck knows? People want other people to be perky.

ANNA: Look. Grief is hard. That's what love does to us. It hurts us, right?

HELENA: I don't think it's supposed to. Not always.

ANNA: Because of death, though. Love always hurts the one that's left behind.

HELENA: Right.

ANNA: You're supposed to grieve for something you loved.

> *HELENA hugs ANNA.*

HELENA: Thank you for meeting me on your lunch break in the freezing cold!

> *ANNA gets a thick manuscript out of her bag.*

HELENA: You'll think this is crazy but sometimes I can still feel Zoë with me…

ANNA: *(Ignoring that, passing the manuscript.)* You're the first person I've given this to.

HELENA: Is this…?

ANNA: I want to hear everything you have to say about it.

HELENA: "Keats' Punctuation"

ANNA: I need to find a snappier title. Any section you don't understand, I want to know about. Because I want it to be accessible, you know? And not just read by other Keats Scholars. I tried to make it...at least...the middle is kind of boring –

HELENA: Don't say that!

ANNA: But the beginning and the end...I tried to get to some place... human.

HELENA: You're so frikkin' incredible, you know that? I am so proud of you. You finished!

ANNA: It's just a first draft –

HELENA: It is a big deal. It is a big frikkin' deal.

> *They hug.*

ANNA: I have to go teach. Don't you have to get back to work?

HELENA: No.

ANNA: How come?

HELENA: Because at five pm today, little ol' Helena has a little ol' audition.

ANNA: Oh that's great!

HELENA: Would you like to guess for what play?

ANNA: No.

HELENA: *A Midsummer Night's Dream.* Would you like to guess for what part?

ANNA: I just don't have time.

HELENA: Helena! Isn't that crazy? Don't you think that *means* something? That *her* name is already *my* name? I already know what it's like to answer as Helena, I mean I know that's superficial but...I don't know. It feels meaningful to me right now. And she's such a strong woman, you know? That's how I see her. Strong. Guess where the production is?

ANNA: Where?

HELENA: Here! Columbia! A student production! Which is great because that means it will really be about the work and it just never is when you're trying to sell tickets, but they don't sell tickets for student productions so...

ANNA: Is it paid?

HELENA sighs. The sigh becomes a stony silence.

ANNA: I was just asking because if it's a graduate thesis production they do pay the actors so —

HELENA: I don't know if it's paid.

ANNA: If it's not you can claim back on your tax return. Call it an in-kind donation.

HELENA: Whatever. Maybe it's paid. Maybe it's not. I'd just like to be working again. Not everything is about taxes, Anna. I don't even do my taxes.

ANNA: Oh.

HELENA: I could hang around after my audition and we could get a drink around here. I frikkin' miss student bars.

ANNA: I can't. I have a date.

HELENA: *(Disappointed.)* Who is it this time?

ANNA: A critic.

HELENA: *(Horrified.)* No…

ANNA: The machine kept matching me with lawyers and bankers. I adjusted my search criteria last week. Now it's matching me with journalists.

HELENA: You know Anna, the hunt for the soul mate, that is a mysterious thing, and I don't care how much you pay this website, the big old American dollar is not going to short cut that process. What if you're supposed to be with a coal miner or something? Or an acrobat? But the machine can't think out of the box, the machine keeps hooking you up with ivy league a-holes.

ANNA: It's my fault. Those are the guys I'm getting because those are the things I said were important to me. Education. Ambition. Money.

HELENA: You said money?

ANNA: Well…sure…

HELENA: *(Pure judgment.)* Wow.

ANNA: If this one's a disaster I'll change my search criteria.

HELENA: The very fact that there are criteria is a problem.

ANNA: An acrobat?

HELENA: I find it really offensive that you would go on a date with a critic. It's the equivalent of dating someone who's trying to kill me. *(Beat.)* Want to hear my audition speech?

ANNA: I have to go. Break a leg.

> *ANNA exits.*

HELENA: Hey Anna!

"I am as ugly as a bear,
For beasts that meet me run away for fear…"

SCENE 5: LINDA'S HOUSE, IRELAND

> *Late at night. LINDA and MAX sit, drinks in hand, staring out into space.*

LINDA: Sean's out tonight. Out on a date.

MAX: That's nice.

LINDA: A girl he met. On the internet.

MAX: On the internet?

LINDA: Not in a dirty way, in an organized way when they give details about the kind of person that they want to meet and –

MAX: I gotcha. Millie's cousin Marion was married that way.

LINDA: Really?

MAX: She was, she met a man through an internet website –

LINDA: That's it. It's a website –

MAX: Enthusiasts of cheese, I think it was –

LINDA: No this is different –

MAX: And they got along and within six months he'd popped the question. Now she's pregnant and they're talking about moving to Greece to set up a B and B.

LINDA: All Sean does now is go on dates.

MAX: Very nice.

LINDA: Tonight he dates a facialist.

MAX: What the fuck is a facialist?

LINDA: They squeeze your face and make it pretty.

MAX: *What?*

LINDA: That's what they do.

MAX: Why would squeezing your face make it pretty? It would make it blotchy I should think.

LINDA: Faces are full of pus.

MAX: Mine isn't.

LINDA: Everyone's is.

MAX: Mine isn't.

LINDA: Every time I talk to him he's going on a date. "Can't talk, Mum. Going on a date." "Getting ready for a date." "Out on a date." He is *obsessed* with the word date. I told him "only the people in the pictures go on dates." He took it the wrong way.

MAX: Kids *always* take things the wrong fucking way. You can't open your fucking mouth without them pointing out that you just *fucked* something for them. Like my girl, Janie. She's got emotional problems.

LINDA: Since when?

MAX: Since her *therapist* said so. And I swear to God, every single time I open my fucking mouth she says I'm belittling her. Every time I use the word "fucking" *she* says *he* says it's aggressive. So now I have to try and not use the word around her. And you know *why* she's got emotional problems? Do you know why every single kid in her generation has emotional problems?

LINDA: They're weak.

MAX: Their expectations are too fucking high! Animals are fucking happy. Not people.

LINDA: I kept Claire and Sean's expectations *very* low. They're happier as adults than they were as children, the only person they have to thank for that is me. There's nothing about it in the books, but there's something to be said for providing an upward trajectory.

MAX: Since Janie's been in counseling the only topic of conversation on offer is "remember when you broke my heart by not taking me fucking ice skating after you promised."

LINDA: Mine still criticize. Well, not Seany so much, course he's not here to criticize, but Claire… "Remember the time," she'll say, "after Dad left and you didn't get out of bed for three days and I had to make the sandwiches?" *(Beat.)* What does she fucking want me to do about it *now*?

MAX: Stop saying "fucking!" You're emotionally damaging me!

LINDA: Claire's not making too good a parent herself. She dropped the baby the other day.

MAX: Whoops!

> *They roar with laughter. Pause.*

MAX: Shouldn't criticize them. Not really.

LINDA: Why not? They sit around and complain about us.

MAX: I'm not saying I couldn't have done better. I'm not saying that. *(Beat.)* No, I am saying that. I will say that. I didn't drink much, worked hard, helped with homework, I mean what do they want? Jesus Christ could have fathered my Janie and she'd have said, "remember that time you were supposed to take me ice skating, but you had to go deal with the loaves and the fishes?" *(Beat.)* And the reason I didn't take her ice-skating was that I had band practice! Had to give it up in the end though, didn't I? And I don't call her up and say "remember when I gave up my rock band because there weren't enough hours in the day with everybody needing something from me! *(Beat.)* It's nice to be drunk. I haven't been drunk in a long time.

LINDA: Millie keeps you on a tight leash –

MAX: She made me promise I wouldn't get stinking. And I am stinking.

LINDA: What does she expect? You and I always got drunk together. Since we were kiddies.

MAX: You've drunk enough booze tonight to sink a bloody battleship.

LINDA: Bollocks. I can drink, and drink, and drink, and drink and it doesn't do a thing to me.

MAX: It's doing something to you, Linda. *(Beat.)* What time is it? I should call Millie.

    He stands.

LINDA: Can't I have you to myself for one fucking night?

MAX: I was just going to go in the other room for a *second...*

LINDA: Does Millie understand that you and I never see each other since she moved you to the other side of Ireland?

MAX: Linda, it will just take a minute.

LINDA: Oh a minute now, is it? First it was a second, then a minute, then you'll be gone for a full half hour, talking to another. *(Worked up.)* I see you once in a fucking blue moon and I can't have you all to myself for one night?

MAX: Ah, you're behaving badly now, that's the alcohol, that's what it's doing to you... *(Beat. He thinks of a solution.)* I'll text her.

    He gets out his phone. He inexpertly texts his wife.

MAX: Its probably better anyway. She'll only be cross at me for drinking.

LINDA: *(Fixing him with a stare.)* What are you telling her?

MAX: I'm writing that I love her.

    LINDA rolls her eyes, but says nothing.

LINDA: Does Millie know? That tonight's the anniversary?

MAX: Of course.

LINDA: The anniversary of my death.

MAX: Don't say that.

LINDA: My ending, the termination of little Linda was twenty-one years
    ago tonight. And back then she was pretty as picture. Remember her?
    A young thing in a yellow dress. And then boom! As old as the cliffs.
    (Beat.) And where's he tonight I wonder?

MAX: Who?

LINDA: The man in the mist. At home with his family? Playing with his
    children?

>   *MAX claps his hands.*

MAX: Don't get maudlin.

LINDA: Get what?

MAX: Maudlin.

LINDA: I don't even know what that means.

MAX: Mournful. Morbid. Melancholy.

LINDA: How'd you ever hear a word like that?

MAX: It's just a word.

LINDA: Think I'm stupid now, do you?

MAX: No.

LINDA: Maudlin. I'm entitled to be maudlin, I think. Tonight. Do you
    mind if I'm maudlin for one fucking night? I never *tell* anyone how I
    feel! I never talk about the nightmares! I never repeat what plays round
    and around in my head. It's a lot of fucking energy to stay silent Max!
    Can I indulge myself a little tonight? On the fucking anniversary!

>   *Beat.*

MAX: Say whatever you want, Linda.

LINDA: I want to die… I want to be dead…

MAX: Always?

LINDA: I don't know.

MAX: I know I made fun of the counseling before but…for you it's different
    It's deserved…I could pay if you'd like to see a person who is trained
    in…your pain, Linda.

LINDA: I don't think…I don't think…I can do it. I had the counseling at the time and it didn't…*(Distress, panic.)* I'm too sad. Everybody says. It's why Martin left. He'd come home, I'd be staring into space. "I'm so sorry, Martin," I'd say. "I'll get myself together." "Don't worry," he'd say. "You're entitled." But I never let him touch me again, and then he was gone.

MAX: Martin was a bastard.

LINDA: Cost me my husband, that man in the mist. And then my son.

MAX: No…

LINDA: He's why Sean left! Now he's out on a date! He'll marry out there and never come back!

MAX: He's a young man, Linda! That's what young men do! They go out in the world! They seek adventure!

LINDA: All the tiny little stones I picked from his tiny little cuts on his tiny little knees and he's gone. Bought a pair of long trousers and off he went across the sea, not a look over his shoulder not a word of apology. You spend every last pence you have on them! The constant buying of things for children! The T-Shirts and posters and key rings, pound after pound after pound and then boom! Grown men and women and you're at their mercy! I wish I hadn't come back! I wish I had jumped! The man in the mist had killed me so what was the fucking point!

MAX: Linda, you wanted to live. You want to live…

LINDA: *(In pieces.)* I'm sorry, Max! I know this must be awful for you!

MAX: *(Grim.)* You're my sister. It's the least I can fucking do.

SCENE 6: KAY'S HOUSE, DC

KAY wears pajamas.

KAY: What the hell are you doing here, Colonel? You're supposed to be in New York.

ADAM: Surprise?

KAY: You're supposed to be spending the night at Anna's.

ADAM: Surprise.

KAY: You said you weren't coming to DC until tomorrow.

ADAM: It is tomorrow.

KAY: It's 4 a.m.!

ADAM: I'm just a little early.

KAY: Something's wrong. I swear to God, I don't see you from one year to the next then you show up like a bad penny and spill your guts.

ADAM: I thought it would be like the old days in Texas. Me knocking on your door in the middle of the night, hoping for...

KAY: *(Playful.)* Hoping for what?

ADAM: Hoping to see you.

KAY: Give me a kiss.

ADAM looks around him. The room is mostly bare.

ADAM: What happened here?

KAY: Everything's in storage. I told you on the phone. I'm taking a trip.

ADAM: For how long?

KAY: A while.

ADAM: You're renting the place out?

KAY: Selling.

ADAM: Where do you plan on living when you get home?

KAY: I haven't made any definite plans.

ADAM: Why haven't you made any definite plans?

KAY: Because it's liberating.

ADAM: Just how sick are you?

Pause. ADAM continues to study the empty space.

KAY: You were going to have a drink in your hand when I told you. *(Beat.)* I have defeated Western Medicine. So I'm headed east. To India. I shall see mystical people. Maybe they'll wave their hands over me and make it all go away.

> *ADAM starts to ask another question.*

KAY: And then I was going to tell you that I don't want to talk about it any more. It's not my favorite subject.

> *Beat. ADAM nods.*

ADAM: I shouldn't have woken you up.

KAY: But you did so why don't you tell me what's wrong? Why didn't you stay at Anna's?

ADAM: It's not important any more.

KAY: Of course it is.

ADAM: Forget it.

> *Beat.*

KAY: So how is Anna?

ADAM: Good.

KAY: Last time I saw you she was at Columbia, right?

ADAM: She's teaching there now. Got her Ph. D.

KAY: *Dr* Anna.

ADAM: She's writing a book.

KAY: What's it about?

ADAM: Nothing. Punctuation. She's been telling me about the damn thing for years, I have no idea what she's talking about.

KAY: Punctuation's important.

ADAM: Is it?

KAY: Sure. Without it nothing would make any sense. Period.

ADAM: Our conversations are a blast. She tells me about her work which I don't understand and I can't tell her about my work because its classified.

KAY: *(Beat.)* Is she seeing anyone?

Adam sighs.

KAY: Aha. Who?

ADAM: A personal trainer. What kind of job *is* that?

KAY: Fitness and such. The two of you probably have a lot in common.

ADAM: I am a colonel in the United States Armed Forces, Kay. I am not a fitness instructor.

KAY: *(Amused.)* Sorry.

ADAM: She brought him to dinner! No warning, just brought him to dinner. I mean, maybe I wouldn't have minded so much if this guy had anything to recommend him, you know. He didn't even tuck his shirt in. He's Irish.

KAY: Sexy.

ADAM: I'm not one of those Americans who's sappy about Ireland. *(Beat.)* I asked if he planned to go back, he didn't even answer. He just shrugged. Language is not his first language if you know what I mean.

KAY: Maybe he was shy.

ADAM: His father's dead. His mother...I could not get a clear picture of the mother. I did gather that she was unemployed.

KAY: Adam. Honey. You're not supposed to like him. He's screwing your daughter. *(Beat.)* Has she ever brought any other boy to dinner?

ADAM: No.

KAY: So this one's important.

ADAM: They were clamped together at this restaurant. Physically clamped. Finally, he goes to the bathroom and she says "for the first time I really understand what you and Mom had."

KAY: Oh boy.

ADAM: And she's glowing, you know? Just glowing. I felt sick.

KAY: Adam...

ADAM: We're strangers! She put her hand on my arm, looked into my eyes, and she was a stranger. And then the personal trainer came back from the bathroom, sat down, stuck his arm around her like she was his property, and I picked up the check.

KAY: Adam...

ADAM: I could hear my dead wife laughing.

KAY: What was she finding so funny.

ADAM: She told me this would happen! "Some day that little girl will be all grown up and you'll have missed her." And she was right. Good for Rosie.

KAY: Adam... It's not too late.

ADAM: Oh I think it is. I've always known that Anna and I had to struggle for conversation a little, I didn't mind. When it was just Anna and me we were both outsiders, you know? Trying to get in. But Anna and another...that makes me the outsider. That makes *me* the stranger. *(Beat.)* On the way here I kept thinking "I should feel young again. Finally, no dependents." But I swear to god I feel a thousand years old.

KAY: You're not a thousand years old, you're a thousand different ages. We all are. Right now you look just the same as when we first met. A frightened man in his twenties.

ADAM: You're hallucinating. What kind of drugs have they got you on anyway?

KAY: You were running from Anna just like now. You said you needed a break from the screaming. I said "Colonel, you're hilarious. Your country needs you and you shoulder the burden. Your family needs you and you head to the nearest bar."

ADAM: *(Irritated.)* Look, don't blame me, Kay. I make the effort. What the hell do you think these dinners are about? Why the hell do you think I fly in to New York every time I have to report to DC even though I hate New York! She hates Texas so I never ask her to come to Texas. It's me that makes the effort! I have been making the effort for years! I show up at the over priced hell-hole that she's picked and I sit there!

> *Beat.*

KAY: Don't show up at four in the morning, ask for my help and then yell at me. I am not a wife. *(Beat.)* It's not too late.

ADAM: It is too late. Rosie was right. I missed her. She passed me by.

KAY: If she passed you by, you know what to do.

ADAM: No. I don't.

KAY: For God's sakes man, give chase!

SCENE 7: AN ART GALLERY

ANNA and HELENA staring at incomprehensibly abstract modern art.

Eventually HELENA begins to study ANNA instead.

HELENA: Miss Anna? You are totally wearing a little outfit.

ANNA: What do you mean?

HELENA: You're wearing a little scarf.

ANNA: So?

HELENA: Your bag matches your shoes.

ANNA: Are you complimenting me?

HELENA: I am complimenting you, absolutely I am. You look incredible.

ANNA: Thanks.

HELENA: When did you become such a *woman*? When did you become such an adult lady? I mean maybe that it's that I haven't seen you in a while but you look so different. I mean you always look beautiful but right now what I'm getting, what you're projecting, what I'm picking up, is that you are an adult suddenly. You look great. You look really put together.

ANNA: Thanks.

HELENA: You look like the kind of lady I have no business knowing. You look like the kind of lady who has stocks.

ANNA: I do have some stocks.

HELENA: *(Flabbergasted.)* From the stock market? Shares? You have shares in things?

ANNA: Sure.

HELENA: What stocks do you have?

ANNA: Most of it's in environmentally friendly waste management.

HELENA: Wow. I am a child. Do you think I'm like a child?

ANNA: No.

HELENA: Really? Even though I dress like a clown?

ANNA: I like how you dress.

HELENA: I'm just so used to seeing you in jeans. Where did these dresses come from all of a sudden. Is it Sean? Does he prefer you in dresses?

ANNA: He's never commented one way or the other.

HELENA: Oh really? He doesn't care what you wear?

ANNA: I don't think so.

HELENA: That's nice. It's so long since I've been in a relationship that I can't remember what it's like. Somehow, in my imagination, the guy says "you must wear *this,* woman! Now suck my cock!" but that's not what it's like, right? That's just my fucked up imagination. Honestly, secretly, I think I'm terrified of men. Even like, with my brother sometimes, he'll be talking to me and all I'll be thinking is "you have a penis, you have a penis" and I find it *terrifying.* You know what I mean?

ANNA: Kind of…

HELENA: No but it's so great about you and Sean. You seem so happy.

ANNA: I am.

HELENA: That's great. Isn't it amazing how we find each other? Like him being Irish and a personal trainer, I mean, that's crazy! He's from Ireland!

ANNA: I know.

HELENA: And a personal trainer! I would never have thought in a million years that you – or in fact anyone I know – could find a meaningful relationship with a personal trainer. But you have. *(Beat.)* Do you guys have sex all the time?

ANNA: No.

HELENA: And you said it was really good, right. You said the sex was good.

ANNA: Sure.

HELENA: Can you see me with a boyfriend? Can you see that in my future?

ANNA: Of course.

HELENA: That's good. Sometimes I find I can't… *(Her voice starts to break a little, tears close.)* picture it as closely as I used to. The only guys that like me are married, or gay. The last time little Helena actually had full blown sex, it turned out the guy was married. Anyhow, let's talk about you, we always talk about me, let's talk about you. You want to?

ANNA: Sure…

HELENA: Talk. I'll listen.

ANNA: Something weird happened last night. My Dad telephoned. Just, he said, to *chat*. I have never heard him use the word chat in his life.

HELENA: Right, you guys don't chat, you have awkward conversations twice a year.

ANNA: Exactly.

HELENA: So how was chatting?

ANNA: It was ridiculous. We have nothing to chat about. Normally I hide that by never shutting up. I saw a fascinating movie I say, I'll say. A student came to me with a fascinating problem. I'm always trying to fascinate him. And I don't think I've ever fascinated him once.

HELENA: God that's so sad.

ANNA: I know. All I do is try to entertain him.

HELENA: Like a geisha.

ANNA: Right. But on the phone, last night, I didn't. There was a lot of silence. *(Beat.)* I didn't tell him the big news.

HELENA: What's the big news?

ANNA: Another publisher passed on my book.

HELENA: *What?* What is wrong with these people?

ANNA: Nobody is interested in Keats' Punctuation. I should have seen that coming, really. I mean I wasn't even interested half the time I was writing it, I wanted to write about Emily Dickenson's punctuation, remember, but then Simon said everyone wrote about Emily Dickenson's punctuation and I just happened to be reading Keats at the time, and now it's five fucking years later and my whole life has been about Keats's punctuation and it looks like it was a waste of time.

HELENA: If no one wants to publish your book that just confirms that it's frikkin' excellent. It's a topsy-turvy universe. If something is worthless, we raise it up. Something of value, we trample it into the frikkin' mud.

ANNA: It's the title, Sean thinks. It's the fucking title. "Keats' Punctuation."

HELENA: Did Sean also tell you that you're a genius and that your book is brilliant?

ANNA: He hasn't read it.

HELENA: What?

ANNA: I told him not to. It would bore him.

HELENA: But you wrote it.

ANNA: But it's not for everybody. Which is why they won't publish it. *(Beat.)* What?

HELENA: I just don't see how you can be with someone who doesn't want to read your work.

ANNA: He read a chapter, I think.

HELENA: *(Shocked.)* How could he only read a chapter of it? It's your brain, it's your heart, it's your soul, how can he – I don't even *know* Sean. I find it really weird that you've been seeing each other forever and I've met him like five times. Does he even like me?

ANNA: Of course he does.

HELENA: Because I kind of got the impression that he didn't like me.

ANNA: When?

HELENA: You remember how I was telling the story about how I got really drunk at my dad's sixtieth birthday party and cried and kind of ruined it for everybody and he just seemed really judgmental.

ANNA: I don't think he was judging you. He was just listening.

HELENA: Even you said he was judgmental, remember. Didn't you tell me that on your first date he totally judged you for being in therapy?

ANNA: I was wrong. That was – that was about something else.

HELENA: You never tell me anything about him.

ANNA: What is it that you want to know?

HELENA: I don't *know*, you just never talk about him.

ANNA: Because there's nothing to say.

HELENA: That can't be true. He's such a huge part of your life! And I totally feel you making him separate!

ANNA: I'm not.

HELENA: Yes you *are!*

ANNA: He works all the time. I work all the time. The little time we have together we want to spend by ourselves. And if I don't talk about him it's because I have nothing to say about him except that I *love* him. And he makes me happy. And it makes you unhappy when I'm happy.

HELENA: I can't believe you would think that.

ANNA: We start talking about me being happy and within ten minutes you're in tears because you're not happy as well. You and me like to talk about our problems. Sean's not a problem so I don't want to talk about him. No one wants to publish my fucking book, let's talk about that. My Dad is calling me on the phone and acting crazy, let's talk about that! This exhibition is horrifying, let's talk about that. But leave Sean alone!

HELENA: Wow. I had no idea you felt this way. Thank you for telling me. This is very enlightening.

> *Pause.*

HELENA: Maybe I do cry a lot because guess what, big surprise, little ol' Helena is an emotional person, – but I think I am also a very joyful person –

ANNA: You are…

HELENA: I am a person of extremes, but do not tell me that I am incapable of celebrating with you. Do not tell me I am the person who can only discuss misery.

ANNA: Not just miserable things. Deep things! Like…art…and…you know… Deep things!

HELENA: But you're in love, Anna! Isn't love deep?

ANNA: It's private. It's private right now.

> *Pause.*

HELENA: But you're happy. And the sex is wonderful.

ANNA: Sometimes we have sex and it's wonderful. Sometimes I never felt more alone in my life.

SCENE 8: A GYM, DUBLIN, IRELAND

> *MAX, sweating, exhausted, is on the running machine. SEAN stands next to him.*

MAX: This woman you're seeing…

SEAN: Anna.

MAX: Do you torture her like this?

SEAN: She has no interest.

MAX: Been going on for sometime now, hasn't it? *(No response from Sean.)* When are we going to meet her? Does she not want to visit this marvelous country of ours?

SEAN: Oh she does. Very much.

MAX: So?

SEAN: I'll never bring a girl home again unless it's to ask her to marry me.

MAX: It must be about that time, isn't right?

SEAN: According to who's timetable?

MAX: Well how serious is it? What are you doing?

> *SEAN speeds up the machine. MAX runs.*

MAX: Isn't this just a metaphor for life? You sweat and you strain and you still end up in the same place. This is giving me an existential crisis! *(Running faster.)* You're a fucking torturer. I had no idea. I had no idea that torturing people was your fucking career of choice…Vanity. One of the seven deadly sins. A man my age is supposed to spread a little.

SEAN: You'd find this easier if you would just shut up.

MAX: I think I might die. Soon. In the next five minutes. I feel it. My death approaches. He's at my back. You're killing your uncle, Sean. Your own flesh and blood. This can't be healthy.

SEAN: It is.

MAX: But I'm about to throw up.

SEAN: You're doing great.

MAX: Oh you're just feeding me your personal trainer bullshit. I'm not an American, Sean. I don't believe I'm the best fucker in the world just because somebody tells me so!

SEAN: Alright, what about this. You're a heart attack waiting to happen! And when you're dead Auntie Millie will say "that lazy bastard. I could have had him for another fifteen years if only he exercised more."

MAX: Fifteen years?

SEAN: Now you know what you're chasing after.

> Pause. MAX runs, more determined.

SEAN: A few more seconds now…

MAX: Fuck you! This is bullshit! This is a terrible way to spend time!

SEAN: Ten, nine, eight, seven…

MAX: I hate you Sean, I hate you Sean!

SEAN: Five, four…

MAX: Fuck you! Fuck me! Fuck everybody!

SEAN: And now we slow down to walking…

> SEAN slows the machine down to a fast walk.

MAX: We don't stop?

SEAN: No. We get our heart rate down, we get our breath back, but we keep going…

MAX: "We" nothing! What are you doing? You get paid for this shit?

SEAN: I do.

MAX: I'm going to be in pain tomorrow, aren't I? This is the last walking I'll be doing for quite some time, isn't that right?

SEAN: Got to push through the pain, Max.

MAX: Listen to you…like a fucking Marine…

SEAN: You're doing great.

MAX: I am not doing great! I am pathetic. The seventeen-year-old Max is watching and he is in tears.

SEAN: You really are doing well.

MAX: What happened to great? *(His breath is steadier now.)* So this girl you've been seeing. We were talking about whether or not it was serious.

SEAN: Her name is Anna.

MAX: Well, you're on the other side of the world, Sean! We've never met her! She's not quite real to us, you know what I mean? Your mother's worried you're keeping her away deliberately.

SEAN: Why?

MAX: She thinks you're ashamed of where you're from.

SEAN: That's ridiculous.

MAX: She gets the impression that Anna is a different sort of person, a posh sort of person. Teaches at a university, doesn't she? Your mother would feel better if she met her, that's all. But if it's not going to last –

SEAN: I didn't say it wasn't going to last.

MAX: Well two years, boy! When I was your age I had two kids already! The time goes by quick, what are you waiting for? A sign from God? If she's not the right fish throw her back in the sea.

SEAN: How do I know?

MAX: How do you know? Do you love her?

SEAN: Aye.

MAX: No but do you really love her, do you truly love her? No, don't make me run!

> *But SEAN has stopped the machine. MAX sees SEAN looks very serious.*

MAX: What? What's the matter with you? *(A beat.)* What Sean?

SEAN: I don't know. She wants to move in together. I don't want to. And if I don't want to then I should end it. But I don't want to end it. I'm a dick. I don't know what I'm doing. She probably wants to have babies. And I'm just...I don't know what to do! I don't want to be the bad guy! But I don't want to end it! But I *should* end it because I'm a liar!

MAX: Who are you lying to?

SEAN: To Anna! I'm lying next to her at night and against my will against my fucking will there's this other girl in my head and I'm thinking that I love her. Or that I loved her. I loved her more.

MAX: Who?

SEAN: Rachel. *(Beat.)* Christ, Max. I'm asleep with one woman I'm dreaming of another.

MAX: I haven't done enough for you, Sean. You had no Dad and I've tried to look out for you but with four of my own and...

SEAN: Max –

MAX: Let me finish. I've been remiss in my responsibilities towards you. A kid needs a father. You need a father, this moment right here is why a child needs a father. Let me be yours. For this moment, let me be yours.

SEAN: Alright.

MAX: Son. You will always think of other women. *(Beat.)* I do, even now. Helen May.

SEAN: You've not been remiss, Max. You had your own family.

MAX: But you are my family.

SEAN: I'm alright.

MAX: I don't know how you did it, but you've grown up fine.

Beat.

SEAN: So who was Helen May then?

MAX: It was with her that I had my first kiss. Beautiful girl. Became a nun.

SEAN: I see you had quite an effect on her.

MAX: We were kids. Running around the playground. The girls would make daisy chains and chase the boys. If they put the chain around their necks they had to kiss them. And us boys off we ran. We ran, but we wanted to be caught. Helen May caught me. So we turned and we faced each other. And I bent forward like I was bowing, you know? And we were making these little Chinese bows at each other. And I closed my eyes and she kissed me. Oh it was delicious. Some nights, Millie is asleep, and I pretend that I seek out Helen May in her nunnery. I call up to the tower! Helen, do you remember me? Run away with me! Millie gives a little snort and awakes. "I can't sleep," I tell her. "Well think about Helen May," she says. "That usually drops you off." *(Beat.)*

SEAN: *(Surprised.)* She doesn't mind it?

MAX: She doesn't mind.

SCENE 9: LECTURE THEATER, COLUMBIA UNIVERSITY

ADAM alone. Awkward. Out of place. The outskirts of a party. HELENA arrives, hurried. She looks disheveled. ADAM is relieved to see someone he knows.

ADAM: Helena!

HELENA: Hey…how are you? Gosh it's been…

ADAM: A long time.

HELENA: Can you believe it? She's totally published! Awesome! Where is she?

ADAM nods off stage.

HELENA: The woman of the hour.

ADAM: I'm just letting her do her thing.

HELENA: How long are you in town for?

ADAM: Just a couple of hours. The timing was off for me.

HELENA: That's so amazing that you flew in!

ADAM: Wouldn't miss it.

HELENA: I'm late-a-roony. I decided to have a catnap and it turned into a sleeporama. I have very vivid dreams, you know, and I was just having this crazy dream that I –

SEAN comes over.

SEAN: Helena. How are you?

HELENA: Honestly, I hate being asked that. People just want you to say fine. It's a lot of pressure. There's so much pressure to be *unreal* with people, you know?

SEAN: Okay…

HELENA: Okay.

SEAN: *(To ADAM.)* Anna told me to check on you. She's in the middle of a very dry conversation about ellipses.

HELENA: Ellipses are fascinating, actually.

ADAM: I don't even know what they are.

HELENA: They're the little dot dot dot at the end of a sentence. They change everything. For actors.

ADAM: Helena, what are you working on now?

A long pause. Gradually it dawns on ADAM that HELENA will not be answering his question.

HELENA: Is there any wine at this shindig?

SEAN: Over there.

HELENA exits towards wine. Pause.

SEAN: Work going well for you, Adam?

ADAM: Very well. *(Beat.)* And yours? Work?

SEAN: Great. Fine. *(Beat.)* I've been taking a class in Karate. I might incorporate it into some of the training.

ADAM: I have a black belt in Karate.

SEAN: Anna told me. You could give me a few pointers, maybe.

ADAM: When I was taught the object was to kill the other person. Different kind of training.

> *The ensuing silence is broken by the SCREETCH of a microphone. Then we hear SIMON's AMPLIFIED VOICE. All our attention is on ADAM and SEAN's reactions.*

SIMON: *(Offstage.)* Welcome everybody, welcome. I won't take up much of your time I just want to say how pleased we are to host this event tonight. Anna –

> *ADAM and SEAN listen, pride on their faces.*

SIMON: – began life as an undergrad here at Columbia. No actually, she began life as a baby. My little joke. Sorry.

> *ADAM and SEAN are unimpressed.*

SIMON: *(Offstage.)* Anna began her *academic* life at Columbia as an undergraduate and I actually had the pleasure of teaching her…she was everything you want a student to be, quick, attentive, studious, curious, passionate.

> *Pride on ADAM and SEAN's face. They even smile at each other.*

SIMON: *(Offstage.)* Anna went on to get her Ph.D here, and to my great delight she and I became more than student and teacher…

> *ADAM and SEAN tense, horrified*

…we became colleagues.

> *ADAM and SEAN relax.*

SIMON: *(Offstage.)* Tonight, we are here to celebrate the book that bloomed from her PhD thesis. *The Grammar of Love: Keats and Punctuation* represents Anna's first academic publication. It's really wonderful and without a doubt one of the most exciting publications to have come out of Columbia all *year*. So, Anna, if you'd like to come up here and say a few words?

HELENA walks up to ADAM and SEAN. We hear ANNA's voice through the microphone.

ANNA: Thanks everyone for coming…I want to thank Simon especially for so much help with the book and the faculty for all of their support and my dad for flying all the way in from Texas and my boyfriend for putting up with me and…you know…thanks for coming…! Drink up!

SCREETCH. The microphone is switched off. ADAM and SEAN are modestly delighted with their acknowledgement.

SEAN: *(To HELENA.)* After this, I though we'd get a drink downtown. I hate student bars.

ADAM: Anna's mother would have been incredibly proud of her. She always hoped to write a book herself.

HELENA: Everyone has a novel in them, right?

ADAM: She never had the discipline to get it out.

ANNA enters.

ANNA: *(Tense.)* That was a horrible speech.

SEAN: No.

ADAM: Short, quick and to the point.

SEAN: You thanked everyone you needed to thank and then you got off the stage.

HELENA bursts into tears and runs off stage.

ADAM: What's the matter with her?

SEAN: This isn't about the dog again, is it?

ADAM: The what?

SEAN: Her dog died a hundred years ago. She's still in mourning.

ANNA: It's because I didn't thank her. She read the book three times and I didn't thank her. I should have thanked her…

SEAN: That's ridiculous.

ANNA: I meant to I just, I was flustered.

SEAN: You've thanked her *in* the book. It's fine.

ANNA: That's why she's crying. Bet you.

SEAN: *(Angry.)* Then she can get over it. Jesus, it's your night.

ANNA: Some night. Could it be any more anti-climactic? Five years of work and this is what I get? Wine, cheese, and a lecture theatre. There's still equations left up on the blackboard for fuck's sake. Sorry, Dad.

ADAM: Come now. *(Beat.)* Come now.

ANNA: Yeah, well now I have to write another one. It never ends. *(Beat.)* I better see if Helena's alright –

SEAN: *Leave* her… It's your night.

> *Beat.*

ANNA: *(To SEAN.)* I am so fucking sick of her – *(To ADAM.)* sorry Dad – *(To SEAN.)* I swear to God it's the one night that's meant to be about me and she dragged me to one side and started telling me her dream, and when the head of the faculty came over to introduce me to some donor or something, she acted really…you know…mad. Like she was mad that the story of her *dream* got interrupted. I mean for God sakes…

ADAM: *(Emphatically.)* She has *aged.* I almost didn't recognize her. How's her acting going?

SEAN: She never works.

ADAM: Didn't you take me to see a play she was in?

ANNA: Ages ago.

ADAM: I thought she was *excellent.*

ANNA: She was.

ADAM: *Really* talented, I thought.

ANNA: What time's your flight?

ADAM: I've got about an hour still.

ANNA: You should go now. Get some food. You can't eat cheese for dinner. I have to stay for the end. I'm sorry it's such a pathetic little gathering, Dad. I told you it wasn't worth flying in for. Oh Jesus, I'm being waved over. *(To SEAN.)* Come with.

They walk off. ADAM alone. He's almost relieved to see a tear stained HELENA.

ADAM: Are you ok?

HELENA: Oh fine. I cry all the time. *(Beat.)* You know, I just woke up I had a really intense dream so…

ADAM: I just remembered. Last time I saw you I was here. You were doing a show with the students.

HELENA: *Midsummer Night's Dream.*

ADAM: That's right! You played Bottom!

HELENA: Right…

ADAM: You were excellent. *(Beat.)* I have to go. It was good to see you, Helena.

> *He leaves.*

HELENA: *(To the audience.)* I had this dream that I passed a store front and there were jellos in the window. I went inside. There was a back room full of children. My Dad was there. He was playing with them. I said surprised. "What are you doing here, Dad?" He was confused, like he didn't understand the question. He was playing cards with a little girl so I let him be. I started talking to a serious little boy. The boy told me he'd tried to kill himself that morning. He told me all the children there had tried to die. And then I remembered that I had tried to kill myself the day before. That's why my Dad was there. He was there for me.

SCENE 10: ACADIA NATIONAL PARK, MAINE

SEAN and RACHEL sitting on a bench. A cold, blowy day.

RACHEL: Smoke?

SEAN: Gave up.

RACHEL: You always were a goody two shoes.

SEAN: Set a good example for my clients. You know.

RACHEL: How'd you find me?

SEAN: Facebook.

RACHEL: You're not on Facebook.

SEAN: I had to join it to find you.

RACHEL: I looked for you there when I joined. But I figured it wasn't very you.

SEAN: So you didn't mind me getting in touch?

RACHEL: No, why should I?

SEAN: Never pegged you for a country girl.

RACHEL: I'm not really.

SEAN: You're married.

RACHEL: Yes.

SEAN: Not a question. Facebook. Tells you everything, really. So much stuff. I had no idea. I had no idea. Ten minutes after I joined three ex-girlfriends in Ireland wanted to know what I was up to. Sending me quizzes to find out which golden girl I'm most like. *(Beat.)* Rose by the way. *(Beat.)* I shut my page down already. *(Beat.)* Anyway, sorry, Who'd you marry?

RACHEL: His name's Devrak.

SEAN: What is it?

RACHEL: Devrak. He's from India.

SEAN: I didn't know there were Indian people in Maine.

RACHEL: Had you ever seriously thought about it?

SEAN: No.

RACHEL: What about you? Married? Girlfriend?

SEAN: Girlfriend.

RACHEL: What's her name?

SEAN: Anna.

RACHEL: Serious?

SEAN: Yup.

RACHEL: Where are you working now?

SEAN: Freelance now.

RACHEL: Still saving to run your own gym?

SEAN: Yes.

RACHEL: You always said it would take years.

SEAN: I was right.

RACHEL: I'm a – oh you already know... Facebook.

SEAN: You're a hairdresser.

RACHEL: Stylist.

SEAN: You never did go back to school then?

RACHEL: No. *(Beat.)* I like cutting hair. I don't talk enough. My boss always tells me to be more chatty. But my regulars, that's what they like about me.

SEAN: That's funny.

RACHEL: What is?

SEAN: That's what my boss used to tell me. That's what I'd tell him.

RACHEL: I think that's why we liked to drink so much together. Loosened our lips.

SEAN: I drink less now.

RACHEL: I was AA all the way, baby. AA. I don't miss any of it. Half the people in my band are in recovery.

SEAN: *(Pleased.)* You're still playing?

RACHEL: Oh yes. We have kind of a following here in Maine. We're what they call "Maimous."

SEAN: How are your parents?

RACHEL: Good. Very good. Retired. I don't know where they are half the time. They bought an RV, travel up and down the country.

SEAN: I remember them saying they'd do that someday.

RACHEL: Some day's here.

Pause. SEAN begins to cry.

SEAN: I miss you. I still miss you. It doesn't go away. Don't say anything back. The last time I saw you, you had tubes coming out of your fucking nose. There were fucking sirens.

RACHEL: I'm sorry.

SEAN: *(Getting himself back together.)* I hate the sound of sirens. Can't stand hospitals. You know who else I think of all the time? Your folks. They hate my guts, I bet.

RACHEL: They don't think about you.

SEAN: I'll never forget your Dad screaming at me in the hospital. He hit me. Did you know that? Or tried to. I jumped back. I wish I hadn't now. I wish he'd hit me hard in the face, sometimes I pretend he did. If I can't sleep, I imagine him hitting me again and again.

RACHEL: He shouldn't have done that. It wasn't your fault. You had every right to dump me.

SEAN: Dump you, hook up with you, dump you, hook up with you, and on and on and on and on…I was a fucking idiot.

RACHEL: Young love. That's what it looks like.

SEAN: I'm so sorry about it.

RACHEL: You don't need to be. It really had nothing to do with you.

SEAN: Oh please –

RACHEL: It didn't. It had to do with me. Honey, back then I was drinking a bottle of vodka a day.

SEAN: I didn't know that.

RACHEL: Well I was. I was a time bomb. That's what my lady said.

SEAN: Your what?

RACHEL: They make you see a shrink if you try to kill yourself. I was a train wreck back then.

SEAN: Not to me.

RACHEL: Yes to you. That's why you kept dumping me!

SEAN: I don't remember. I don't remember why I broke it off. I keep asking myself why.

RACHEL: What you said was…we need to grow up.

Pause.

RACHEL: Does your girlfriend know you came?

SEAN: Her suggestion. She said – she kept using this stupid word.

RACHEL: What word?

SEAN: It doesn't matter. It's silly.

RACHEL: What word?

SEAN: Traumatized.

Pause.

SEAN: What did your lady say about me?

RACHEL: Not much. We talked about my family mostly.

SEAN: Oh.

Pause.

RACHEL: But she said when I think of you, and I do think of you, it's just a fantasy of escape. The Sean I think of doesn't exist anymore. He's gone. And the Rachel you're thinking of doesn't exist either. Not really. She's long gone.

Pause.

SEAN: I don't exist?

RACHEL: Neither do I.

SCENE 11: ADAM'S HOUSE, TEXAS

Christmas Eve. ANNA holds a notebook. ADAM studies her. Very anxious.

ADAM: I don't know what to say. Do you want to call Sean? What can I do? Anna? I don't know what to say…

ANNA hurls the notebook at ADAM who has to dodge to avoid it.

ANNA: You can stop staying *that!*

ADAM: Hey!

ANNA: Asshole!

ADAM: Do you want to call Sean?

ANNA: Why would I want to call Sean?

ADAM: To comfort you…

ANNA: God I hate you! I have worked so hard not to hate you and now I give up. I hate you.

ADAM: I haven't done anything! I didn't even know she kept a journal!

ANNA: Of course not! Apparently you paid her no attention at all!

ADAM: I don't know what she wrote in there, but obviously it's just one half of the truth. The truth exists between two opposing viewpoints, don't forget that, don't ever forget that.

ANNA: Patronizing. She said you were patronizing. She captured you perfectly. And I've been ignoring –

ADAM: What? No –

ANNA: – Ignoring who you really were because I thought it was her, that it was her death that made you –

ADAM: Anna…

ANNA: She hated you!

ADAM: No! Not always.

ANNA: And you let me believe that it was a love story!

ADAM: It was! It…Anna you're not…

ANNA: What?

ADAM: *(Angry.)* Will you let me think? Will you just let me think? *(Beat.)* I have sensed from you a misunderstanding about the nature of the marriage for some time now and… *You* tell me how I was supposed to *correct* something like that? You got it all built up in your head. Not to blame you, not to blame you, but you must see that… Anna, every couple has their problems, you're a big girl now, you know that. I'm sure you and Sean have your problems, it doesn't mean... Please don't be so upset... Jesus Christ, Anna! I didn't know it was up there! I kept all her things in case you wanted to go through them some day! If I thought there was anything in there that would have upset you, I would have burned it! As would she! *(Uselessly completing his sentence.)* Have... I know she wasn't happy. There was a period where she was not happy. Neither was I. Is that what upsets you? What did she write? How unhappy was she?

ANNA: Read it!

ADAM: Anna it was a different time, it was a difficult time, men and women spoke to each other in different ways. Anna will you look at me, please? Let's talk about this. I don't want this to... please do not let this... I have been trying very hard to... It's Christmas Eve. Come on now. This is our first Christmas together for a long time, and it's supposed to be... we were having a very nice time I thought... and Sean is flying in for New Year. This is supposed to be a new fucking era or whatever. Jesus! Why is it always like this! Why is it always such a fucking drama?

ANNA: What?

ADAM: Eventually! Why does everything always turn into such a fucking drama! You're just like your mother, you know that? You're just like her right now. I want calm. Let's just calm down.

ANNA: "Adam is so distant from me, I can't bear it. Why did I marry a stone?" She wanted a divorce? You wanted a divorce? And then she got cancer and died? *That's* the story of my mother? Do not touch me! Don't you touch me! She says she thinks you cheated on her. Did you?

ADAM: We both screwed around.

ANNA: *(Broken.)* With who?

    Beat.

ADAM: *(Very nervous.)* There was this one woman –

ANNA: *(Panic.)* I don't want to hear it.

ADAM: For God sakes, Anna! We weren't saints. Your mother in particular was an extremely free spirit. I don't know what period of time that journal covers but... We did love each other. And we loved you. And you didn't hear the fights because we fought in the yard. I did grieve. I don't know what she wrote about me, but I tried. I really did. It just... I was away so much. And at the beginning, when I came home... food on the table and pretty dresses... Everyone was a homemaker in Texas. I got offered a post in Japan. I wanted very much to take it. I thought it would be good for you. See the world. Learn Japanese. What a wonderful childhood, I thought. Your mother refused. That was the beginning of a coldness. And something got broken. No more pretty dresses. Suddenly not a happy woman, not a happy woman, suddenly. Suddenly she wants more. More than the house, more than the baby. And then the eighties, the nineteen eighties... When I first served women weren't even allowed in active combat. Now... And they're good at it! It's the darndest thing. Rosie used to tell me "there's not so much difference between a man and a woman." I laughed in her face. And now. What do I see? In combat, with a gun, the one could be the other! And she told me all this. She told me years ago. I was limited. Anna, I admit it. I limited her. I see that now. But we were kids! You're in your thirties, you and Sean are only moving in together now! Please don't take this so hard.

ANNA: I'm packing my bags and I'm going to the airport and I'm waiting for a flight home.

ADAM: Don't do that...

ANNA: I thought the reason you were so cold and distant was because you were crippled with grief. But I was wrong. You're just cold and distant. I've put so much energy into trying to reach you. Being early to our dinners. Dressing up for you. Always trying to entertain you. No point. She married a stone.

> *She exits.*

ADAM: Anna!

SCENE 12: A PSYCHIATRIC WARD, NYC

> *HELENA in an enormous hospital gown. SEAN visiting her.*

SEAN: How are you?

HELENA: That's a joke, right.

SEAN: Right. *(Beat.)* I brought you some books and some magazines and stuff.

HELENA: Thanks.

SEAN: Although I see they're not short on board games here. *(Beat.)* And this is chicken soup and some chicken sandwiches. I thought the food here would probably be pretty awful.

HELENA: You made these?

SEAN: Yes. I cook.

HELENA: I forgot. Anna said. You're really good at it.

SEAN: Anna doesn't eat enough. Always picking at things. Works too much. *(Beat.)* She wanted to be here. I was the one who told her to wait until I'd checked on you. Her plane had only just landed there when she got your message.

HELENA: Where's she gone this time?

SEAN: Some conference in France. She's giving a paper.

HELENA: She travels all the time now.

SEAN: Yup. I've barely seen her since we moved in together.

HELENA: She's busy, busy, busy. I had to talk to a psychiatrist this morning so that he could medicate me. I'm currently medicated, I don't know if you can tell. And he said I simply have too much time on my hands. As simple as that. Simple, simple, simple. I said to him "are you saying that if I worked in a bank none of this would be happening" and do you know what he said? "I'd put money on it." And I said "then you'd lose your money, doc, because if I worked in a bank then I *would* kill myself."

SEAN: They are going to let you out again, right?

HELENA: Exactly. I checked myself into rehab but I can't check myself out. I have to be released into somebody's care. My Mom is driving up from Arlington. Tomorrow.

SEAN: Don't you hate your Mom?

HELENA: Yes.

SEAN: That doesn't sound like a good plan.

HELENA: I don't have a fucking plan. I have to be released into someone's care.

SEAN: What about me and Anna?

HELENA: What about you?

SEAN: There's our care.

HELENA: It's too much.

SEAN: It's fine.

HELENA: No. It's too much. I should go home. My parents have money. They can pay to get me some…whatever it is I need…-

SEAN: I'm free all day. If you want company.

HELENA: What will we talk about?

SEAN: Did Anna tell you about the journal?

HELENA: Her Mom's journal? Uh huh.

SEAN: She won't talk about it. She's gone silent. Like a ghost.

HELENA: That's how she was when I first met her. Like a ghost. Her mom had just died. She appeared at boarding school. A mystery. Never said a word to anyone.

SEAN: How did you get her to open up? She said you guys used to talk to each other after lights were out, that she'd cry in your arms.

HELENA: I asked her lots of questions, I guess. I don't really remember. We were both always the last people picked for softball. It was a common bond.

SEAN: I ask her questions. She says she doesn't want to talk about it.

HELENA: Push her. You have to push her.

> SEAN sighs.

SEAN: Sorry. You don't want to hear about our problems.

HELENA: I do. It's comforting. What's the worst thing? What's the worse thing about where you guys are at right now?

SEAN: The not knowing. Not knowing if we're going to end up together. We've been together so long and we're totally lost.

HELENA: That sounds awful.

SEAN: It's like floating on a sea, scanning the horizon for land and you know it's out there but... No plan. It feels like we're drifting. In the land of not-knowing.

HELENA: That's where I live.

SEAN: Hi.

HELENA: Hi.

SCENE 13: A HOSPITAL BED, DC

KAY's propped up but her eyes are closed. Somewhere a machine beeps. ADAM watches her. Silence for a while, then...

KAY: Just, Christ, say something. Don't just sit there and watch me die.

ADAM: I thought you fell asleep.

KAY: No I didn't, although with your conversation I might as well have.

ADAM: I'm sorry.

KAY: Talk. Tell me something classified. Come on. My lips are sealed. I'll take it to the grave.

ADAM: The government was responsible for 9/11.

KAY: Really?

ADAM: No.

KAY: *(Amused.)* You're such an asshole.

> *Pause.*

ADAM: Are you in pain?

KAY: There's no pain. They've got me on all sorts of wonderful things. The only problem is I'll be asleep any second. I drop off, just like that.

ADAM: That's ok. I'm here for a while. I took a few weeks off.

KAY: Why did you do that?

ADAM: Why do you think?

KAY: I haven't got a few weeks.

ADAM: Who knows with you? You're a miracle.

KAY: Not any more.

ADAM: Always.

KAY: I don't want you here. Getting mushy.

ADAM: I won't –

KAY: I'm going out of this world the way I came in. All by myself. That's the way I want it. And don't you feel sad, or bad, or anything. I'm off to see the end of the world.

ADAM tries to control his emotions.

KAY: How's Anna? Give me a final installment.

ADAM: Barely talking to me. I told her I was coming East but…it's probably just a coincidence but she had to go to a conference. Toronto. She's been giving a lot of papers this year. Doing incredibly well.

KAY: At least you skipped New York. That must have made you happy.

ADAM: No, no. I flew in to New York anyway. Saw Sean. Gave him another karate lesson. He's a good man, a very good man. He's clearly devoted to her. Rosie would have approved, he's very much a new man. He does nearly all of the cooking, he told me. Loves to cook.

KAY: He sounds like quite a guy.

ADAM: He is. I really think he is.

KAY: I'm glad. I always wanted everything to work out great for her. It had to be so tough losing her mother like that. *(Beat.)* I don't even know what she looks like.

ADAM: Would you like to meet her?

KAY: What real, live, in person?

ADAM: Yes.

KAY: I thought she wasn't talking to you.

ADAM: I could try.

KAY: I don't need to meet her. I like thinking of her knocking them dead in Toronto with a man in her kitchen waiting for her to come home.

ADAM: But I'd like you to meet her.

KAY: Too late.

ADAM: Do you want to see a photograph?

He gets a book out of his bag – ANNA's book. ANNA's picture is on the dust jacket.

KAY: That her? This her book?

ADAM: Yes.

KAY: Boy. Weighs a ton.

ADAM: I know.

KAY: You can tell her some time that when she died her hair blue I was the one who told you to get over it. *(Beat.)* Now get her book off my chest before it stops my heart completely.

ADAM takes the book.

ADAM: Can I hold your hand?

KAY: What do you think?

Long Pause. He takes her hand.

SCENE 14: ANNA AND HELENA ON THE TELEPHONE

HELENA is calling. She's in North Carolina.

ANNA: *(To HELENA.)* Hey!

HELENA: Hey! I didn't think you were going to pick up.

ANNA: I just got in. How is it?

HELENA: I've moved to a town that only has seven hundred and forty people in it, how do you think it is? *(No response.)* I feel so weird being back in the *South*, because as you know I have a lot of *shame* about it…

ANNA: Yeah, I just walked through the door. I heard your message. Your message said "help."

HELENA: You know what? I was trying to be funny. But I guess that's not so funny.

ANNA: It frightened me.

HELENA: Oh honey, I'm sorry. It's okay. I'm okay here. I love it. I can tell I'll love it. You know what? It is so beautiful. The trees around here, and the mountains – they are just gorgeous. And there are *stars*. You can see stars out here, Anna. I'm going over to my front door right now and…I'm looking at stars.

> *She opens her front door. Sure enough, stars. She sits down on her doorstep looking up.*

ANNA: When does school start?

HELENA: Tomorrow. A lecture. "Fundamentals of Massage: The Science of Touch."

ANNA: The *science* of touch. I like it.

HELENA: How are you?

ANNA: Working like crazy.

HELENA: How's Sean?

ANNA: Fine.

HELENA: Just fine?

ANNA: Yeah.

HELENA: So you guys are great?

ANNA: I'm worried I want to break up with him.

HELENA: Huh…

ANNA: I catch myself imagining he's having sex with someone else and I burst in and then I'm allowed. I'm allowed to leave him. The other day I was teaching and I suddenly imagined he had cancer, he was dying, and I was happy! Because then I could meet somebody else. I feel like I'm going to throw up?

HELENA: Are you okay? Anna?

ANNA: It's just...my heart's pounding.

HELENA: Are you sitting down?

ANNA: No.

HELENA: Sit down. And breathe. *(Beat .)* Are you sitting down? Are you breathing?

ANNA: I actually feel like I'm going to have a panic attack...

HELENA: Honey? Are you sitting?

ANNA: Yes! I'm sitting. Sorry.

HELENA: That's ok.

Silence. ANNA breathes.

ANNA: I am freaking out. I am freaking out. What if I want to break up with him?

HELENA: Can you talk? Do you think you can talk about it without having a panic attack? Or should we just stick with breathing? Because I can sit here on the other end of the phone with you and just breathe. I have got no problem with that. I have got all night.

ANNA: Everything's fine, between us, nothing's happened, it's just...I can't bear for him to touch me. Not at the moment. I sleep pushed up against the wall.

HELENA: You don't need to make a decision about anything right now. When your body's ready to make a decision it will make a decision. It will stay or go. You don't need to over think it.

ANNA: Okay. I don't want to talk about it any more, okay?.

HELENA: No problemo. How's the new book coming? Emily Dickenson?

ANNA: No time to write it. People keep asking me for articles about Keats. He's become my life partner. Could I be any more fucking esoteric and obscure?

HELENA: It's not just about Keats. It's not just about grammar. It's about art. It's about indicating, right, indicating, what is it you say in your book? That "seemingly insignificant details result in beauty!" I mean, that's what you're devoting your life to! To beauty! And if we don't have

beauty then what's the point of progressing! What's the point of recovering from cancer? What's the point of anything?

ANNA: God, I love you.

SCENE 15: A THRESHOLD, IRELAND

ANNA and LINDA sit with their backsides squarely inside the house and their legs outside. Bright sunlight. LINDA might wear sunglasses.

LINDA: The weather's not always like this, you know. This is very unusual weather for Ireland.

ANNA: That's what Sean said.

LINDA: You've been very lucky weather-wise.

ANNA: Yup.

LINDA: I must say it's been a pleasure meeting you. You're very nice.

ANNA: Thank you.

LINDA: No really. You're very, very, nice. I hope you'll come again.

ANNA: I hope so too.

LINDA: We've been like ships in the night, haven't we? All Seany's fault. You're a pleasure, you've been a pleasure. I was really nervous before you came, you know? I was incredibly nervous. The night before you arrived, I was up all night worrying about how to pretend to be a totally different person for a week but then you came and I hadn't the energy and then we had a little drink and we got on fine, didn't we?

ANNA: Absolutely.

LINDA: I shall miss you.

ANNA: It's not over. There's still two more days.

LINDA: Sean will be back with the sandwiches soon. Won't he be surprised? Seeing me on the front step.

ANNA: How are you feeling?

LINDA: Fine. I feel fine. That Xanax really is something.

ANNA: I'll leave you a few.

LINDA: I would never have thought that a tiny little pill could have such a huge effect. I mean, I'm not one hundred percent, you know. I wouldn't say that. I know that I'm frightened in my head. But my heart... steady as a rock. Incredible.

ANNA: I use them for flying.

LINDA: How do you get them?

ANNA: My friend Helena gave them to me.

LINDA: Is that legal?

ANNA: Absolutely not.

LINDA: Did your friend Helena not want to keep them for herself?

ANNA: No. Her mother, who is a psychiatrist, mails them to her. But Helena won't take them because she thinks it's her mother's way of trying to control her.

LINDA: Interesting people you know out there. *(Beat.)* I honestly can't believe I'm sitting on the step. If a neighbor walks by they'll shit.

ANNA: Is it people you're frightened of, or space?

LINDA: Oh I don't know. It's that there's a world out there. *(Beat.)* The attack was so long ago, I wonder if maybe even that has nothing to do with it. Maybe I was always to end up this way. Born with a deficiency of something.

ANNA: You haven't ended up this way. It's where you are right now.

LINDA: My brother says it would have been easier on me if they'd caught him. But they never did. I was no help at all. He was all a haze to me, you see. It was a day like this, a rare day, a warm day, and I fell asleep, and by the time I woke up again the mist was coming in, the light was leaving, and...I couldn't give the police a single detail. They said it was shock. They said he shocked all the details out of my head. My pretty little head. I overheard the doctor and that's what he said. He said "the bastard shocked every detail out of her pretty little head."

ANNA: I can't imagine...

LINDA: So no he was never caught.

ANNA: Most, I believe, aren't.

LINDA: That's right. Running free. When I can't sleep I imagine they found the one who did it. I get a telephone call. "Hello Linda," they say. "We've found him." So I go down to the station. They take me to a black room. A cell. He's chained up. Handcuffed. And they leave me alone with my man in the mist. And I walk up to his chair and I… Oh Lord. If you knew…you'd be amazed with the kind of things my imagination comes up with. Still. A long time ago. No need to be maudlin.

    Pause.

ANNA: After lunch, Sean wants to take a walk along the cliffs. He says there's no view more beautiful.

LINDA: It was always his favorite place.

ANNA: So he's says.

LINDA: *(Meaningfully.)* I know he really wants to take you there. *(Beat.)* There's heather, purple for miles just about. And you walk and you walk and there's only sea ahead of you. You're standing on an edge of the world. *(Beat.)* Shall we go in, have a nice cup of tea?

ANNA: I thought you wanted Sean to see you on the step. *(Beat.)* You'll make his day. *(Beat.)* I bet Claire would do this with you, if you wanted her too. Once in a while.

LINDA: Don't get your hopes up. You're not The Miracle Worker.

ANNA: Listen, I'm an American. I am terminally optimistic. I want to you to visit us in the States.

LINDA: *(Scoffing, but pleased.)* Visit you in the States. Have we not established that I'm bat shit crazy?

ANNA: Maybe one day you'll find yourself on a plane to America. See where we live. You've only seen a photograph of our apartment. And our apartment has only seen a photograph of you.

LINDA: A photograph?

ANNA: Sure. You're on the bookcase.

LINDA: What am I doing there?

ANNA: You're framed.

Pause.

LINDA: Fresh life. That's what you are.

SCENE 16: THE WOODS OF NORTH CAROLINA

HELENA marches, intrepid, through the woods. Finding a clearing, she stops and prepares herself and the space for meditation. Ready, she crosses her legs, closes her eyes and begins.

Enough silence to hear silence. Then a growl. The growl comes from a BEAR. HELENA opens one eye. She sees nothing troubling. She resumes her meditation.

Behind her, GIDEON enters. He has a rifle pointed beyond HELENA, off stage. HELENA hears GIDEON's footsteps, opens her eyes again, sees the gun.

HELENA offers up an earsplitting scream. Confusion.

GIDEON: Shhhh!

HELENA: What the fuck do you want? What the fuck do you want from me?

GIDEON: Ma'am…ma'am…

HELENA: I knew it! I knew it that one day I'd be raped!

GIDEON: Get down on the ground. I need you to stay very quiet.

HELENA: I bet you do you filthy son of a bitch!

GIDEON: There is a bear behind you.

> *HELENA whirls around and sees the bear. She screams again, even more loudly if possible and then throws herself to the ground and curls up into a tiny little ball.*

HELENA: Oh my God, oh my God, oh my God…

GIDEON: Stay calm now…

HELENA: Is this because I have my period?

GIDEON: This is because we're walking about where bears live.

HELENA: Is he still there?

GIDEON: It's a lady bear and yes she is. She's just watching us.

HELENA: Are you going to kill her?

GIDEON: Only if she charges.

HELENA: So we just wait?

GIDEON: That's right. That's what we do for the minute.

> *Beat.*

HELENA: Now what's happening?

GIDEON: Not much. She's just looking right at you.

HELENA: At me?

GIDEON: That's what she's doing right now.

HELENA: Can I look at her?

GIDEON: Sure. Sure you can. Just don't make direct eye contact.

> *From her fetal position, HELENA sneaks a peek at the bear.*

GIDEON: You know what we're going to do? We're going to back away slowly...

> *HELENA gets up, cautiously, staring at the bear.*

HELENA: I am making eye contact...

GIDEON: Ma'am, she's going to perceive that as a challenge –

HELENA: She's looking at me, I'm looking at her. "for I am as ugly as a bear, for beasts that meet me run away for fear." But she's not ugly. And she's not running away.

> *HELENA is crying. But for the first time in her life she cries tears of joy.*

HELENA: You're not ugly...

HELENA starts walking towards the bear.

GIDEON: Lady –

HELENA: We're not ugly...

GIDEON: Woman, get away from that bear, she'll rip your fucking head off.

HELENA: I don't think so…

>   *GIDEON shoots, HELENA charges him.*

HELENA: No!

>   *She knocks GIDEON to the ground, landing on top of him. This is not an un-erotic moment for either of them.*

GIDEON: There now. She's taking off.

HELENA: Are you blind? We were communing. I was communing with her and you betrayed the *trust* –

GIDEON: No…

HELENA: Yes.

GIDEON: I just saved your life, you crazy bitch.

HELENA: My. What happened to ma'am?

GIDEON: I just saved your life, Ma'am.

HELENA: Helena.

GIDEON: Helena. Gideon.

HELENA: Nice to meet you, I suppose.

GIDEON: You were not having a moment with that bear.

HELENA: No, I was. It was quite a profound moment actually. Until you spoiled it with your gun.

GIDEON: *(Grinning.)* Are you on 'shrums? Can I have some?

HELENA: You can make fun all you want but I looked in her eyes and she looked into my eyes and it was… it was life changing actually. I saw total acceptance. And she was feeling some –

GIDEON: Bears feel only three things. Hungry. Sleepy. And like they need to take a shit. They're a lot like men in that way.

HELENA: Oh God.

GIDEON: What?

HELENA: I hate it when men limit themselves like that. You can be so much more. You can be sensitive, and loving and complex and broken and …

GIDEON: *(Slowly.)* I find you *fascinating…*

HELENA: You do?

GIDEON: Where you from?

HELENA: I was living in New York but I moved out here just a few weeks ago.

GIDEON: That's a change of pace.

HELENA: Yup.

GIDEON: Well I've been out here fifteen years and they still call me a newcomer.

HELENA: What does that make me?

GIDEON: A baby.

HELENA: Where'd you move from?

GIDEON: Mississippi.

HELENA: I was also raised in the South.

GIDEON: No kidding, you're a Southern girl?

HELENA: Arlington, VA…

GIDEON: Well Helena, the South welcomes you back home. Welcome home.

> *HELENA kisses him on the lips.*

GIDEON: Me and my wife should have you over for dinner some night.

> *Pause.*

HELENA: Wow, you're married. That is great, that is so great. When did you get married?

GIDEON: Going on twelve years now.

HELENA: High school sweethearts?

GIDEON: Met in a bar.

HELENA: Any kids

GIDEON: Six.

>*Beat.*

HELENA: Six? You have six kids?

GIDEON: Ben, Megan, Rachel, Christian, Nick, and little Bethy.

HELENA: There's really no common ground here. Wow. Can I ask you something?

GIDEON: Shoot.

HELENA: How old are you?

GIDEON: I'm thirty-four.

HELENA: I'm thirty four.

GIDEON: Something in common, then.

SCENE 17: LINDA'S HOUSE, IRELAND

>*Lunchtime.*

LINDA: Anna is just lovely.

ADAM: Oh, I like Sean *v*ery much. Great guy.

LINDA: Good kids.

ADAM: Yes they are.

LINDA: I need to talk to you about the wedding. Before they get back. To get to those cliffs you have to walk.

ADAM: Anna said it's quite a way.

LINDA: Twenty minutes across the heather.

ADAM: Anna said you're a little agoraphobic.

LINDA: That's right.

ADAM: I was surprised when they told me where they were getting married. Seems a little selfish of them.

LINDA: No, they asked me. When they came back to tell me they were getting married, Sean said "Mammy we'd like to do it on the cliffs". And what could I say? I said "I think that's perfect."

ADAM: Are you concerned you won't be able to…should we push for a change of venue, do you think? After all the weather is against us anyway.

LINDA: No. I will walk on my two legs to those cliffs and I will stand there and watch my son marry. I promise you that. I wanted to tell you I was afraid. I might need your arm. I might need a man on steady legs beside me, understanding. My brother will be there but so will his wife. He'll be taken up with her, she'll probably be complaining about getting her heels stuck in the mud or something.

ADAM: I'd be happy to.

LINDA: Maybe take my arm or something.

ADAM: No problem.

LINDA: Thank you. Sean said you've traveled all over the world, seen all kinds of things, fought all kinds of battles you're not even allowed to talk about. He looks up to you. *(Beat.)* I expect you're almost never afraid.

ADAM: I was afraid ten minutes ago. I was afraid to ring your doorbell. A strange country, a strange house.

LINDA: It's kind of you to tell me that.

ADAM: I was afraid to get on the airplane. Afraid to come. All by myself. No wife. No…no other person. I will be grateful for your arm on the day of the wedding.

LINDA: I used to go to the cliffs all the time when I was a girl. Sean's right. It is the most beautiful view in all the world. *(Beat.)* I was raped there when Sean was eight years old. That was the last time I went.

ADAM: Do the kids understand what they're asking you to do?

LINDA: Not at all. They know that it happened. They don't know where. I would never tell them. This man, he took away many things from me, he never knew, I think, he was taking. There was a child. I aborted the child. The church aborted me. My husband left. My son and daughter grew up with a useless mother and no father at all. But I would not let this man destroy Sean's favorite place in all the world. And now I'm going back to watch my son marry there. And perhaps now *I* win.

SCENE 18: LINDA'S HOUSE, DONEGAL

LINDA, ADAM, MAX, HELENA all talking loudly, on top of each other, as big families do. That's the important thing. A cacophony.

MAX: It's going to rain –

HELENA: But Anna says –

LINDA: Sean is dead set on –

MAX: The forecast says rain, my darlings.

LINDA: What does it matter if people get wet? It's a tiny wedding.

HELENA: These are friends! They won't care if –

ADAM: But you have to consider, people have flown in –

HELENA: Is there a way we can erect a tent?

MAX: Not by tomorrow morning.

LINDA: The weather forecast isn't always right, you know. In fact it's always wrong!

Blackout. The sound of bells, not wedding bells, but a clock striking the time. Then, a howling wind.

SCENE 19: THE CLIFFS OF DONEGAL

We see the people we know – ADAM, LINDA, and MAX, standing in raincoats. The rest of the CAST is on stage, as WEDDING GUESTS.

HELENA fights to make herself heard above the wind and rain.

HELENA: Hello, I'm Helena and I will be officiating today. This is the first time I have done this so as you can imagine I am both excited and a little nervous – much as I imagine Anna and Sean are. It is after all the first time that they have done this too. I am not here as a representative of any church, or of any state. I have not been arbitrarily ordained on the internet. I am here not to marry them but to witness with all of you as they choose to marry each other. And what we are witnessing is the birth of a new family.

The wedding scene remains, at least at first, but what we hear, and probably see, is ANNA and SEAN late at night, their first real conversation.

SEAN: Tell me about where you grew up. The place you were born.

ANNA: Countryside.

SEAN: Yeah?

ANNA: Tall grass. Watercolor colors. That kind of thing. A lot of space. A lot of sunshine. A lot of play. I was a happy child. I didn't see my father much —

SEAN: How come?

ANNA: He's in the military.

SEAN: Army?

ANNA nods.

ANNA: When I did it was a treat, and when he was gone I had my mother all to myself. That's what every child wants anyway. I was lucky. Very, very lucky I think. Of course that's what made it so hard when she died. That she was my best friend. My therapist says —

SEAN: You have a therapist?

ANNA: Uh huh. *(Pause.)* This is New York City, that's what we do.

SEAN: Sure.

ANNA: Wow.

SEAN: What?

ANNA: You're making me feel really uncomfortable.

SEAN: Why?

ANNA: Because I say I have a therapist and a fucking cloud covers your face like —

SEAN: No.

ANNA: Yes.

SEAN: I've dated a lot of crazies.

ANNA: Were they in therapy?

SEAN: No.

ANNA: There you go.

> *Pause.*

SEAN: I'm sorry. I interrupted. What does your therapist say? About your mother?

ANNA: Never mind.

SEAN: I'm sorry.

ANNA: She said that my mother died before I had a chance to rebel against her. So it made her death particularly…

SEAN: Sure. *(Beat.)* My father died of a heart attack when I was eighteen.

ANNA: I'm sorry.

SEAN: I hadn't seen him for years. He left my mother. I think I stopped loving him. When he died I felt sad. But relieved almost. Free.

ANNA: I don't like the word "crazies." I like the word "troubled." You've dated a lot of *troubled* women.

SEAN: Have I?

ANNA: Apparently. *(Beat.)* I'm not troubled any more. Fragile sometimes, but I'm not troubled.

SEAN: That's nice.

ANNA: Tell me about where *you* grew up.

SEAN: Town. Covered in mist usually. Small town. Stony. Grey. Near the sea.

ANNA: Happy?

SEAN: No. Not me. I wasn't. Sometimes I was. But mostly sad. My mother was very sad you see. Something bad happened to her and she never got over it. So when I was growing up the sadness was like the mist, you know. Fucking everywhere.

ANNA: It's awful, isn't it?

SEAN: What is?

ANNA: Getting to know someone.

SCENE 20: TWO FIGURES, BRIEFLY ILLUMINATED

ANNA and SEAN are the only people on stage. They are somewhere quiet.

SEAN: A few drops of rain never hurt anybody.

ANNA: Could you even hear what you were agreeing to?

SEAN: I could hear. Could you?

ANNA: Yes.

SEAN: It was perfect.

ANNA: It was perfect.

Pause.

SEAN: I wish we didn't have to die.

ANNA: We won't. Not for a long time yet. Not for a long time.

END OF PLAY.

MIDDLETOWN

WILL ENO

Will Eno lives in Brooklyn. He is the recent recipient of a Residency 5 Fellowship at the Signature Theatre, where his play *Title and Deed* premiered in May 2012. His play *The Realistic Joneses* had its world premiere at the Yale Repertory Theater, in April 2012. His play *Middletown* was a winner of the Horton Foote Award and was produced at the Vineyard Theater in New York and Steppenwolf in Chicago. His play *Thom Pain (based on nothing)* was a finalist for the 2005 Pulitzer Prize and has been translated into many Romance languages and several Slavic ones. His work is published by TCG, DPS, Playscripts, Inc., and Oberon Books, in London. Other work has also appeared in *Harper's*, *The Believer*, and *The Quarterly*.

INTRODUCTION

Precious little is known of the dramatist's early life. It is understood, however, that while still in grammar school, young Wilton Eneaux (or, "Williston," as he was affectionately referred to by a phalanx of sisters and brothers as well as mothers and fathers, not to mention the family's shuffleboard tutor), evinced an exceptional fondness for dogs of every variety and that, a decidedly aimless, mayhaps even pathological child, subject to periodic bouts of weeping and pouting, the once-and-future playwright appeared to "find himself" when placed in charge of the naming of the ever-growing population of stray canines which strolled freely and peaceably among the struggling olive groves Father Eneaux had planted as a joke. There is no doubt that – for an all too brief while – a rusticated existence suited the emerging artist well. Classmates report, sniggeringly, that Wilton played an adroit game of quoits and gave every evidence of enjoying the eviscerating of weeds he happened upon wherever his larksome wanderings took him. But "the farm," or "here," as the family spread was affectionately referred to by the tradesmen who saw to the maintenance of its piteously dwindling supplies of firewood and baling wire, proved too constricting a setting for an artist to really go ahead and emerge. Wilton collected comb, hairbrush, and a favorite stick into a pillowcase and, accompanied by his pet suet (he'd named it Raoul in honor of the hounds Emily and Alice), bid "the farm" or "here," adieu, this in 1991, three weeks shy of his fourteenth birthday, thereafter traveling, penniless but with the sturdy suet at his side, by raft, to the mainland, which locals affectionately referred to as America. Halifax lay behind him – also France and the rest of Europe, whereas before him the theater and its insistent claims upon incipient genius now beckoned, plus called. Will (teenage Eneaux had abandoned his given name and adopted, in its stead, the name of his namesake) underwent not the first difficulty in establishing himself with... Okay, that's it – introduction, preface, foreword's over. Nothing should come between the work and those who would enter it. No notes, no mediation, no nothing – except, in this instance, the undersigned's irrelevant statement that he loves Will Eno and all Will Eno has wrought.

Gordon Lish

On November 3, 2010, *Middletown* premiered at the Vineyard Theatre (Douglas Aibel, Artistic Director; Jennifer Garvey-Blackwell, Executive Director; Sarah Stern, Associate Artistic Director) in New York City. It was directed by Ken Rus Schmoll; the set design and costume design were by David Zinn, the lighting design was by Tyler Micoleau, the sound design was by Jill BC DuBoff; the properties master was Lily Fairbanks, the production stage manager was Charles M. Turner III. The cast was:

PUBLIC SPEAKER	*David Garrison*
COP	*Michael Park*
MECHANIC	*James McMenamin*
MRS. SWANSON	*Heather Burns*
JOHN DODGE	*Linus Roache*
LIBRARIAN	*Georgia Engel*
TOUR GUIDE	*McKenna Kerrigan*
MALE TOURIST	*Ed Jewett*
FEMALE TOURIST	*Cindy Cheung*
GREG	*David Garrison*
AUNT	*Johanna Day*
SWEETHEART	*Olivia Scott*
FREELANCER	*Ed Jewett*
MAN	*Pete Simpson*
WOMAN	*Cindy Cheung*
LANDSCAPER	*Pete Simpson*
MALE DOCTOR	*David Garrison*
FEMALE DOCTOR	*Johanna Day*
ATTENDANT	*McKenna Kerrigan*
ATTENDANT #2	*Cindy Cheung*
JANITOR	*Pete Simpson*

Offstage voices of:

COP'S RADIO	*Johanna Day*
GROUND CONTROL (possibly seen onstage)	*Pete Simpson*
INTERCOM	*Johanna Day*
RADIO HOST (science show)	*Ed Jewett*
RADIO HOST (classical music show)	*McKenna Kerrigan*

Middletown opened at Steppenwolf Theatre Company (Martha Lavey, Artistic Director; David Hawkanson, Executive Director; Joy Meads, Literary Manager) on June 26, 2011. The director was Les Waters; the scenic designer was Antje Ellermann, the costume designer was Janice Pytel, the lighting designer was Matt Frey, the sound designer was Richard Woodbury; fight choreography was by Matt Hawkins, casting was by Erica Daniels, the stage manager was Laura D. Glenn, and the assistant stage manager was Michelle Medvin. The cast was as follows:

Alana Arenas
TOUR GUIDE, SWEETHEART, ATTENDANT 2, INTERCOM

Brenda Barrie
MARY SWANSON

Molly Glynn
FEMALE TOURIST, ATTENDANT, WOMAN ON DATE

Tim Hopper
PUBLIC SPEAKER, MALE TOURIST, GREG, FREELANCER, MALE DOCTOR, RADIO SCIENCE SHOW HOST

Ora Jones
AUNT, FEMALE DOCTOR, LANDSCAPER, JANITOR, GROUND CONTROL

Martha Lavey
LIBRARIAN

Tracy Letts
JOHN DODGE

Danny McCarthy
COP

Michael Patrick Thornton
MECHANIC

CHARACTERS
(in order of appearance)

PUBLIC SPEAKER	male, 40s-60s
COP	male, 30s-50s
MECHANIC	male, late 20s-30s
MRS. SWANSON	female, late 30s
JOHN DODGE	male, late 30s-40s
LIBRARIAN	female, 50s-60s
TOUR GUIDE	female, 20s-30s
MALE TOURIST	30-40s
FEMALE TOURIST	30-40s
GREG	male, 40s-60s
AUNT, FEMALE	40s-50s
SWEETHEART	female, 12-16
MAN	20s-30s
FREELANCER	male, 30s-40s
WOMAN	20s-30s
LANDSCAPER	male, 20s-30s
MALE DOCTOR	40s-50s
FEMALE DOCTOR	40s-50s
ATTENDANT	female, 20s-30s
ATTENDANT #2	female, 20s-30s
JANITOR	male, 30s-50s

ALSO, OFFSTAGE VOICES OF:

COP'S RADIO	female
GROUND CONTROL (possibly seen onstage)	male
INTERCOM	female
RADIO HOST, SCIENCE SHOW	male
RADIO HOST, CLASSICAL MUSIC SHOW	female

There is opportunity for double-casting of roles, but this should be done as unobtrusively as possible, and not for the purpose of commenting on the nature of any of the characters.

STAGE SETS

ACT ONE:
Window of Mrs. Swanson's house and Window of John Dodge's house
Library
Town Square
Seating for Intermission Audience

ACT TWO:
Window of Mrs. Swanson's house and Window of John Dodge's
house
Entrance and Lawn of Middletown Hospital
Doctor's office
John Dodge's hospital room
Loading Dock behind hospital
Mrs. Swanson's hospital room

A natural and unforced symmetry might exist between aspects of the sets in the
first act and second act. Specifically, between the Swanson and Dodge houses,
in the first, and the Swanson and Dodge hospital rooms, in the second; and,
between the Town Square and the Hospital Lawn and Entrance.

PROLOGUE

PUBLIC SPEAKER: Ladies and Gentlemen, Esteemed Colleagues, Members
of the Board, Local Dignitaries, everyone really, stockbrokers,
dockworkers, celebrities, nobodies, Ladies, Gentlemen, all comers,
newcomers, the newly departed, the poorly depicted, people who are
still teething, who are looking for a helping verb, the quote beautiful,
the unquote unbeautiful, whose bones are just so, whose veins are just
so, the drunk, the high, the blue, the down, *los pueblos, los animales,*
foreigners, strangers, bookworms, those whose eyes are tired from
trying to read something into everything, those at a crossroads, in a
crisis, a quandary, a velvety chair, the dirty, the hungry, yes, we the
cranky, the thirsty, the furious, the happy, who are filled with life,
bloated with it, gorged on words, and of course the bereaved, the
bereft, and let's not forget the local merchants, the smiling faces, the
placeholders, us, all we people slowly graying, slowly leaving, who make
all this all possible, this activity, this festivity, this hope, this dream
dreamt with open eyes, with closed eyes, friends of the deceased, the
diseased, friends of the disowned, and of course also healthy friendly
people with great skin and congenital heart defects, sports fans, sufferers
of autism, down-and-outers, non-believers, animal lovers everywhere,
real people people, with doubts, without certainty, with nothing else
worth mentioning, the majority of us, silent, stifled, delinquent, in the
background, barely hanging on, running out of time, hope, air, heart,
nerves, chances, money, blood, friends, courage, faith, hair, time, teeth,
time, time, health, hope, all of it, all of it, those *sans* everything, those
avec nothing, who can't stand it any longer, who never really could,
gentle gentle people, infinitely injured people, lost souls, ghouls, ghosts,
descendants, shades, shadows, future ancestors, Ladies, Gentlemen, I
know I'm forgetting somebody, friends, likenesses, darknesses, citizens,
people, hopeful people, hopeful people, everybody, every last lone dying
and inconsolably lonely person, fellow human beings, breathing people,
breathers, breathers...welcome. The fire exit's over there. I think you can
also get out this way.

SCENE 1

*Average evening. Middletown. COP enters and strolls across the dimly
lit stage. He comes to the window of a house, upstage. Through it,
illuminated, MRS. SWANSON is seen unpacking boxes, hanging a
painting on the wall, etc. COP stands outside, looking in. He strolls a
bit more, comes to another window of another house, upstage. Inside,
JOHN DODGE, illuminated, is seen sitting at a table, building a
pyramid of playing cards. COP stands outside, looking in. He strolls
a little more, twirling his police baton. He arrives at MECHANIC,
who is sitting on a bench, downstage, drinking out of a bottle in a
paper bag. MECHANIC eats something and throws the wrapper on
the ground, as COP nears. MECHANIC hides the paper bag upon
seeing COP approach.*

MECHANIC: Evening.

COP: Maybe. *(Referring to the bottle.)* I saw that. You think I'm a cop. I look
like a cop, I walk like a cop, so, you figure, case closed: I'm a cop.

MECHANIC: You're not a cop?

COP: No, I am a cop. You were right.

MECHANIC: Well, that's what I —

COP: *(Interrupting.)* That's what you thought. Everything is as everything
seems, I guess. Good for everything. What about you?

MECHANIC: What do you mean?

COP: What about you?

MECHANIC: I don't know. I mean, who knows, you know?

COP: No. What are you doing here?

MECHANIC: I don't know, I just went to the store. Later tonight, I thought
I might —

COP: *(Interrupting.)* Forget about before and after. I mean now.

MECHANIC: Well, I don't know, because I was —

COP: *(Interrupting.)* You don't know because you don't know. That's the
trouble, the beauty, the trouble. So let's just leave it at that. *(Motioning*

to the wrapper MECHANIC threw on the ground.) I think you dropped something. (*MECHANIC picks up the wrapper.*) The problem with people like –

MECHANIC: (*Interrupting.*) I was just sitting here, minding my –

COP: (*Interrupting.*) Don't interrupt.

MECHANIC: (*Long pause, as MECHANIC waits and does not interrupt.*) Was there something else you were –

COP: (*Interrupting.*) I thought I said, don't interrupt. You know what, I should just goddamn… (*Long pause. To AUDIENCE.*) Welcome. Hi, hello. Welcome to the little town of Middletown. Ordinary place, ordinary time. But aren't they all? No. They are not, all. (*To MECHANIC.*) Say something nice.

MECHANIC: (*To both the audience and to COP, with some unease.*) I'm just sitting here. I don't know what else. Um… (*He tries to think of something else.*)

COP: (*Pause. To audience.*) Right. Anyway, Middletown. Population: stable; elevation: same. The main street is called Main Street. The side streets are named after trees. Things are fairly predictable. People come, people go. Crying, by the way, in both directions.

MECHANIC: Ain't that the truth.

COP: (*Immediately.*) Why don't you get out of here.

MECHANIC: (*Defensively.*) Why? I'm not doing anything.

COP: And that's a reason you should stay? Let's go, move.

MECHANIC: Where?

COP: A different bench, I don't know, another perspective. Just not here, okay? In fact, you know what – here, allow me. I want to help you make a little speech. (*COP moves behind MECHANIC and begins to choke him with his baton, pulling it with both hands against MECHANIC's throat, from behind. MECHANIC struggles, unable to breathe, unable to get free.*) Say, "I just went to the store." Say, "This is my hometown." Say, "My life's a mystery to me." Say it! Be a good human. Be filled with humility. With wonder and awe. Awe! (*MECHANIC tries to speak, but is unable to breathe. COP continues to choke him.*) It's not easy, is it. Well, that's life. Listen, I'm sorry for what I'm still doing to you. Truly. But, don't worry. It'll be over in three, two, one... *(COP continues choking MECHANIC for three or four more seconds, and then releases him. MECHANIC tries to breathe, tries to recover. He begins to exit. To MECHANIC.)* Hey, no, I didn't mean you had to – *(MECHANIC mutters something. To MECHANIC.)* Wonderful, great. *(Brief pause. To AUDIENCE.)* Excuse me. I'm not exactly sure what I was hoping to.... I apologize. I was just trying to imitate nature. Anyway, welcome. Honestly. Middletown. *(COP exits.)*

SCENE 2

> *Morning. The library. LIBRARIAN is at her desk, on the front of which is a sign that reads* INFORMATION. MRS. SWANSON *enters.*

MRS. SWANSON: Good morning. I was hoping to get a library card.

LIBRARIAN: Good for you, dear. I think a lot of people figure, "Why bother? I'm just going to die, anyway." Let me just find the form. *(She looks through some paperwork.)*

MRS. SWANSON: I wanted to learn more about the area. Do you have any books on Middletown?

LIBRARIAN: I should certainly hope so – let me take a look. *(She searches on her computer, believes for a moment that she's found something.)* And... voilà. No, sorry, we don't. There's a wonderful book called *Yesteryear in Today's City of Tomorrow*. But it's out. It's due next Tuesday. *(MECHANIC enters.)* Hello.

MECHANIC: *(Passing through. His voice is somewhat hoarse.)* Hi.

LIBRARIAN: *(Searching on her computer.)* Here's something from the Chamber of Commerce, just to give you a general sense. *(She reads from the screen.)* "Middletown was built on the ruins of other older Middletowns, and, before them, a town called Middenton, which was named for being between two other places, both unknown and now incidentally gone." *(Stops reading.)* That doesn't sound right. "Incidentally gone." Anyway *(She returns to reading.)*, "A thousand years ago, the area was home to the Chakmawg Indian and it was called Inpetway, which no one knows what it means, but it might have meant, 'You are far away' or, 'Between the snowing.' The Chakmawg had a highly developed culture and they thrived in their time, until they disappeared, forever. New residents arrived and looked around." *(Stops reading.)* That's not much of a sentence. But I guess it still helps to give us a picture – people kind of lost and smiling. But, okay, let's see, *(She re-finds her place in the text and continues reading.)* "...arrived and looked around. Today, Middletown is a beehive, a human beehive, of activity and business. Many come to raise families and watch, swollen with civic pride, as their baby draws its first breath of local air. Also, drawn by the excellent clouds and the mostly silent nights, many come here to quietly retire. Middletown. We've got you coming and going."

MRS. SWANSON: That's from the Chamber of Commerce?

LIBRARIAN: I know. There's quite a lot they didn't mention. There's the library, here. And of course, the people. Which is what most places are made out of, if you think about it.

MRS. SWANSON: I guess. I'll wait for that other book. *(Brief pause.)* We just moved here.

MECHANIC: *(Looking through a magazine, far from the LIBRARIAN's desk.)* I'm listening in on your conversation.

LIBRARIAN: *(LIBRARIAN and MRS. SWANSON briefly look over at MECHANIC.)* Sorry. You were saying?

MRS. SWANSON: My husband and I just moved here.

LIBRARIAN: Well, welcome. Is it just you two?

MRS. SWANSON: It's just us. He travels. But we're here now. I am. We're trying to start a family.

MECHANIC: "Come on, family – start! Start, you bastard!"

LIBRARIAN: *(To MECHANIC.)* Shhhh. *(To MRS. SWANSON.)* Well, welcome to you both. That's wonderful. How long have you been trying?

MRS. SWANSON: Almost a year now.

LIBRARIAN: And I imagine it must be about the same for your husband. Well, good. Something you both can work on. Good for you. The world needs another person.

MECHANIC: *(Again, from across the room.)* Whatever you do, don't have an only child. They're the worst. Or so I've been told. Every time you hear a little noise, some little singing or humming, you look over, and there it is again, the same only child. *(Brief pause.)* I'm just being me.

LIBRARIAN: Don't mind him, he's only... *(To MECHANIC.)* You're just responding to things around you, aren't you, dear.

MECHANIC: Basically. *(Very brief pause.)* Hey, just did it again.

LIBRARIAN: *(To MRS. SWANSON.)* Is there something else I can help you with?

MRS. SWANSON: Do you have books on children? You must. On childbirth and children?

LIBRARIAN: We do. They're in the business section – I've never known why. I'll show you.

JOHN DODGE: *(Enters.)* Hi. Quick question. Books on gravity.

LIBRARIAN: Hi, John. *(To MRS. SWANSON.)* Let me just get him squared away. One second. *(Searching on her computer. To JOHN DODGE.)* Books about gravity. Let's see. We have two: *The Silent Killer* and another one called *Laws of the World.*

JOHN DODGE: The second one.

LIBRARIAN: That just came back. Let me go see if it's sitting on a roll-y cart somewhere. *(She exits.)*

MRS. SWANSON: Gravity. *(Brief pause.)* Hello.

JOHN DODGE: Hi.

MRS. SWANSON: We just moved here.

JOHN DODGE: That's great. Who's we?

MECHANIC: They're trying to start a family.

MRS. SWANSON: Yes, we are, *(To MECHANIC.)*, thank you. We is my husband and I. *(MECHANIC drifts off. To JOHN DODGE.)* You live here, obviously.

JOHN DODGE: That I do. Is it obvious? Ten years, now. Ten, fifteen years. In fact, I think we're talking fifteen, twenty years, now. Time, you know? "Whooooosh." "Clank."

MRS. SWANSON: I guess. And what do you do?

JOHN DODGE: More like, what *don't* I do.

MRS. SWANSON: Okay, what *don't* you do?

JOHN DODGE: *(Brief pause.)* You originally asked what *do* I do. So I'll
answer that. I do paperwork, lawn work, plumbing, sometimes some
house painting. I've worked graveyards, regular hours, happy hours.
Sure, sometimes, I'll just stare out a window, let a year go by, two years.
For instance, right now, I'm kind of between things. I'm between two
crappy jobs, I'm sure – I just don't know what the second one is, yet.
Give a call. I'm also trying to catch up on some reading. You might say
I'm bent on self-improvement, although I'm sure there's a better phrase.
(Brief pause.) What about you? Wait, let me guess. *(A pause, perhaps ten
seconds, in which JOHN DODGE stares at MRS. SWANSON and she waits
for him to guess.)* Yeah, I give up – no idea.

MRS. SWANSON: *(Following the above line very quickly.)* I used to manage a
restaurant. Before that I worked in a bank. Just jobs, you know. When
we get settled, I might do something else.

JOHN DODGE: You sound like me.

MRS. SWANSON: No, I don't. I do?

JOHN DODGE: Sort of. Not really. I hate how I sound. You don't sound like
me.

LIBRARIAN: *(Enters, with book.)* Here we are. Speaking of gravity, you
might be surprised to know we have a real astronaut from here.

MRS. SWANSON: I am. Wow.

JOHN DODGE: I bought a tandem bicycle from him. He was really friendly
when I brought it back.

LIBRARIAN: Oh, he's a complete gentleman. He has one of those haircuts.
He said he wouldn't be able to see us, way up there, but that he'd think
about us. Can you imagine? All that splendor, all that wonder and
beauty, and all you can say is just, "Houston this," and "Houston that."
To be so far away, with such a little vocabulary. *(She stamps the book
for JOHN DODGE.)* And then there's John, here, with his handyman
work and now his reading. Such *lively* people, our townspeople.
Always trying different things. Always occupied, somehow. *(To MRS.*

SWANSON.) And now you, too. *(Hands JOHN DODGE the book.)* There you go. Bye, John.

JOHN DODGE: Thanks. Bye. *(To MRS. SWANSON.)* Nice talking to you. Here's my card.

MRS. SWANSON: *(She looks at it.)* This says "Lucy Graves Associates: If you need help, we can help."

JOHN DODGE: Yeah, that's wrong, that's someone else's card.

MRS. SWANSON: Okay. *(Pause.)* Well, so, then, how would I get in touch with –

JOHN DODGE: *(Interrupting.)* Here, why don't I just write my name and number on that one. *(He does so.)* There we go. Problem created, problem solved. Bye. *(Exits.)*

MRS. SWANSON: Bye.

LIBRARIAN: *(To MRS. SWANSON.)* Now, you wanted books on children. What, specifically?

MRS. SWANSON: Health. Pre-natal health. And also maybe wallpapering. We want to get a room ready.

LIBRARIAN: It's so exciting. A room. Wallpaper. I love the patterns. Little flowers or fire engines – it's almost too much. Let me show you. *(They exit.)*

MECHANIC: *(Moves downstage and stands very still, looking through the audience.)* I was nervous, earlier. I don't know why. Well, I do know – for part of it, I was being choked. And I'm nervous now, now that I think of it. But, I'm nothing special, post-natally speaking. I fix cars, I try to. I get hassled by the cops, try to maintain a certain – I don't know – sobriety. Sometimes, I volunteer at the hospital, dress up for the kids. It was part of a plea deal. But, what isn't. Nothing really crazy to report. Except, I found this rock once, everyone. What I thought was a meteorite. I brought the thing into the school, here. The kids ran it through all these tests, tapped on it, shined lights at it. I found it in a field. It looked special. Then the astronaut here told me it was just a rock. Said it was probably from, at some earlier time, another slightly larger rock. His name is Greg Something. I had ideas about getting famous, getting on local TV with my meteorite. When it turned out to just be a rock, I thought I could still make some headlines with it if I threw it off a bridge, hit some family in their car and killed everybody. But then I figured, you know what, forget it, that's not me. So now some family's driving around, not knowing how lucky they are, not knowing how sweet it all is. Just because. *(Very brief pause.)* Wait, hang on a second. Do you... *(Pause. He stays very still and listens intently.)* I thought I heard something. *(Listens again for a moment.)* I'm still not convinced I didn't. Weird. Anyway, that was just a little local story. Although, you know, it almost had outer space in it. *(Brief pause.)* I wish that lady luck, with the family. People don't stop to think of how lucky they are. I do. And, I've realized, I'm not that lucky. But I get by. If I had more self-esteem, more stick-to-itiveness, I might have been a murderer. I was a child once. Like everybody. Some worried mother's son or distant father's daughter, sneaking around with a dirty face and an idea. My hand was this big. *(With thumb and forefinger he indicates the size of an infant's hand. About an inch and a half.)* I was somebody's golden child, somebody's little hope. Now, I'm more just, you know, a local resident. Another earthling.

    MECHANIC exits as LIBRARIAN returns to her desk.

MECHANIC: Bye.

LIBRARIAN: Were you looking for anything, in particular?

MECHANIC: No, I'm good. But thanks.

LIBRARIAN: Okay. *(She returns to working at her desk. Lights down.)*

SCENE 3

Same stage-set as in Scene 1. JOHN DODGE's house and the SWANSON's house. COP enters and strolls across the dimly lit stage, in the opposite direction of his earlier stroll. We briefly see MRS. SWANSON and JOHN DODGE in their windows, getting up to get a glass of water or something simple like that. COP speaks into his two-way radio.

COP: All units in the vicinity: see the man. See the man. See the woman. See the streets and houses, the shadows, the words that don't rhyme. All quiet here, over. No News is Good News, over. But there's no such thing as No News, over. Try to see my point. Just look at yourself, over. See the Universe. See a tiny person in the middle of it all, thrashing.

See the bright side. Try to look at the bright side. *(Brief pause. To AUDIENCE.)* Sometimes I'll talk like this, over the wire. Just to see if anyone's listening.

COP'S RADIO: *(Female voice.)*

(Very brief pause.) Someone's listening.

COP: Well, there you go. Now I know. *(Into two-way radio.)* Hi, Susan. Sorry. All clear.

> *He turns down radio, strolls. He comes to the window of JOHN DODGE's house. He stands outside, looking in. JOHN DODGE, illuminated, is inside, tossing a ball up and down, making notes. COP strolls to the window of the SWANSON house. MRS. SWANSON, illuminated, is inside reading. She stands, referring to her book and moving her hand over her belly.*

COP: *(He turns to AUDIENCE, moves downstage. Gently.)* I do like this time of day: night. All the people. All their bones and arteries and personal problems. Beautiful animal: the Person. Dark. *(Pause.)* I was too rough with that guy, earlier. I think I embarrassed him. Regrettable. I'm not myself. Sad stuff at home and I haven't been sleeping, but, I guess we all have a story. Once upon a time, Once upon a time, and so on, The End. *(Brief pause.)* I try to uphold the law, keep some order around here, but, I have my moods. I just remember screaming "Awe" at the poor guy. Hard word to scream. It just sounds like a sound. And you can't bully people into feeling something, anyway. Oh, well. *(Pause.)* We once almost had a Glass Museum, here. It would have been called the Middletown Glass Museum. Fact. *(Brief pause. He looks back toward the windows.)* Behold. You know, just, look. *(In their separate windows, we see JOHN DODGE, illuminated, tossing a ball up and down, making notes; and, MRS. SWANSON, illuminated, reading. She stands, referring to her book and moving her hand over her belly.)* This is what life is like, here, right now. *(Brief pause.)* Looking in people's windows at night makes you feel lonely. Lonely, but, lonely along with the people in the windows. Along with the whole world, the whole lonely billions. It feels sort of holy, in some screwy way. Fact. *(Brief pause.)* Fact.

SCENE 4

Bright daylight. Town Square. TOUR GUIDE is holding a clipboard and some maps. She is standing before a simple block of granite, which measures 4' by 4' by 4', and features a small plaque bearing an inscription in unreadably small letters. She checks her watch. A tourist couple arrives. MALE TOURIST has a camera hanging around his neck.

TOUR GUIDE: Morning. Are you here for the walking tour?

FEMALE TOURIST: We are. Hi.

TOUR GUIDE: Great. Hi. Have you done walking tours before?

MALE TOURIST: *(Looking at the monument.)* We went to Rome, last summer.

TOUR GUIDE: Oh. I bet you saw some serious monuments there.

MALE TOURIST: The whole place is history.

FEMALE TOURIST: We walked everywhere. We saw all the famous things. A lot of the ancient inscriptions are chipped off or just kind of worn away. And they're in Latin, so even if they were readable, you can't really read them.

MALE TOURIST: It's a dead language.

TOUR GUIDE: *(Referring to the monument.)* Well, this is in English, so people can enjoy it for years to come.

FEMALE TOURIST: What about when English dies?

TOUR GUIDE: Oh, I think English'll be around for a pretty long time.

FEMALE TOURIST: I doubt the Romans thought Latin was going anywhere, either.

MALE TOURIST: We went to Holland, two summers ago. Holland was a world power, a glorious empire, ruthless. *(Brief pause.)* We loved those "stroopwafels." They're, like, the local yummy snack. Ruthless empire; yummy snack. People change. Empires, too, is my point. So, ergo, I'm wary of monuments.

FEMALE TOURIST: He likes statues of horses, but, just the horse, no rider. Ergo... *(Small shrug.)* you know?

MALE TOURIST: I used to gamble – the ponies, trotters. I kept scribbly notebooks and had big dark circles under my eyes. Lost my job, my previous wife – not a long story. But, anyway, yeah *(Gesturing toward monument.)*, this makes me feel sort of sad and beautiful, sure, but not *that* sad and beautiful. *(Brief pause.)* Look at us. No, really look at me and her.

FEMALE TOURIST: Just because we don't look like pilgrims doesn't mean we're not pilgrims.

MALE TOURIST: I can see why you'd think we're just yahoos on vacation. But, we're serious people.

TOUR GUIDE: No, of course you are. *(Brief pause.)* I'm not sure what you – I mean, I don't know... I give this tour every day. I'm normally thinking about lunch or looking for another job – I'm not really focused on the next ten thousand years. What can I say? We don't have any other statu—

MALE TOURIST: *(Interrupting.)* I'm not trying to be difficult.

FEMALE TOURIST: *(Looking at monument.)* I sort of like it. It reminds me of my dad. *(They all look at it for a moment. To MALE TOURIST.)* But I can see what you're saying. *(To TOUR GUIDE.)* I guess we kind of like a strange angle on things. If we go to the opera or something, sometimes we specially request Obstructed View seats. It somehow adds to the whole experience.

MALE TOURIST: And they're cheaper.

FEMALE TOURIST: We love a bargain. You know that saying, "Politeness doesn't cost you anything"? Sometimes, that's what we'll do for the weekend. Just go around being polite.

MALE TOURIST: We've saved a fortune.

FEMALE TOURIST: But, so, yeah, I guess we just like some perspective.

MALE TOURIST: That's right. Perspective.

TOUR GUIDE: Sure, of course. *(Brief pause.)* I grew up here. *(Referring to monument.)* This thing was just always – I don't know – There. I'd see it in the rain and snow, serving its purpose. So that we remember, I guess. In general. So that we have memories.

FEMALE TOURIST: That's a thought.

TOUR GUIDE: I haven't traveled, ever. I'll walk around town, is about it. I'll notice a building or something. I'll look at people. I don't know. I grew up here. I thought this was the world.

MALE TOURIST: Of course you did. But, hey, let me get a quick picture of you being wrong. *(He snaps a photo of TOUR GUIDE.)*

FEMALE TOURIST: We always sort of want something more, I guess because there's a long history of death in both our families. I guess we like things that are potentially monumental, but that aren't necessarily monumentalized, yet.

TOUR GUIDE: Well, then, I don't know – *(Looking around.)* I guess then maybe that's everything else. Technically. *(Referring to the monument.)* Other than this.

FEMALE TOURIST: I guess.

TOUR GUIDE: I don't really know what you want.

MALE TOURIST: Just, something, you know. You're the one with the clipboard. *(He takes a photograph.)*

TOUR GUIDE: Well, okay. Take the air. I wrote on it in school. Take a deep breath. *(They do.)* A hundred years ago, someone was digging a hole here, for this very monument, and he rested on his shovel and sighed. You just inhaled a molecule of the air that shoveler exhaled, in that quiet sigh long ago.

FEMALE TOURIST: *(Inhaling again. Slightly surprised, as if she's sensed that particular molecule.)* Oh yeah.

MALE TOURIST: *(Inhaling again, he feels he's also sensed one of the ancient molecules.)* Definitely.

TOUR GUIDE: Yeah. I mean, think of how personal everything is, ultimately – these little sighs, going around in time and space. But then, think of a beautiful sunset on Earth, before human beings had ever evolved. It just beautifully sets. No one there to say, "Oooh" or "Ahhh," or something breathy like that. It just sets, and then it's night, nothing personal. *(MRS. SWANSON enters.)* Morning. *(To the group.)* Beneath us, okay, the dirt the sighing man was digging into? It's layers of fossils and broken pottery and things they think had religious value.

Maybe some sad little instrument, way down, a hollow bone with three holes in it. Down we go. Maybe a tooth or a piece of cloth. It's people strewn all the way through. Some of the dust on my shoes is from outer space; most of the rest is dead human skin. *(JOHN DODGE enters, opposite side of the stage, carrying a plastic shopping bag. He stops and looks inside it, checks his pockets.)* And there's a person, looking for something in a bag.

FEMALE TOURIST: It sort of completes the scene.

TOUR GUIDE: Sort of.

MALE TOURIST: *(Taking a photograph of JOHN DODGE.)* Look at him. Classic.

MRS. SWANSON: *(She leaves the group, saying "hi" to them as she goes.)* Excuse me. Hi.

TOUR GUIDE: *(To MRS. SWANSON, as she moves away.)* Hi. Bye. *(Brief pause.)* You know what – there's a meadow we could walk to. Just nice grass and trees, nothing noticeably historical going on.

FEMALE TOURIST: We got married in a meadow.

TOUR GUIDE: Then this'll bring back some memories.

MALE TOURIST: It really will. "Married in a meadow."

TOUR GUIDE: Okay, then. Onward. *(They exit.)*

SCENE 5

MRS. SWANSON, who has been standing off to the side, perhaps trying to remember JOHN's name, perhaps checking her hair, etc., approaches JOHN DODGE.

MRS. SWANSON: John? We met at the library. You gave me your –

JOHN DODGE: I remember. Sure. Hi. *(Still looking around.)* I think I bought something and left it at the store. That wasn't a very smart investment.

MRS. SWANSON: I've done that – it's so stupid. Hey, are you hungry? *(She sits down on a bench.)* I have some little sandwiches. I'm really hungry.

JOHN DODGE: That'd be great. *(Still thinking about whatever he lost.)* Damn it. *(Brief pause.)* I'm sorry – I would love a sandwich. *(He sits.)* Thanks.

MRS. SWANSON: Was that a tour going on?

JOHN DODGE: I'm sure it was something.

MRS. SWANSON: Here. *(She hands him a sandwich.)*

JOHN DODGE: Wow. They are little.

MRS. SWANSON: I have more.

JOHN DODGE: No, they're great, thanks. *(Brief pause.)* God, I had the worst night. Almost non-stop meaningful silence. Worst morning, too. Don't get married, that's my advice.

MRS. SWANSON: I'm already married.

JOHN DODGE: Oh, that's right, I forgot. Well, I hope you brought a good book.

MRS. SWANSON: I didn't know you're... Are you married?

JOHN DODGE: I was. All I remember is lying in bed, listening to the breathing. That's not true. We had some pretty good times. Probably my best. Yeah.

MRS. SWANSON: I'm sorry.

JOHN DODGE: It's sad. You sit around reading the side of a cereal box. Half the dishes are gone, half the cups, you eat everything out of a dented can, no more pretty shoes by the door, and, that's your little half-life. *(Brief pause.)* Definitely don't get divorced. I know, I'm all over the place on that one. *(Brief pause.)* Sorry. Are you getting settled here?

MRS. SWANSON: I am. We are. More and more. This is all a big change.

JOHN DODGE: What?

MRS. SWANSON: Here. And the whole idea of children.

JOHN DODGE: It is. I have two nieces.

MRS. SWANSON: Oh, how great – girls.

JOHN DODGE: They are great. You know what – it's just one niece, I think. The other one is her friend. I'm a terrible uncle. But, I don't know, I still feel like a nephew. Time, you know. "Buzzzzzzz." "Plink."

MRS. SWANSON: You said that the day we met.

JOHN DODGE: Something like it, I'm sure. It's a theory of mine.

MRS. SWANSON: It's not really a theory. You're just making different sounds with your mouth.

JOHN DODGE: So are you.

MRS. SWANSON: True. "True." *(Brief pause.)* How's gravity?

JOHN DODGE: It's all right, I guess. *(Brief pause.)* What?

MRS. SWANSON: You were reading a book about gravity.

JOHN DODGE: Oh, right. That's over. I just kind of lost the... you know. I mean, do I really need to know about that? Anyway, now, I'm taking this course on watercolor painting.

MRS. SWANSON: You're quite a Renaissance man.

JOHN DODGE: It's not really a course. It's just the directions that came with the paints.

MRS. SWANSON: Well, still, it sounds great.

JOHN DODGE: It's not. It's just some other thing.

MRS. SWANSON: I would think you'd make a really good uncle.

JOHN DODGE: I would too, but, yeah, no. I get, I don't know – I panic. Who wants a panicky uncle? I don't know. I get anxious, you know? I forget everybody's name and birthday and get all nervous and worried I won't recognize people.

MRS. SWANSON: I feel that way sometimes.

JOHN DODGE: Me too.

MRS. SWANSON: *(Brief pause.)* So, Bob is finishing up some things with work and our old house. He just started up in a new position. He should be here soon. I still don't really know the place. It can get lonely, can't it.

JOHN DODGE: Yeah. You get the mail, it's a clothes catalog. Maybe you leaf through it, maybe think, "Hey, I could buy those pants." Then you think, "But then it'd just be me, again, in a different pair of pants." Then you go out and walk around, and that's your day, time for bed.

MRS. SWANSON: That's kind of gloomy. I like looking at catalogs. Things aren't so bad. I visit Bob here and there, if he's at a convention or something nearby. He's in sales.

JOHN DODGE: I always wanted to be in something.

MRS. SWANSON: Yeah? Well, I'm sure you'll, you know....

JOHN DODGE: Yeah? That's nice. Thanks.

MRS. SWANSON: *(Brief pause.)* I've been having trouble sleeping.

JOHN DODGE: Oh, God – night-time. Daytime, too. I'm like, "Enough – I get it." *(Brief pause.)* I read articles about identity theft and I actually get a little jealous, you know? "Just take it," you know. "Good luck, fella." Sometimes, I think I should just go quietly retire, you know, alone in the bathroom, with an X-acto knife. But then I start up some dumb project or get a book about some idiot thing.

MRS. SWANSON: *(With real sympathy.)* John.

JOHN DODGE: You have a nice voice, um... I'm sorry...

MRS. SWANSON: Mary.

JOHN DODGE: Mary, of course. I like it.

MRS. SWANSON: We all have our dark nights. We're probably never as alone as we think.

JOHN DODGE: Yeah, no. We hope. *(Brief pause.)* I heard what you said. It probably seemed like I didn't, but I did. I'm really sorry you can't sleep.

MRS. SWANSON: Me too. No, thank you. *(Moved, by even this very small kindness.)* I know you're just making sounds with your mouth again, but, thanks.

JOHN DODGE: I haven't asked you a lot about yourself.

MRS. SWANSON: Is that...are you asking now?

JOHN DODGE: No, or, I don't know – I just suddenly tried to picture you not sleeping. Sometimes you get used to the words for things, and then you suddenly remember the things. And so I suddenly saw you, the real Mary, not a word, staring out a window, or crying or reading, whatever you do.

MRS. SWANSON: I do read, sometimes. Or, yeah, sometimes, cry. That's nice of you to – it's nice you would picture me. In tears, or reading. *(Brief pause.)* Night is hard, you know? It gets so quiet. I never know what I'm supposed to be listening to. *(Brief pause.)* But it does give me time to catch up on my needless worry.

JOHN DODGE: *(Small laugh.)* I do that – what you just did.

MRS. SWANSON: What?

JOHN DODGE: Use humor to try to distance myself from the pain.

MRS. SWANSON: I was using humor to try to be funny.

JOHN DODGE: Yeah, no, that's something different. *(Brief pause.)* If you ever need any help, I'm pretty good with the needless worry.

MRS. SWANSON: The other night, I couldn't stop thinking, "What if my taste buds stop working?"

JOHN DODGE: Massive heart failure in a public place.

MRS. SWANSON: You can do better than that. Plus, that's really more of a guy thing.

JOHN DODGE: Cancer, in the privacy of your own home.

MRS. SWANSON: Now you're talking. The old standby. And, yes, good – something for the ladies.

JOHN DODGE: *(Without having laughed.)* It's good to laugh. *(Brief pause.)* I like that thing you said – "dark nights."

MRS. SWANSON: I guess all nights are dark, but you know what I mean. *(Brief pause.)* Oh, I almost forgot. I'm hoping you can come have a look at something.

JOHN DODGE: I'd love to. What?

MRS. SWANSON: A plumbing thing. I think it's just a clogged drain.

JOHN DODGE: I was thinking maybe it was a painting or a sunset or something.

MRS. SWANSON: No. *(Small smile.)* Sorry.

JOHN DODGE: Yeah, I'll take a look. I could use the work. Not that I'd charge you. *(He gets up.)* Speaking of not making any money, I should get going. Hey, what's today?

MRS. SWANSON: Tuesday. *(Or whatever the actual day is.)*

JOHN DODGE: Oh, shit. I thought it was Monday. *(Or whatever the actual day before would be.)*

MRS. SWANSON: Sorry, again.

JOHN DODGE: I probably would have found out eventually.

MRS. SWANSON: I'll give you a call. Bye, John.

JOHN DODGE: Bye, Mary. It was really nice talking.

MRS. SWANSON: It was. Thank you. We should – yes. Definitely. Bye, see you later. *(He exits. She begins to exit, then sits back down, lights fade.)*

SCENE 6

LIGHTS suggest evening. LIBRARIAN, with her purse and some books, enters.

LIBRARIAN: *(To AUDIENCE.)* That book came back today. I was just reading. Here: *(She reads, periodically clarifying terms for the AUDIENCE.)* "Life had gone on. Several moons had passed." *(Clarifying.)* Several months. *(She reads.)* "The medicine man" – a medicine man is a doctor – "The medicine man shook his feathers. The villagers stood, shivering. A star shone over Inpetway." That's here. It was. *(She reads.)* "The medicine man spoke in difficult ways of difficult things, in the worried vocabulary of medicine and night. The villagers listened quietly, and quietly misunderstood. The sick man listened, and quietly got worse." For "sick man," just think of anybody, an average person. A child has written in the margin here: "anxiety, sickness, death, spiritual." *(She quickly shows us.)* She writes in these wonderful loopy letters in a bright red pen. At least, I think it's a girl. *(She reads.)* "The medicine man continued – differently, now. His calm eyes sparkled slowly, as he turned to the blushing woman there." The "blushing woman" is probably a bride or a woman falling in love. *(She reads.)* "He spoke now in simple ways of simple things. He asked the moon to be beautiful. He asked the sun to come to warm the unborn child and the born mother. He asked the people to be human and the animals to stay animals. He asked the Universe to expand. He said, deeply, to all of them, "Great things. Oh, Great things. Someone is born, someone will die, both are you. Unwind, unknow." The same little girl has written a question mark, here. *(Brief pause.)* I read once the question mark comes from a musical notation used in Gregorian Chants, to signal that the phrase should have an upward intonation, that it should rise upward, to heaven. Imagine this little red one here – no sentence, no question, just a little red question mark, by itself – rising up to heaven, to God. Imagine the look on His face. *(Leafing forward a few pages.)* Later, she's written the word "atmosphere." And here's a barrette she used for a book mark. Ah, literature. *(Brief pause. Looking up.)* It's a beautiful night. Whether or not there's anything up there.

SCENE 7

GREG is seated in a chair, tilted sideways, facing the AUDIENCE. He is in a space capsule, floating. The following lines are amplified, with some static and perhaps some delay, as though a radio transmission. GROUND CONTROL may be seated on stage, perhaps facing away from the AUDIENCE.

GROUND CONTROL: Cormorant Nine. *(Pause.)* Cormorant Nine. This is Ground Control, Houston. Do you read? Do you copy?

GREG: This is C-9. Copy. Sounds like you're in my living room. Over.

GROUND CONTROL: The things we can do. Go ahead, C-9. How's life?

GREG: What a view, is one thing. I've heard about it. But, what a wonderful... I never knew how round round was, Houston. God. All this space, it's just pure majesty, it's endless, majestic. But it's cold, it's almost just raw data, raw mathematics. Then you see little planet Earth and – my God, she's just so welcoming and good. Seems like a symphony should be playing. It, wow, it's just this beautiful fragile thing, something a happy child would draw. It's so blue. Houston.

GROUND CONTROL: *(Indistinct sentence. Something like, "Fivv – . Gull sensor. Ooh min. Ive.")*

GREG: Repeat, please.

GROUND CONTROL: Fifty-one degrees. Angle sensor arm, two minutes forty-five.

GREG: Copy. Arm is in position. *(A short indistinct sentence.)*

GROUND CONTROL: What's that? Didn't catch that.

GREG: *(Pause.)* Sorry?

GROUND CONTROL: Go ahead, Greg.

GREG: Oh. I'm just trying to picture life, back home in the old hometown. There's a guy there I remember, thought he found a meteorite, once. It was normal sedimentary rock, just made from dead animals and plants crushed together. He was disappointed. Shouldn't have been. I was never crazy about him, I think he bashed my mailbox in, but, he shouldn't have been sad. That rock, that guy who found it, the field he found it in, all these things are miraculous because all these things are earthly. The words he used to refer to it, the breath it took to make the words, all of it. Just sacredly and profoundly and mysteriously – well, yeah – earthly.

GROUND CONTROL: Are you getting mystical on us, Greg?

GREG: I'm just looking and talking, Houston. I didn't prepare anything.

GROUND CONTROL: Just giving you a hard time, partner.

GREG: Okay.

GROUND CONTROL: Looking good. Go ahead.

GREG: I'm done. But I just have to say, it doesn't look lonely from up here. Everything looks right-next-door. It's where you're sitting, right now. How 'bout that. You're breathing the Earth's atmosphere. You got mountains and clouds, oceans. People out doing things together. Inexpressible, you know. How'd we get so lucky? *(Brief pause.)* I probably sound like a real cliché. Me, with my chiseled features and the flight suit, waxing all poetic. Waxing all fragile and religious.

GROUND CONTROL: All right, Greg. *(Brief pause.)* Synchronize, one seven six.

GREG: Synchronize.

GROUND CONTROL: Copy. *(Pause. Garbled static.)* Say again, Cormorant Niner?

GREG: I didn't say anything. Go ahead, Houston.

GROUND CONTROL: Roger. No matter. Looking good. We do recommend P65 alignment, plus point two two.

GREG: Thank you – P65, plus point two two. *(Brief pause.)* I'm looking out at the world. I'm thinking about people. I can't tell you what this is like. Over.

GROUND CONTROL: Copy.

GREG: Maybe everybody knows what this is like.

GROUND CONTROL: Maybe they do. Wunderbar, Greg. Looking good. We have no abnormalities. Over.

GREG: Roger. Oxygen is good.

GROUND CONTROL: Whoa – fuck. Sorry. I almost spilled something.

GREG: Careful, down there.

GROUND CONTROL: Yeah, I know. All right, partner. Come home soon.

Static. Static fades.

SCENE 8

The SWANSON's kitchen. JOHN DODGE is working on the kitchen-sink drain. He is lying on the floor, periodically ducking in and out of the cabinet, and therefore periodically inaudible. At the top of the scene, JOHN DODGE is on his back, his head and upper torso hidden in the cabinet. MRS. SWANSON is at the kitchen counter.

MRS. SWANSON: No, seriously, John, thanks for helping out. Bob and I are grateful.

JOHN DODGE: *(Appears from under the sink to grab a wrench.)* No, it's no trouble. When does he get here?

MRS. SWANSON: Any day, I hope. It's crazy. We used to just be regular people. We said "good night" and "good morning," every day. All of a sudden we're so modern. It's funny. *(Brief pause.)* Have you always done this kind of work?

JOHN DODGE: God, yeah. In fact, I've been thinking about that philosophy thing about how you can't step in the same river twice. It turns out you can. Sometimes, I feel like I should just... I don't know. I try, you know, but some days it all just seems like the,... *(Disappears under the sink. Indecipherable end to the sentence.)*

MRS. SWANSON: I know. I know what you mean. Everything suddenly looks like it's spelled wrong, or something. Like, even your own name looks like a typo.

JOHN DODGE: Yeah, exactly. I'm always getting, I don't know, I told you this, I get these awful panic attacks. They're actually how I stay in shape. It's a mess. Enough about me, and how I sometimes get claustrophobia and can't swim. *(Indistinct short question: an indecipherable version of "So how does it feel being pregnant?")*

MRS. SWANSON: What?

JOHN DODGE: *(Repeated mainly as before.)*

MRS. SWANSON: Oh. It's so new. I don't think I could even describe it. I'm really excited. But it's almost like it's just words, at this point.

JOHN DODGE: *(Indistinct medium-length sentence. An indecipherable version of "It's probably just words at every point.")*

MRS. SWANSON: You're probably right – it's just words at every point. It scares me, though. Having a baby. The words seem so tiny and quiet, compared to the truth of it. Compared with if you really try to picture it. Not to mention, just, the whole thing. I mean, do I look like the kind of person?

JOHN DODGE: *(Indistinct sentence: an indecipherable version of "I think you're quite intoxicating.")*

MRS. SWANSON: Well, thank you, John. I don't think I've ever been called "intoxicating" before. That's very flattering.

JOHN DODGE: *(Appears.)* I hope you don't think of me as just some kind of a... I don't know. Because I have so much going on inside me. A lot of different.... *(Brief pause.)* You know, people laughed when I said I wanted to get a law degree.

MRS. SWANSON: You have a law degree?

JOHN DODGE: Me? Oh God no. People really laughed, though. *(Brief pause.)* I've wanted a lot, out of life. First, air and milk, and then it just kept going.

MRS. SWANSON: Well, you've gotten a lot, too, haven't you? In life?

JOHN DODGE: I had shingles, once. I'm kidding. Well, no, I'm not, actually – I did have that. Good argument for death, by the way – shingles. Nice reminder your skin's an enemy.

MRS. SWANSON: Your skin's probably your best friend.

JOHN DODGE: For a while, sure. *(Very brief pause.)* I have a kind of serious mind/body problem. But, I know what you're saying. I try to be grateful for what I have.

MRS. SWANSON: Good. I wish I had more gratitude. When you think of all the miracles it takes just to sit in a chair. A billion things going right, just to sit here. And do nothing. And watch you work. Miracles.

JOHN DODGE: You get used to them, though. That's the sad thing. You look around: miracle, miracle, miracle. It's tiring. It's sad. Or scary. *(Indistinct short sentence.)*

MRS. SWANSON: That's kind of extreme, isn't it? But, I guess, to be completely honest, it's always an option.

JOHN DODGE: *(Indistinct short sentence. Indecipherable version of: "Except for the fact that I'm afraid of dying.")*

MRS. SWANSON: *(Laughing.)* You can say that again. Oh, Johnny Boy, you can say that again.

JOHN DODGE: *(Appearing from under the sink.)* That "I'm afraid of dying"?

MRS. SWANSON: I thought you said something different.

JOHN DODGE: No. *(He removes a handful of sludge from the drain, puts it onto a piece of newspaper.)* There.

MRS. SWANSON: Yuck. Is that the problem?

JOHN DODGE: Yeah.

MRS. SWANSON: What is it?

JOHN DODGE: Just years of stuff. Sort of a metaphor for, yeah, no – just years of stuff, gunk. *(He stands up, and is slightly disoriented.)* Whoa. I stood up too quick. My whole life, I don't think I ever stood up at the right speed. All life long, John Dodge in the wrong. "All life long," wow, that's hard to say.

MRS. SWANSON: No it isn't.

JOHN DODGE: *(Effortlessly.)* "All life long." No, you're right – it isn't. I think I better sit down for a few seconds. *(He sits down.)* One one-thousand, two one-thousand, three one-thousand. Okay. *(He stands up, same disorientation.)* Wow. Did it again.

MRS. SWANSON: *(She takes his hand.)* Maybe you're just a dizzy person. They say some people have trouble with the Earth's, you know, with the rotation.

JOHN DODGE: Yeah, maybe that's – yeah. *(Brief pause.)*

MRS. SWANSON: John.

JOHN DODGE: Again, she says, in her nice voice, "John."

MRS. SWANSON: *(Small slightly nervous laugh.)* Well, what am I supposed to say? *(Brief pause.)* Are you all right? *(She lets his hand go. Very brief pause.)* We haven't known each other very long, but, do I seem different?

JOHN DODGE: How?

MRS. SWANSON: I don't know. Somehow. Inside.

JOHN DODGE: Yeah, I don't know. Kind of. Yeah, you do.

MRS. SWANSON: *(Small smile.)* Good.

JOHN DODGE: Change.

MRS. SWANSON: I know.

JOHN DODGE: You smiled when you said "Good." That says a lot about you. You look really well. I bet you'll be a radiant mother. *(Pause.)* I don't have anything, Mary. Sorry, big change of topic, but – I don't.

Look at me. I have a bunch of hobbies I quit and some overdue books I never read. I don't have anything.

MRS. SWANSON: Yes, you do. Come on. Yes, you do.

JOHN DODGE: Mary, I don't.

MRS. SWANSON: Maybe you're not looking hard enough.

JOHN DODGE: *(Pause. Short indistinct sentence, somewhat clearly vocalized.)* Mome gavnerma thurn.

MRS. SWANSON: What?

JOHN DODGE: Just joking, because of the – *(He points to the cabinet.)* Remember when you couldn't hear me?

MRS. SWANSON: Oh, right. *(She covers her mouth and says an indistinct line, about five syllables long, perhaps something like "Gabralldee yo fon gerg fonderall.")*

JOHN DODGE: Hmm. I never thought of it that way. *(They share a little laugh. Very brief pause.)* Mary, I'm looking as hard as I can. *(Lights down. MRS. SWANSON and JOHN DODGE remain, for a moment.)*

SCENE 9

COP enters darkened stage with powerful flashlight. Perhaps he comes into the AUDIENCE. Behind him, INTERMISSION AUDIENCE enters and is seated, facing actual AUDIENCE.

COP: *(He shines the light into the face of an actual AUDIENCE member. Moves the light to another AUDIENCE member, and then another.)* Don't worry. People always look so worried. *(Shines light around the stage.)* We got a report of some problem, down here. Some trouble. A scream, maybe a loud sigh, a couple of sighs, something. I'm sure it's fine. Just normal people being human in the night. Inner life meeting outer life. Bang. Kapow. But, yeah. Nothing to worry about. *(He shines the light back over the stage.)* Sleep tight, pretty Middletown. All is well. *(Flashlight goes out. COP bangs it on his leg a couple of times. It comes back on.)* There we go. *(Brief pause.)* Okay. Pray the Lord your soul to keep. Something like that. Whatever makes you feel calm. *(Brief pause.)* Just be all right. *(He exits.)*

SCENE 10

The INTERMISSION of this play. Lights that suggest house-lighting come up. Recorded applause. The INTERMISSION AUDIENCE, seated on stage, applauds. It is made up of FREELANCER, MAN and WOMAN (on a date), SWEETHEART (a young woman with a mild mental disability) and her AUNT. Some have programs for "MIDDLETOWN". Almost all of SWEETHEART's lines are said very loudly, but not shouted. FREELANCER is writing in a notebook.

AUNT: *(Brief pause.)* I should have brought a sweater. Are you cold, sweetheart?

SWEETHEART: Feelings.

AUNT: Remember, we're inside. *(To others.)* Excuse me. *(To SWEETHEART.)* Would you like some candy?

SWEETHEART: "What about when English dies."

AUNT: Nice and quiet, dear. *(Gives SWEETHEART some candy.)*

FREELANCER: That's from the play. *(He writes.)*

MAN: *(Standing and stretching.)* Excuse me. *(He exits.)*

AUNT: *(To FREELANCER.)* You're very busy.

FREELANCER: I'm writing a book on being an audience member. Originally, I wanted to be an autobiographer.

AUNT: Oh?

FREELANCER: Yeah. But then I had to sit down and ask myself, "Seriously? Me?"

AUNT: What do you like to go see?

FREELANCER: Oh, God, anything and everything. I've seen horses being born, Egyptian tombs being exhumed. I've gone whale watching, I watched my poor mother die, saw a Hindu bathing festival, a total solar eclipse, you name it. Mainly plays. Sometimes, I have anxiety attacks when the curtain goes up.

WOMAN: I always want to cry at the end. When you see the actors smiling and bowing in the light. Dead kings waving to their wives and girlfriends.

SWEETHEART: "Be a good human."

FREELANCER: That was in there, too, right at the beginning. I have the worst memory. But I like to write down lines. *(As he writes down the line. To AUNT.)* Your daughter has an amazing memory.

AUNT: She certainly does. She's my niece.

FREELANCER: Well, she has a very good memory. *(To SWEETHEART.)* What's your first memory, ever? *(Long pause. No response from SWEETHEART.)* It's hard, isn't it. *(Brief pause.)* I was always sitting somewhere. I was born in the audience.

AUNT: *(Brief pause.)* I like when plays have a break in the middle. Once, we met an oceanography student. *(To SWEETHEART.)* Remember, he painted the garage? It's nice.

FREELANCER: It's funny, though. Since you don't know the end, you're not sure what you're in the middle of. Hey. *(Pleased with the thought, he writes it down.)*

MAN: *(Enters.)* Much better. Are we talking about the play? Let me ask, so the town is like a –

AUNT: *(Interrupting.)* The town is called Middletown. But it has other names.

MAN: Yeah, I got that. But the people are –

AUNT: *(Interrupting.)* I think the main two are having a romance. They represent the future, I think.

MAN: Thanks. I really enjoyed that.

WOMAN: I had a neighbor like the John guy. If you talked to him, he would listen so hard, but you weren't sure what he was listening to. He finally left or something bad happened. It was really sad. He didn't have anybody. At least, the guy in the play has the lady who just moved in.

AUNT: Mary.

SWEETHEART: "Houston."

AUNT: *(To SWEETHEART.)* Houston is in Texas.

SWEETHEART: "Your daughter has an amazing memory."

FREELANCER: *(Standing, stretching.)* My back is killing me. I think it's growing into the shape of a chair.

SWEETHEART: "I have the worst memory."

WOMAN: *(Brief pause.)* You know what's funny? So, everything, in a way, is still going on. Time's going by, in the town, at the library, in outer space, here – all over. In a fictional way, of course, but, at the same time, like, non-fictionally, too.

MAN: Relativity.

WOMAN: *(Brief pause.)* Is that your contribution?

MAN: Yeah. Just, everything's all... I don't know – Sir Albert Einstein.

WOMAN: I don't think he was ever knighted, but, okay. *(To AUNT and FREELANCER.)* But, do you know what I'm saying? Something's coming.

AUNT: But we don't know what.

WOMAN: Neither do they. They're right in the middle of some life in some town – you know, in a way.

AUNT: They deserve something good. We all do.

SWEETHEART: "Life."

AUNT: It's quite a topic, isn't it. I think she's pregnant, Mrs. Swenson. There's always a glow, a kind of shadow. You can tell.

FREELANCER: It's always a possibility.

MAN: So is suicide.

WOMAN: Where did that come from?

MAN: I don't know, my mouth? Where does anything come from? Where do crocodiles come from?

FREELANCER: Dinosaurs. But where do dinosaurs come from? And so on, down the ages. Until we're asking, "Where did nothing come from?" King Lear has an answer. King James has another.

MAN: I was just floating it out there. I don't know – somebody said "possibilities." *(Brief pause. Shaking his foot.)* Man, my foot is totally asleep. It must be bored.

FREELANCER: This one culture whose name I forget thought the soul was in the feet. Other peoples have located it in the hands, or the eyes, the heart, all over the whole body.

SWEETHEART: "Peoples."

WOMAN: *(To SWEETHEART.)* Yeah. *(Brief pause.)* It's funny. The Soul. The Afterlife. We say words like that like we say words like Shoe and February. But, just honestly, just imagine, for one second.

MAN: It changes things. Life.

WOMAN: Mm hmm. *(To FREELANCER.)* And it's like the thing you said. You don't know what the end is, so how can you know what you're in the middle of? They don't know what happens to you when you die, so how can they know, really, what happens to you when you're born?

FREELANCER: A serious mystery, then the middle part, then another mystery. Very good. *(He gestures that he'd like to write this down. To WOMAN.)* May I?

WOMAN: Please. *(FREELANCER writes.)*

MAN: Hey, so, where's the husband, anyway? Is he supposed to represent something?

AUNT: Just a regular human being, I think. Maybe they have weekends together. People always figure something out. We're always scurrying around, looking over our shoulders, figuring something out. People. *(Brief pause.)* We saw a play once that had an angel in it. A school production or some kind of community thing. Remember?

SWEETHEART: "Just a regular human being, I think."

WOMAN: *(To SWEETHEART.)* You get everything word for word. It's a real gift. *(No response.)*

FREELANCER: It's strange, though. It's like a museum exhibit about the last ten minutes. But it is – you're right, she's incredible. What a thing. Language, you know. Repeatability. Time, grammar, us. Weird.

WOMAN: Is, Was, Will be.

FREELANCER: That pretty much covers it. *(Brief pause.)* I've been all over the world.

AUNT: *(Musingly.)* "Is, Was, Will be."

WOMAN: *(Nodding.)* Story of my life.

FREELANCER: I've seen so many things. Huh.

MAN: *(Having noticed the armrest of his chair is loose.)* Look at this. *(He holds up the detached part.)* This just comes completely off. *(He reattaches it.)*

FREELANCER: All that travel, all the cathedrals and wonderful meals and evening light and people dying, and what are my findings? What's my conclusion? "Huh."

AUNT: *(Looking in her purse.)* Usually I'll pack a little something to eat.

SWEETHEART: "Huh."

FREELANCER: Yeah. Exactly.

SWEETHEART: "People always look so worried."

FREELANCER: They do. Right. The cop said that.

SWEETHEART: People know what happens.

FREELANCER: *(Wondering whom SWEETHEART is quoting.)* Who said that?

AUNT: *(Leafing through her program.)* People are born, people die. *(Patting SWEETHEART on the knee.)* We'll go to that nice place you like, after. We can do the treasure map on the placemat. I've always loved those. *(The lights on the INTERMISSION AUDIENCE dim three times, signaling the INTERMISSION is ended.)* And here we go. Exciting.

> Lights down as house lights come up.
>
> End of ACT ONE.
>
> INTERMISSION.

ACT TWO

Months later. Middletown.

SCENE 1

MECHANIC enters the dimly-lit stage, from the opposite direction that COP came from in Scene 1, and comes to the window of JOHN DODGE's house, in which we see JOHN DODGE, illuminated, staring out intently. He cleans a piece of lint off the glass with his finger, revealing that he was just staring at the pane of glass. MECHANIC crouches nearby.

MECHANIC: *(He imitates the sound of a crow.)* Ca-caa. Ca-caa. *(JOHN DODGE barely reacts, except to shake his head in a very small way, as if quietly but deeply pained by the sound, and then moves from the window. MECHANIC moves across stage, to where MRS. SWANSON, visible in her window, is looking at herself in a mirror. She is very pregnant. MECHANIC makes a heavy long breathing sound.)* Hhhhaaahh. Hhhhaaahh. *(Crow sound, again.)* Ca-caa. *(MRS. SWANSON moves toward the window, looking frightened. MECHANIC hides.)*

MRS. SWANSON: *(Muffled.)* Is someone there? *(She moves from the window.)*

MECHANIC: *(He steps out of his hiding place. To AUDIENCE.)* Just some regular sounds from nature. Probably nothing to be too afraid of. *(He makes a few long whooshing sounds like the ocean or the wind in the trees.)* Whhhshhhhhhh. Whhhshhhhhhh. That's my impression of a cell dividing – or, I don't know, metastasizing. Same thing, probably, for a while – until it isn't. I learned that word through relatives. *(Brief pause.)* By the way, I started drinking, again. I don't know if people know that I'd stopped for a while? I did. Everything was better. But I decided to start up again. You might be asking yourselves: "Why?" *(Pause. He stays still and looks through the AUDIENCE, suspiciously, but also with a kind of open curiosity.)* That was a little chance to let your minds wander, to let you come up with some reasons for me. *(Another pause, same as above.)* That was some time just for you. *(MECHANIC takes a sip from a bottle.)* Away! *(Pause. He slowly exits.)*

SCENE 2

Entrance and lawn of Middletown Hospital. Bright day. A sign that says "Emergency" is staked into the grass. LANDSCAPER is on his knees on the grass, preparing to plant a tree, a young sapling. COP enters and quietly approaches LANDSCAPER from behind. COP holds his hand out in the shape of gun, aimed at the back of LANDSCAPER's head.

COP: Bang!

LANDSCAPER: *(Startled. Recovers.)* Jesus. Hey.

COP: I could have killed you, just then.

LANDSCAPER: And that's somehow my fault?

COP: Planting a tree?

LANDSCAPER: Great work – you solved the case of what I'm doing.

COP: Don't be smart.

LANDSCAPER: Done.

COP: How's my sister?

LANDSCAPER: She's good. She wants you to come over for dinner, next week. We finished the new patio and we're having a cookout. *(Some business with the tree.)*

COP: Sounds good. *(Very brief pause.)* What type is it? Elm?

LANDSCAPER: White Ash, I think. Although it could be a Green Ash. They're surprisingly hard to tell apart.

COP: Fair enough. *(Brief pause.)* Pretty day.

LANDSCAPER: *(Looking for a place to plant the tree.)* Where do you think this should go?

COP: I don't know – somewhere. *(Brief pause. Shaking his head, contemplatively, somewhat disdainfully.)* People.

LANDSCAPER: I know. *(Brief pause.)* Actually, I don't know. What, specifically, about people?

COP: Just: people. The things they do. You think you know people. You don't. You think you caught some non-suicidal gleam in their eye. You didn't. You never know what people are going to do.

LANDSCAPER: *(On the COP's lines above, he picks a spot on the grass, stands straight and still. Immediately after the COP has finished speaking, LANDSCAPER gently sways for a few moments, his eyes closed, pretending he's a tree, making the sound of wind in the leaves.)* Whhhshhhhhhh. Whhhshhhhhhh. This feels good, right here. What do you think about here?

COP: It's got potential.

LANDSCAPER: *(Digging, preparing.)* So they just wheeled some guy past here. He lifted his head up, you know, "Wait, wait, one more look." That was a sight. Then a pregnant lady went in, crying, trying to carry all her stuff. She looked so lonely, which, you know, when you think about it, she totally isn't. It made me wish the thing was already done. I think it'll be soothing, you know, this tree, just nice for people. Bald kids going in on sunny school days. Shattered families leaving in the rain. Just a good old sturdy old tree. Year in, year out – a good tree.

COP: Sure.

LANDSCAPER: Maybe someday some young lovers'll carve their initials into it. *(He pinches the tree, not even an inch in diameter, with thumb and forefinger.)* Into this. Pretty incomprehensible: The future.

COP: There are some guidelines, some givens.

LANDSCAPER: Yeah, maybe. *(He begins to dig.)* I buried some sunglasses around back, this morning. Just to give somebody something to find, someday. *(He strikes something with the shovel.)* Hey, what's that? *(Picks up the object, which is a rock.)* I always think it's going to be gold or a skull or something. *(Brief pause. Holding up the rock.)* Alas. That's got to be a really old word: "Rock." *(He carefully sets the rock aside.)*

COP: It fits pretty well, doesn't it.

LANDSCAPER: It sounds like a name the rocks would've picked out themselves. Same thing with Tree. *(He digs up another small rock and places it on top of the other and looks at the two rocks.)* There. A monument to the moment of its own construction.

COP: A rock a person put on top of another rock.

LANDSCAPER: There's that word again. It's got a real honest ring to it: "rock." "Person," on the other hand – I'm not so sure. It feels sort of last-minute, doesn't it? Sort of fleeting? "Person."

COP: Sounds like an average-paying job.

LANDSCAPER: It does. "I'm a person. Been one for years, now. It's okay. The benefits, and so on. Of course, I'm not going to do it forever."

COP: This isn't really my kind of conversation.

LANDSCAPER: No?

COP: Yeah, not really. In fact, I've got to go in here. It's potentially a crime scene, if you can believe it. Tell my sister I said hi. I'll see you later. *(COP exits, to enter the hospital.)*

LANDSCAPER: See you later, person. I mean that in all the best ways. *(He digs up another rock, and places it on top of the others, making a tiny snowman or a semi-human statue.)* Rock. Tree. *(He pokes in the dirt.)* Worm. *(Stands up straight, leans on his shovel and sighs.)*

SCENE 3

MALE DOCTOR's office. MRS. SWANSON and MALE DOCTOR. MRS. SWANSON is very pregnant. MALE DOCTOR, though entirely compassionate, is also very busy, and he speaks quickly.

MALE DOCTOR: *(He is periodically writing, filling out forms, and referring to notes throughout this scene.)* There's a problem – no, sorry, there's no problem. That's "Swenson." You're Swanson. Sorry. Now, we did some more tests on your little man. Everything looks very good. His Babinski Reflex, for example.

MRS. SWANSON: Is that where you –

MALE DOCTOR: *(Interrupting, nodding.)* Right – that's where we stroke the foot to see if the toes curl. We do this with sound and tiny beams of light. We can do almost all these tests prior to the actual birth, now. It's incredible. In a few more years, people won't even have to be born. Anyway, he was magnificent. The first expressive gesture. From that little curl of the toes to all of the world's bibles and languages, it's just a matter of time. Everybody watched on the monitor. You probably heard a cheer go up from the other room. It's like a space launch. Long way away, but, he could be a tiny little Beethoven, your boy. Get him a fun little drum or a bell. Now, will the father be in the room with you?

MRS. SWANSON: He said he would, yes.

MALE DOCTOR: Good. It's good to have someone. This is literally going to be the first day of the rest of your baby's life. Linguistically, you'll want to start him out small. Simple words like hi and juice and tree and bye-bye. Say whatever you feel. Most of it happens on a vibrational level, anyway.

INTERCOM: *(A brief staticky buzz. A voice comes over the office intercom.)* I'm sorry, Doctor – I have Mrs. Swenson on the line.

MALE DOCTOR: *(Brief pause. To INTERCOM.)* Tell her I'm very sorry. I'll have to call her right back. *(To MRS. SWANSON.)* Excuse me. That's a sad story. But, back to you. We'll generate a birth certificate, of course. That'll start up the paper trail. Do you have a name?

MRS. SWANSON: We're thinking possibly "John."

MALE DOCTOR: "John" is perfect. Biblical, one syllable, no complicated back-story, just "John." "John Swanson." It's like a little poem. *(Very brief pause.)* What else?

MRS. SWANSON: Can I ask you... sorry, this is so general, but... I mean, what should I do? How should I be?

MALE DOCTOR: Those are great questions. And here's my answer. Love is all. It sounds so simple, I know, but, give him love. Without it, he'll just go around the world saying different things and seeing this and that and none of it'll make any difference. You've seen the type. Out in the rain, just kind of rattling around in their bodies. But, it's easy. This is the time for smiles and simple rhymes. Let's see you smile. *(MRS. SWANSON smiles. He barely smiles.)* Great. Wow. Did you see? You made me smile, too. Let's be honest, part of the whole great March of Humanity is just swinging your arms and walking, just smiling and moving forward. One other thing is: you never know. So be forgiving, of yourself, of him, of nature, everything. Nature is so insane, it's so rough, and we're just humans, just these chatty mammals with different names and colorful clothing. So, forgiveness, forgiveness and love, and you're all set. Now, I'm speaking quickly, and I'm sure there's a lot of huge gaps in my thinking. Apologies, I'm sorry, I make this speech a lot.

MRS. SWANSON: No, no, it's great, it sounds completely unrehearsed. Thank you. I'm grateful for anything. It's good to hear these things. *(She rubs her eye.)*

MALE DOCTOR: Does your eye itch?

MRS. SWANSON: A little. Is that a problem?

MALE DOCTOR: Just for you. Because it itches.

MRS. SWANSON: Oh, right. Is there anything else I should do? In the first little while?

MALE DOCTOR: Just hold him tight, hold the little human tight. Sing as much as you can. After the first few weeks, the amniotic fluid will drain from his ears. Before that, mercifully, everything is just a muffled kind of music. Same as in the womb. Right now, to him, most words probably sound a lot like the word "mother." Or "hearth" or "Earth," something indistinct like that, sort of rounded off. Who knows what shamanistic sense he's making of it all, you know? *(He speaks toward her belly.)* "Mahherhm. Herhomm. Mome gavnerma thurn." As far as he knows, the whole world is a soft little murmur of gentle intent. His instinct is going to be to trust life. His actual animal instinct – I never get over this – is to hold your hand. He's in there, right now, listening, forming, waiting to hold your hand. Wow, huh? Neither science nor religion has yet undone the wonder of the crying baby in air and light, grasping onto a finger.

MRS. SWANSON: You make it all sound so noble. Which it is, which I'm sure it is. *(Brief pause.)* I'm sort of alone, in this, at the moment. I'm sort of afraid, sometimes. It's hard to believe so many women have done this before.

MALE DOCTOR: Oh, but they did. And they were scared. And they did great. So be scared. Be yourself. You look great. You look like someone's mother. Don't forget – it's so easy to forget, but – everyone in the world was born. Try to name someone who wasn't? You can't. So just be a part of the whole crazy thing. The rest is details, little tests, taps of a tiny hammer. Oh, take one of these. *(He hands her a tiny white cotton hat.)* I get these free. Isn't it great? Did you ever see a tinier hat? Anyway, don't worry, why worry, come on, it's life. It's just good old life, been going on for years. *(Brief pause.)* It's a lot, all at once, isn't it.

MRS. SWANSON: Well, it's just all sort of surreal.

MALE DOCTOR: It is. But it's also sort of real. But, you're right, it's strange. A little person inside you is going to come out of you.

MRS. SWANSON: It's almost vaudevillian.

MALE DOCTOR: It is, yes. *(He doesn't laugh.)* That's very funny. But let's not overthink it. This is one time it makes good sense to just sit back and breathe and try to believe in miracles.

MRS. SWANSON: All right, I will. *(Brief pause.)* What happens to you when you're born? *(Very brief pause.)* Does it hurt?

MALE DOCTOR: Okay. Distress is certainly the first event. I'm sure there's a lot of pain, maybe even infinite pain, seeing as all we've known before has been infinite warmth. Even the gentlest birth must feel like a car crash. We'll probably never know the full effect. It could be the full effect is our life, our personality. Then it's over. He'll fall asleep in your arms, on your chest. He'll grasp your finger, because that's what the deepest thing in him tells him to do. It's so beautiful, it's so mysterious. You won't believe it. We have three.

MRS. SWANSON: Congratulations. That must be great.

MALE DOCTOR: It is. They are. My wife – her name is Jen – she said she forgot the pain, the worry, everything, the second she saw our firstborn. And she suddenly understood this word she'd been hearing all her life – Love. I felt it, too. You can't really describe it. As for the actual birth, we were worried, too, but, no surprises.

MRS. SWANSON: I'm glad. *(Brief pause.)* What about yours?

MALE DOCTOR: What, my own birth? Oh. I don't know. I'm sure it was fine.

MRS. SWANSON: Were you close to your mother?

MALE DOCTOR: I don't know, yeah, you know – just regular mother and son. She's still with us. Great lady. *(Very brief pause.)* What else, anything else?

MRS. SWANSON: I'm sure, but nothing I can think of.

MALE DOCTOR: I see you brought some stay-over things. Good. You're going to be great. Now, I'm sorry, please, excuse me. I really have to return this phone call. Go take a stroll. Walking is good. It's what we do. We hold hands and we walk. Activity can help the labor along. All right?

MRS. SWANSON: Thank you. Yes. Thanks.

MALE DOCTOR: Good. Perfect. Sorry I have to rush.

MRS. SWANSON: No, I appreciate your time. If I think of anything or if I have any – you're busy, sorry, thanks. Bye.

MALE DOCTOR: Great. Sorry. See you soon. *(MRS. SWANSON exits. MALE DOCTOR begins looking through some paperwork.)* Now, Swenson, Swenson... Swenson or Swanson? *(Quickly checks some other paperwork.)* Swenson. One vowel away. Ahhhh. Eeee. Owww.

SCENE 4

Hospital room. JOHN DODGE is in bed.

FEMALE DOCTOR: *(Enters. Checks chart at the foot of the bed, etc.)* How are you feeling?

JOHN DODGE: *(Quietly.)* Okay, I think.

FEMALE DOCTOR: Good. *(Pause.)* Sorry. This is difficult.

JOHN DODGE: I know. *(Brief pause.)* What is?

FEMALE DOCTOR: Well, we don't know each other. Of course. So it's hard to know how to begin.

JOHN DODGE: *(Pause.)* Are you going to try? *(Brief pause.)* I know what you're thinking. I'm not this kind of person.

FEMALE DOCTOR: What kind of person?

JOHN DODGE: I'm normally just a face in the crowd. In fact, I'm normally just home, by myself. Just a face in my house. Which is fine, normally. I don't think that – I don't know.

FEMALE DOCTOR: Go ahead, what were you going to say?

JOHN DODGE: Maybe I'm imbalanced. Or, I was. But I don't think I'm suicidal, deep-down. Even though, I mean, here I am, yes. And I think I'm probably making you feel uncomfortable.

FEMALE DOCTOR: I'm sure that's a little true. Thank you for your consideration. It's complicated.

JOHN DODGE: It is. I didn't know what I was doing. It was like this cloud came over me, this big dark idea.

FEMALE DOCTOR: And that was what?

JOHN DODGE: That I wanted to be an emergency, somehow. I always felt like one, deep-down. I've got all these weird problems. I get nervous in certain weather. Sunlight reminds me of this great woman I knew. My heart races, I get these twitches in my elbow, my mind races. *(Brief pause.)* It always scared me there was even a word: Suicide. It scared me they even had a word for it. And then, suddenly, there I am, you know, on my kitchen floor, like a crazy person, right in the thick of that word.

FEMALE DOCTOR: Forgive me, but, you used some kind of a knife?

JOHN DODGE: A house-painting tool. Like, a scraper thing.

FEMALE DOCTOR: That sounds dirty.

JOHN DODGE: What do you mean?

FEMALE DOCTOR: That it might have had dirt on it. Germs.

JOHN DODGE: Maybe. Probably. *(Pause.)* I pictured everybody with their eyes all red, saying funeral stuff like, "We hardly knew him." And, in reality, they kind of didn't. I never thought I'd have a lonely life. I do, it turns out. Like, medically lonely. Like I've got sad genes. Like, what's that word? *(Very brief pause.)* I don't know. I'm sure there is one.

FEMALE DOCTOR: I'm sorry.

JOHN DODGE: Please don't worry. I know I'm not crazy. I'm just sad. And not even that much, right now. I even feel hungry. That must be a good sign. *(Pause.)* I keep explaining, but – I wanted to see if I had a survival instinct. It was a stupid way to find out, but I did. And I'm glad. And I'm better, I think. Not fine, but, better.

FEMALE DOCTOR: That's the thing.

JOHN DODGE: It really is. *(Brief pause.)* What do you mean?

FEMALE DOCTOR: Well, we're not sure. Now, I just want to take a look at this. *(She puts on rubber gloves and pulls up the cotton mask hanging around her neck. She gently opens the surgical gauze covering the wound on his wrist.)*

JOHN DODGE: It smells really bad.

FEMALE DOCTOR: That's bacteria. It could just be topical. But we're concerned. We're worried you might have something serious.

JOHN DODGE: Me?

FEMALE DOCTOR: An infection. We want to be cautious.

JOHN DODGE: Okay. Is "we" you and me?

FEMALE DOCTOR: All of us here. We might need to do a biopsy. I'll have them dress this again. *(She gently replaces the bandage.)*

JOHN DODGE: Isn't there something you can give me?

FEMALE DOCTOR: We have you on an anti-toxin named Neovitamole. *(Brief pause.)* This is just a precaution, but, is there anyone you want us to contact?

JOHN DODGE: *(Pause.)* Can you give me more of that stuff, just to make sure?

FEMALE DOCTOR: You're at the maximum. It's doing what it's going to do.

JOHN DODGE: What's it doing? What do I have?

FEMALE DOCTOR: I don't want to overwhelm you with details. You're showing signs of an infection, which we're trying to identify, and then, when we do, we can treat it.

JOHN DODGE: I'm having some trouble with my legs. And, my stomach's been… I've had diarrhea.

FEMALE DOCTOR: They told me. It can also strain the breathing, which is the big danger, if it's what we're worried about.

JOHN DODGE: It's curable, though, right?

FEMALE DOCTOR: We have high hopes on the Neovitamole. We'll see, fairly soon. It works quickly when it works. If not, there are other treatments. Some are somewhat radical, but they've been effective.

JOHN DODGE: What are they? No, forget it. You'll tell me when you tell me. *(Brief pause.)* What happens when you die?

FEMALE DOCTOR: You don't need to think about dying.

JOHN DODGE: But what happens? Do you think.

FEMALE DOCTOR: A few things. Dying, from the outside, from the bodily perspective, it's not very pretty. Nobody looks very peaceful, as far as I've seen. We have stories of people seeing white light and feeling an angelic serenity. But these are stories from the people who lived, so they might be just describing what it's like to almost die and then live. So we don't know. *(Brief pause.)* I was just speaking with a patient who's about to give birth.

JOHN DODGE: I guess that about covers it.

FEMALE DOCTOR: Those are just two events. There's a lot in between.

JOHN DODGE: I've always been afraid that shame would be the last thing I felt on Earth. No angelic stuff, no light – just weird pain, and shame that I was sick. And that I'd feel alone, no matter who was there. I've always been afraid of that. And now I just don't want to die like some dirty animal, with my teeth showing and some crazy look in my eye. *(Brief pause.)* I'm sorry to talk like this.

FEMALE DOCTOR: No, it's good. In fact, we have someone here who's wonderful. Once we clear up this other thing, I think it'd be good for you to meet with her. Just to talk.

JOHN DODGE: I'd like that. *(Brief pause.)* I guess this is a real irony. Me being here. How I got here.

FEMALE DOCTOR: Irony is a people thing. Nature is very frank. You're here, and we're taking care of you, is the point. Just this morning, my son Eric, he's seven, said, "The sun doesn't know it's hot, right? It just goes around being orange."

JOHN DODGE: I don't want to die. God. I don't want to be in a hospital.

FEMALE DOCTOR: It's going to be okay.

JOHN DODGE: Oh, it is? For who? *(He becomes nauseous.)* I'm getting this wave. I feel sick. I'm sorry. I think I'm going to be sick.

FEMALE DOCTOR: I can walk you to the bathroom, but it's better to stay still. *(She gets him a plastic bag.)* Use this, if you need it.

JOHN DODGE: Is this the medicine or the thing?

FEMALE DOCTOR: The nausea? It could be both.

JOHN DODGE: When is it supposed to... God....

FEMALE DOCTOR: Just try to relax. Try to breathe. We're doing everything we can do.

JOHN DODGE: I don't want to be here. I don't want to be sick. *(Brief pause. The nausea is passing.)* Okay. All right. I think I'm all right. Sorry. I'm sorry.

FEMALE DOCTOR: I'm going to get you something for your stomach. *(Referring to the call button by the bed.)* Ring if you need anything or if there's any change.

JOHN DODGE: I made a mistake.

FEMALE DOCTOR: Don't worry about that. Just think ahead. Think about simple true things.

JOHN DODGE: Okay. I'll try. The sun is orange.

FEMALE DOCTOR: That's the spirit. Think of good things. I'll come through again soon. *(FEMALE DOCTOR exits.)*

JOHN DODGE: I'm thinking of good things. *(JOHN DODGE covers his face with his hands, perhaps begins to quietly cry.)*

SCENE 5

Loading dock behind HOSPITAL. There are cardboard boxes and bags of garbage lying around. MECHANIC is looking through them, examining little bits of trash. FEMALE DOCTOR enters and stands on the raised loading dock.

MECHANIC: Sorry. *(He begins to leave.)*

FEMALE DOCTOR: No, help yourself. I doubt there's anything good.

MECHANIC: I'm just looking around.

FEMALE DOCTOR: I used to smoke. I still come out here and just stand around for five minutes and think about cigarettes. Don't you volunteer, here?

MECHANIC: Yeah. I'm also a... I collect stuff.

FEMALE DOCTOR: Oh?

MECHANIC: Yeah. Just any kind of, like,... honestly, I'm basically looking for some pills or something. Do you think there's anything in here for a headache? A serious one?

FEMALE DOCTOR: I don't, no.

MECHANIC: Probably not. You look important, up there. Like a person who saves lives. Very, you know –

FEMALE DOCTOR: *(Interrupting.)* I'm not going to give you any pills.

MECHANIC: Oh. You still look – you know – you look really –

FEMALE DOCTOR: *(Interrupting.)* Thank you. Careful you don't cut yourself. You can get botulism.

MECHANIC: That's a good name for a disease.

FEMALE DOCTOR: Isn't it. I always thought it sounded like a philosophy of really bad choices. People think it's not around anymore, botulism, but it is, it's alive and well.

MECHANIC: I'll be careful. *(Brief pause.)* Today's my birthday.

FEMALE DOCTOR: Happy birthday. *(Nodding back toward hospital.)* Someone's about to have a birthday in here.

MECHANIC: I guess it's pretty common. *(Brief pause.)* I was a perfect baby.

FEMALE DOCTOR: I don't think I've ever heard anyone say that.

MECHANIC: Yeah. I just... I was all ready. For the world.

FEMALE DOCTOR: Surprise.

MECHANIC: Yeah.

FEMALE DOCTOR: It's not rare, but, it's very lucky – to be a person, just a regular person. Did you know when you combine an egg cell and a sperm cell, there's more ways they can combine, more particular kinds of people that can result, than there are atoms in the Universe?

MECHANIC: I love facts like that. *(Very brief pause.)* I used to be seven pounds, eight ounces. Now look at me. *(Brief pause.)* I think I disappointed everybody when I was born. If they'd just been expecting a little animal that needed air and food, then I think I would've been pretty impressive. There was no way I could live up to all that want and need, me and my seven pounds, eight ounces. I think being born hurt my feelings. *(Still looking around.)* My head is killing me.

FEMALE DOCTOR: I'm sorry. *(Brief pause.)* Can I ask you, this'll sound silly, but, what do you want out of life?

MECHANIC: Are you kidding?

FEMALE DOCTOR: Just for fun.

MECHANIC: Okay. I want, out of life, for this headache to go away. And, then, just, I guess, to know something. At the risk of sounding like some fuck-up pawing through the garbage for drugs: I want to know Love. I want to calmly know love on Earth. And to feel beautiful. *(Pause. He starts looking around, again. No trace of amusement.)* Thanks. That was a lot of fun.

FEMALE DOCTOR: Pretty good answer. *(Brief pause.)* I ask people sometimes and they say they don't know. You'd think we'd take the time. We have answers for so many things. How many atoms in the Universe, how black holes are made. *(Pause.)* I'm sorry, I don't mean this to be embarrassing. *(She takes a vial of pills out of her jacket pocket, double-checks the label, then pours some on the ground.)* Sometimes people spill things, back here. You're not driving, are you? *(He shakes his head "no.")* Happy birthday.

MECHANIC: *(Picking up the pills.)* Yeah, you too. Thanks.

SCENE 6

Hospital room. JOHN DODGE in bed. ATTENDANT 2 enters and performs some routine task. She smiles at JOHN DODGE, who smiles back, as she exits. MRS. SWANSON, on a stroll down the hall, appears at the door.

MRS. SWANSON: John? I don't believe it.

JOHN DODGE: Mary. Hi. Wow. Let me sit up. *(He lifts himself up in bed.)*

MRS. SWANSON: *(Laughing sympathetically.)* Oh, no. Look at you. What happened? *(She enters.)*

JOHN DODGE: A couple things. Look at you. I could ask you the same thing.

MRS. SWANSON: This is so funny. I kept thinking I'd see you.

JOHN DODGE: I know, me too. I was always looking. I thought I saw you a couple times.

MRS. SWANSON: I almost called when it was so rainy. Remember all that rain? Our basement flooded.

JOHN DODGE: I almost called you, a few times. I'd, I don't know, I had really thought we'd have more of a relationship.

MRS. SWANSON: Well, we did. We do.

JOHN DODGE: Not a relationship, but, I mean, just, I don't know, I thought I'd see you.

MRS. SWANSON: And, here I am. Ta da!

JOHN DODGE: I mean before. I guess I just thought we had a chance.

MRS. SWANSON: A chance of what?

JOHN DODGE: Oh, I don't know. Just a chance.

MRS. SWANSON: *(Very brief pause.)* Well, I guess we always do, right?

JOHN DODGE: You're nice. *(Brief pause.)* You're so big. You look really great.

MRS. SWANSON: Today's the day, I hope. What about you? Are you okay?

JOHN DODGE: Yeah, no, I'm fine, it's just something stupid. I cut myself.

MRS. SWANSON: Making a birdhouse or a canoe or something? One of your projects?

JOHN DODGE: No, just, I don't know, around the house.

MRS. SWANSON: Do you have a cold?

JOHN DODGE: Do I sound stuffed up? I think I'm just tired. Good place to get some quiet, anyway.

MRS. SWANSON: I don't know how quiet it'll be for me.

JOHN DODGE: Oh, you'll be great. It's really nice to see you. Wow. *(Pause.)* This is going to be dumb. Don't make fun of me.

MRS. SWANSON: What?

JOHN DODGE: *(Trying not to cry.)* Mary, sorry, can you hold me? Just for a – can I hold you?

MRS. SWANSON: I'm not sure how holdable I am. *(She sits on the bed.)* But I can give you a hug. *(They hug. It's deeply comforting and possibly even romantic to JOHN DODGE, nice but slightly uncomfortable for MRS. SWANSON.)*

JOHN DODGE: Mary.

MRS. SWANSON: *(She sits on the bed, as before.)* It's good to see you.

JOHN DODGE: It feels really good to see you. The people are nice here, but I don't really know anyone. So is your husband here?

MRS. SWANSON: Can you believe it, he isn't. He's trying to get a flight, right now. *(She notices his bandaged wrist.)* Oh, no – you cut your arm? What did you do?

JOHN DODGE: It was stupid.

MRS. SWANSON: Oh, John – did you do this?

JOHN DODGE: Partly, yeah – I don't know. Yes.

MRS. SWANSON: Why? That's a stupid question, I'm sorry. But, why?

JOHN DODGE: A couple things. A lot of things. It was a mistake.

MRS. SWANSON: God. I wish I'd known. I don't know what I could have done, but…I just wish…

JOHN DODGE: Yeah. I wanted to call. I don't know what I would've said. But, I'm all right. *(Brief pause.)* If Bob doesn't make it, I can try to be there, in the delivery room. If you need someone.

MRS. SWANSON: That's really sweet. Thanks, John. I don't want to be alone in there. You're really thoughtful. *(Brief pause.)* It might not be good, though, because you're…if it turns out you do have a cold.

JOHN DODGE: Okay. But, I don't think I do.

MRS. SWANSON: It's really nice of you to offer. *(Pause.)* I'm sorry, I've got a lot on my mind.

JOHN DODGE: Yeah.

MRS. SWANSON: *(She gets up from the bed.)* It's so good seeing you. They said activity was good. I was walking up and down the halls.

JOHN DODGE: I know, I can't believe it. *(Brief pause.)* All these time. I mean, all these months.

MRS. SWANSON: The sink still drains like a dream. *(Brief pause.)* Remember you unclogged our sink?

JOHN DODGE: *(Long pause. He's dozed off. He opens his eyes. Quietly.)* Hey, Mary.

MRS. SWANSON: Hey. You need some rest. And, John, I should keep walking. They say activity is good.

JOHN DODGE: *(Somewhat hazily.)* Sorry. God, I'm really tired. They've got me on this really serious stuff – it makes me so sleepy. *(Very brief pause.)* It's so great that… Good old Mary.

MRS. SWANSON: Rest up and I'll see you soon, all right? Oh, here's some news, wait until you hear, you'll love this: we think we're going to name him John.

JOHN DODGE: *(He hasn't heard.)* All right, Mary. It's really good to – I keep saying that, sorry. See you later, Mary. *(He begins to doze off again. She leaves the room.)*

MRS. SWANSON: Did you hear what I – . Rest up. Bye, John. *(In the doorway, only partially visible to the AUDIENCE, MRS. SWANSON doubles over. In pain.)* Oh. Sorry? I think this is… John, can you call someone? Can you ring your call thing? John? *(He's asleep.)* Someone? Somebody? I'm sorry, hello!? *(ATTENDANT arrives, mainly out of view and out of earshot, and helps MRS. SWANSON off.)*

JOHN DODGE: *(Pause. He gets out of his bed. Stands, turns, and faces out. He reaches for the bed, and steadies himself with it.)* Was someone… hello? *(Brief pause. Quietly.)* Hey, look at me. *(Lights down.)*

SCENE 7

Entrance and lawn of Middletown Hospital.
The tree is planted. MECHANIC, looking haggard, is sitting on a bench, staring at the pile of three rocks. He sips from a bottle in a paper bag. LIBRARIAN comes out of the hospital entrance.

LIBRARIAN: You've found a nice spot.

MECHANIC: *(Referring to the rocks.)* I'm just looking at this.

LIBRARIAN: Maybe it's a sign.

MECHANIC: Maybe it isn't a sign. *(Pointing to sign that says EMERGENCY.)* Maybe *this* is a sign.

LIBRARIAN: Maybe they're both signs. I'm here visiting a friend.

MECHANIC: I'm here, being difficult.

LIBRARIAN: You were always kind of a suspicious package. *(Brief pause.)* I remember when you were little. Remember that? You wrote an essay for Middletown Day called "This Whole Hamlet is Shaking." I had it hanging up at the library for years. I still remember the first sentence. "If this were…" no. "If Middletown was a horse instead of a town, it would be better for everyone and I would ride it off into the sun." Was that it?

MECHANIC: Wow. Yeah, that sounds right. It's always surprising when people remember something. I had to read it in front of everybody. I was shaking myself. It gave the thing an air of, like, I don't know – it made it more believable.

LIBRARIAN: I remember. They put your picture in the paper.

MECHANIC: Yeah. The color came out funny. All I was was the shape of a kid, with blurry teeth and hair.

LIBRARIAN: You could still tell you were happy. You looked very proud.

MECHANIC: I probably was. *(Brief pause.)* I think someone scared my mother, before I was born, a lot. So all the blood I got was shaky blood. Jumpy blood from my jumpy mother. And I want other people to enjoy the same experience. That's probably why I wrote that thing.

LIBRARIAN: I thought it was big of you. To stand up there and shake and say what you think and feel. We all have our ideas. Some people say the secret to life is being able to live in the middle of all our different ideas about life.

MECHANIC: Some people don't say anything.

LIBRARIAN: True.

MECHANIC: I didn't mean anything. Forget I said that.

LIBRARIAN: Okay. *(Brief pause.)* My mother used to sing "You Are My Sunshine" to me, at night. And then she'd sing, "Kentucky Moon," in the morning.

MECHANIC: That's nice. Mine was on her own. She tried, I think. Just bad luck, I guess. A world full of fathers out there, but try to find one when you need one. I don't know. They do all their magic in the negative, anyway. My father was a speech impediment, is how I usually think of him. He came by once with a doll and some wrong-sized clothes.

LIBRARIAN: My father was very tall. He felt that posture was very important.

MECHANIC: Oh, yeah? *(Nodding towards the hospital.)* I forget, do they have food in there?

LIBRARIAN: There's a little snack bar. I had a good soup, the other day.

MECHANIC: It's weird. *(He takes a couple pills.)* I've taken a lot of these. It's weird to be alive. I know it's supposed to be really important and great. But, here's my philosophy. I'm sitting outside. I'm wearing this shirt and these shoes. It's this certain weather. This is my body, that's yours, end of story.

LIBRARIAN: I can't argue with that.

MECHANIC: Thank you. *(Pause.)* Is this all right?

LIBRARIAN: Of course. I'm just here, waiting.

MECHANIC: Can I ask, did anyone ever explain things to you? Other than stuff about posture? Like, like, really sit down and just say, "Okay, You: here's how this whole thing works"?

LIBRARIAN: *(Brief pause.)* There's an Indian prayer I always liked. I had it up on the wall, too. "If it's raining, it's not snowing. If it's snowing, the deer are thin. If the thin deer are sleeping, it is sunny. Hold the hand of your love and wait for the moon. Some things we are never to know. Listen to the brook." It's sort of woodsy, but, I always liked it. I don't know if I have it word-for-word.

MECHANIC: It's nice. "Listen to the river." That's good. We did Indians in school. I did a re-enactment. People clapped and my mom cried. That felt good. *(Brief pause.)* There're people like me in the world, I think. You don't hear much from us because we usually don't say anything. But we're out here, trying to get a hold on the whole thing. It's like, I don't know, it's like trying to fix a moving car.

LIBRARIAN: I think we're born with questions and the world is the answer.

MECHANIC: Yeah? I guess there're a lot of different ways to go. Some people love God. I have a neighbor who kayaks every weekend. *(Pause.)* You're not going to ask me what I want out of life, are you?

LIBRARIAN: *(She shrugs and smiles, and shakes her head, as if to say, "I don't know, should I?")*

MECHANIC: *(Pause. Trying not to cry.)* I just wish I got somewhere, you know? That I was born, and then I grew, somehow. I'd like people to look at me and feel wonder. I'd like people to look at me and say, "Wow. Look at that guy." I'd like to look at the sky and just think, "Hey, look at the sky." *(Pause.)* What kind of soup was it?

LIBRARIAN: Tomato. Did you ever think you might be a normal person?

MECHANIC: Maybe. I don't know. Bad news for normal people. *(Brief pause.)* I took a ton of those pills.

LIBRARIAN: Are you all right?

MECHANIC: Yeah.

COP: *(COP enters, from hospital entrance.)* Hi, afternoon. *(To MECHANIC.)* You again, in the wild, again, with your pupils all constricted. You're Craig, right?

MECHANIC: Did you get a call to come down here and strangle me?

COP: Why would – no. They want you in there.

MECHANIC: Why don't you like me?

COP: *(To LIBRARIAN.)* What's this?

LIBRARIAN: He's not feeling well. Be gentle.

COP: *(Gently.)* Okay. Craig, I'm sure you'll be fine. You've been really good about showing up for these. They want you in there, okay?

MECHANIC: Okay. *(He slowly gets up, begins to slowly enter hospital.)*

(To LIBRARIAN.) Good luck with your friend. *(Exits.)*

LIBRARIAN: Bye, Craig. Thank you.

COP: I think he wrote the dirty word on the sign coming into town. I'm sorry, I never liked his attitude. Like he's always thinking there's somewhere better to be than here.

LIBRARIAN: Maybe there is. A lot of people probably feel that, sometimes.

COP: Maybe. Probably. Ah, God, I don't know – I'm sorry. I don't even know the guy. I guess I'm not feeling very patient.

LIBRARIAN: I'm sorry about your mother, Robert.

COP: Thanks, Judith. Thanks for coming.

LIBRARIAN: You made a beautiful speech.

COP: I didn't prepare anything. I thought I'd just go up there and talk.

LIBRARIAN: Well, it was lovely. Everyone cried and felt so close to her.

COP: I almost cried. I had a hard time not crying.

LIBRARIAN: You were a good son.

COP: *(Brief pause.)* It was hard. They had her on everything, at the end, so she wasn't very clear. She did these things with her hands. My sister thinks she was playing piano in her mind. Remember she used to teach music? It made us happy to think that's what was happening, that she was playing some song in her head. We were happy she had things to do, even though there was nothing to do in there.

LIBRARIAN: It was good you could be with her. She was a wonderful woman.

COP: She was almost our oldest resident. *(Brief pause.)* A few days before, I was here visiting, and she asked me, "What does this actually mean?" and she held up her middle finger. It was so funny. I said, "Mom, where'd you see that?" It was on some show that had couples working out their problems. She couldn't work the remote to turn it off. But, so, I told her it means, "I don't like you." Then I felt so terrible, almost sick, for even saying those words to my mom, even though I was just explaining. I just wanted to get her flowers and make her laugh and help her get back home and feel peaceful.

LIBRARIAN: I'm sure she knew how you felt. That's a sweet story. *(Pause.)* People know what happens.

COP: Yes, they do.

LIBRARIAN: It seems so original, when it happens to us.

COP: I like the natural order of things, but, yeah, it's hard. When we were leaving, after, her doctor said, "See you later." My sister and I had a laugh about that, over breakfast. Yes, we shall. Sorry – how are you?

LIBRARIAN: I'm fine, thank you. *(Brief pause.)* Mary Swanson is supposed to be having her baby, today.

COP: From over on Oak Street, right? Number 31?

LIBRARIAN: Yes. Mary. That's funny – is that how you remember people?

COP: What? The address? Yeah, I guess. Just a habit. If I know the address, the general layout, then I can sympathize. *(Brief pause.)* Toward the end, I sat with my mom and we listed stores we'd been to. Isn't that sad, that one day, there's going to be a last store you ever went into?

LIBRARIAN: It is. But isn't it great to think there was a first? *(She thinks for a moment.)* Frank's Superette.

COP: Frank's Superette.

LIBRARIAN: *(Brief pause.)* Look at this pretty tree.

COP: Yeah. It's nice. I like trees. Everybody does, I'm sure, but, yeah, me too. *(Brief pause.)* I should get back in here. Will you be at the library tomorrow?

LIBRARIAN: I will.

COP: I'll come in and say hi.

LIBRARIAN: I'll say hi, back.

COP: Thanks, Judith. Thanks. *(COP enters the hospital.)*

SCENE 8

MRS. SWANSON's hospital room. MRS. SWANSON is in bed. ATTENDANT enters with a pitcher of water.

ATTENDANT: Make sure you drink some water. Even if you're not thirsty. *(Does some quick business, chart-checking, etc.)*

MRS. SWANSON: Okay.

ATTENDANT: How are you? *(Pause.)* Can I get you anything?

MRS. SWANSON: Oh, sorry. No. Thank you. I was just thinking about everything.

ATTENDANT: Everything, wow. That's good to do, sometimes. And sometimes it's good to just look out a window. Everything's going to be fine. I'll be up again with some food in just a bit.

MRS. SWANSON: Food.

ATTENDANT: Not hungry?

MRS. SWANSON: I don't know. I'm just kind of... God.

ATTENDANT: You're kind of God? Very nice to meet you. I have a cousin who's a huge fan. It'll all come back, your appetite and everything. *(Checking her forehead for fever.)* Do you feel all right, otherwise?

MRS. SWANSON: I just thought everything would be different.

ATTENDANT: And it isn't?

MRS. SWANSON: People had trouble with travel arrangements. My husband and one of my brothers. Whatever was going to happen, I just didn't think I'd be alone.

ATTENDANT: They'll get here. Don't feel alone. You're not alone. Just rest. *(Motioning toward a call button.)* Ring, okay. If you need anything.

MRS. SWANSON: I will, thanks. *(ATTENDANT exits.)* I'm not alone.

SCENE 9

JOHN DODGE'S hospital room. JOHN DODGE is lying in bed. COP enters.

JOHN DODGE: *(Somewhat scared and confused. His voice is slightly hoarse.)* I'm sorry. Am I not supposed to be –

COP: *(Interrupting.)* It's okay. Hi. I'm Sergeant Hollingsworth. I don't know if you remember, I came to your house when the ambulance was there.

JOHN DODGE: Sorry, I thought I was in the wrong room. *(Brief pause.)* I remember. It was busy, but I remember you.

COP: I wanted to let you know there won't be any charges filed here. The arrangement is you'll do some community service when you get better and that you'll agree to get some help, some counseling.

JOHN DODGE: Thank you.

COP: Does that sound all right?

JOHN DODGE: Have you talked to them, here?

COP: No. Why?

JOHN DODGE: I don't know.

COP: Does it sound all right?

JOHN DODGE: Okay.

COP: *(He puts some papers by the bed.)* Look at these. They need to be signed. The address to send them to is up at the top. Are you feeling better?

JOHN DODGE: I think I'm losing my voice.

COP: Well, you were a real mess. *(Brief pause.)* You look better.

JOHN DODGE: Did you tell Stephanie?

COP: Who's Stephanie?

JOHN DODGE: I don't know. I'm sorry. She's from when I was little. *(Brief pause.)* I don't hear any voices in my head. Should I be hearing any voices?

COP: Are you all right?

JOHN DODGE: I think so.

COP: Just rest up and listen to your doctors.

JOHN DODGE: I will.

COP: Life can get tough. It's tough for everyone. You know that, right?

JOHN DODGE: Yeah.

COP: I get moody. I get sad. People don't think of cops as moody. *(Gesturing toward his gun, notebook, flashlight, etc.)* Look at all this stuff I have to walk around with.

JOHN DODGE: It's a lot of stuff. *(Brief pause.)* I just want to be a regular living person.

COP: You will. I have to be back for something else, tomorrow. I'll stop in.

JOHN DODGE: Stephanie is from when I was little. I was little.

COP: Stephanie. Okay. *(Brief pause.)* I'll have them stop in and check on you, okay? Have a look at those papers and send them back.

JOHN DODGE: Are you leaving?

COP: Yeah, I've got to go. See you later.

JOHN DODGE: Okay.

COP: So, one part of the community service thing is managing the community garden on West Street. Building little stuff and just making sure everything's all taken care of. They said you're good with stuff like that.

JOHN DODGE: Yeah, I like stuff like that.

COP: Well, then, get better. I think they give you a uniform or something.

JOHN DODGE: That'd be good. I like working outside.

COP: All right, then. I'll see you later. *(Exits.)*

JOHN DODGE: Bye.

SCENE 10

MRS. SWANSON's room. MRS. SWANSON sitting up in bed. Warm light.
FEMALE DOCTOR enters with the tiny baby, swaddled in a blanket.

MRS. SWANSON: *(With nothing but love.)* Ohhh.

FEMALE DOCTOR: *(She gently hands the baby to MRS. SWANSON.)*
Somebody needs you.

MRS. SWANSON: I missed him so much. Was he fussing?

FEMALE DOCTOR: He just wants his mommy. *(She pulls up the blanket, to cover the baby, which makes a small sound.)* Take the cloth off him. There you go. As much skin-to-skin contact as possible. Just let him feel you holding him. Look at you both. You're like a Renaissance painting.

MRS. SWANSON: He feels so nice.

FEMALE DOCTOR: Everything's fine. He's a very healthy baby.

MRS. SWANSON: Oh, good. Lucky boy. My lucky healthy boy.

FEMALE DOCTOR: I'll leave you two.

MRS. SWANSON: Thanks, Julie. Thank you. *(FEMALE DOCTOR exits. Softly.)*
Johnnie. There you go. That's nice. Hello, John. Easy. Hello. Welcome to the world, little boy. How does it feel? I wonder what you're feeling. There you go. Ssshhh. What are you feeling on Earth?

SCENE 11

Follows quickly on Scene 10. JOHN DODGE's hospital room. JOHN DODGE is lying in bed. Occasional sounds of labored breathing. Suddenly, he goes into small convulsions. A muffled and very congested scream. This should all be protracted, irregular, underplayed, difficult to watch. He's dying like an animal. A desperate look toward AUDIENCE and then he is still. Lights down.

SCENE 12

Follows quickly on Scene 11. MRS. SWANSON and the body of JOHN DODGE are visible, though in darkness, on the stage. The playing area should be unspecific, empty. MECHANIC enters, dressed as a Chakmawg Indian, with headdress, war paint, bells attached to his boots. His movements are somewhat slow but precise. He begins a ceremonial American Indian chant and dance, in the tradition of the Apache or Sioux. It's haunting and beautiful and strange in melody. It slowly builds in intensity, as he becomes more possessed and more convinced of his expressiveness. He continues, to his physical and emotional limit. Pause.

ATTENDANT: *(Enters.)* Craig?

MECHANIC: *(This line is spoken indistinctly.)* I was beautiful.

ATTENDANT: Did you just say you were beautiful? *(MECHANIC nods.)* Well, then, I'm sure you were. Everything fits okay? *(Pause. He nods.)* You're going to be in pediatric, today. The kids love to see the Rain Dance. Just move around, ring the bells. I don't know if you did any of the reading I gave you? Just be spiritual. Don't use "to be" verbs. No is, was, or, will be. Too many tenses gets confusing. They're just kids. Keep it simple. You know? "It rain and children grow strong, like tree. Sun cross sky many time. Brave and squaw laugh, touch noses. Life never die. This land never die." Something like that. Sound good? They'll love it. Okay? *(Brief pause.)* Did you just wake up? Are you okay?

MECHANIC: Yeah.

ATTENDANT: Are you going to be all right? *(He nods.)* All right. You'll be great. They're just kids. Smile and go around in circles and they see the history of the world. They're just like us, except smaller. Okay?

MECHANIC: Yeah.

ATTENDANT: Okay. Me go do some filing. Me want leave early, play tennis, before sun go away. Thanks, Craig. *(She exits.)*

MECHANIC: *(He moves downstage. Brief pause. As if a soliloquy.)* Me. *(Lights down.)*

SCENE 13

JOHN DODGE's hospital room. Lights up on the body of JOHN DODGE, under a sheet. ATTENDANT and ATTENDANT 2 are taking care of the room, unplugging equipment, etc. Lights will remain up on the body, throughout the rest of the play.

ATTENDANT: The coroner is on his way.

ATTENDANT 2: Dr. Elliman? He's nice.

ATTENDANT: His son goes to school with my daughter.

ATTENDANT 2: *(Referring to a file that's hanging at the foot of the bed.)* Does this stay with the patient?

ATTENDANT: Yeah.

ATTENDANT 2: It's so quiet.

ATTENDANT: I think bodies soak up sound. Listen. *(To JOHN DODGE's body.)* We are in a room. You are a body. I am wearing these clothes. *(To ATTENDANT 2.)* Do you notice that? *(Again, to JOHN DODGE's body.)* This is the sound of my voice. This is the language I use. You are far away. Where are you? What are you feeling? *(Brief pause. To ATTENDANT 2.)* It sounds funny, doesn't it.

ATTENDANT 2: I guess. It's weird. Did you talk to him, before?

ATTENDANT: A little. He was worried about a library book. He was sad but he tried to be good-natured.

ATTENDANT 2: I came in once to change something and he said, "If I had flowers, I'd give them to you."

ATTENDANT: That's sweet. *(One last bit of business.)* I think that does it. *(She checks a schedule.)* Now I think we have to go up to five. *(They exit. ATTENDANT 2 lingers by the door.)*

ATTENDANT 2: *(To JOHN DODGE's body.)* Goodbye, person. That was nice about the flowers. I hope you're not sad.

SCENE 14

MRS. SWANSON's hospital room. She is lying in bed with the baby on her chest, under the covers. LIBRARIAN is sitting by the bedside, gazing at the baby. There is a radio in the room.

LIBRARIAN: Ohh. Look at his little mouth.

MRS. SWANSON: I know. I still can't believe it. Little mouthie.

COP: *(Enters. Quietly.)* Hello. Are you…is everyone dressed? Hi. Congratulations. I'm Robert Hollingsworth. Judith was telling me. I'm really happy for you. I'm over on Pine Street, near the river.

MRS. SWANSON: Thank you, Robert. I'm Mary Swanson.

LIBRARIAN: He's a beautiful boy. Just perfect. He's sleeping.

COP: That's the life.

MRS. SWANSON: Thank you for visiting. It's nice to have people. *(Small sound from the baby as she re-adjusts him on her chest.)*

COP: Yeah, no, of course. I had to be down here, anyway.

SWEETHEART: *(FROM INTERMISSION AUDIENCE)*

> *(Enters from the AUDIENCE.)*

COP: Hello, sweetheart. How did you get up here? Are you lost?

SWEETHEART: No.

MRS. SWANSON: Do you want to look? *(She folds back the blanket a little.)*

SWEETHEART: *(She comes closer and leans in to look at the baby.)* Hi.

MRS. SWANSON: He says, Hello. He says, How are you?

SWEETHEART: Fine.

LIBRARIAN: Well. This has been quite a day. *(SWEETHEART takes a glance across the stage at the body of JOHN DODGE. Looking at the baby.)* Doesn't he look peaceful.

COP: Yeah. *(To MRS. SWANSON.)* Why don't we… we should let you be.

LIBRARIAN: Yes, you should rest up.

COP: *(Exiting with SWEETHEART.)* Congratulations, again.

LIBRARIAN: There's a radio. Would you like some music?

MRS. SWANSON: That might be nice.

LIBRARIAN: I'll leave you this and you can find something. *(She gives MRS. SWANSON a remote control.)* Okay, darling. I'll see you tomorrow. *(She exits.)*

MRS. SWANSON: *(To the baby.)* Those were our neighbors. *(She turns on the radio. It's a program about science.)*

RADIO: "…with a mass more than three times the weight of the sun, of such gravity that it collapses into a black hole. The structure of a black hole is very simple. There is the surface, and the center, or singularity, from which no light can escape. If my friend Sally could watch from a safe distance beyond the event horizon and see me fall into a black hole, what would she see? Sally would see me falling, slower and slower. It would appear that I'll never quite reach the center. If I were waving, she would see me wave, slower and slower. "Bye, Sally." *(JANITOR enters JOHN DODGE's room, rolling a large trash can on wheels. He empties the trash can at the foot of bed, and lines the trash can with a new trash bag.)* For me, the fall would only take a short time. Years would pass, where she was. Eventually, it would look to her as if I had stopped, mid-fall. She would see my hand in the air, my flailing legs, my smile, all frozen – all motion would stop for her. This is because the light from me takes so long to escape. Finally, it will cease altogether. By then, Sally's great-great-grandchildren will be very old people. And I will still be falling, will still be waving good-bye. Next week, we'll visit with a giant tortoise who has an interesting story to tell, if he could speak. He's over a hundred years old! We'll also talk with a man and woman who doubt almost everything they've ever" – *(MRS. SWANSON changes radio stations with the remote control. On the new station, the last thirty seconds or so of the choral part of Beethoven's Ninth Symphony is playing. After about five or ten seconds, ATTENDANT 2 enters to refill a water pitcher. ATTENDANT 2 gives a little wave to the baby, and then exits. MRS. SWANSON listens to the end. A sedate female voice comes on.)* That was the 'Symphonie Number Nine', in a recording from 1981 of the Philharmoniker – *(MRS. SWANSON turns radio off.)*

JANITOR: *(Enters.)* Evening.

MRS. SWANSON: Hello.

JANITOR: Don't mind me. *(He empties the trash.)* Wow, is that a baby?

MRS. SWANSON: This is "John."

JANITOR: Excellent. Congratulations.

MRS. SWANSON: Thank you.

JANITOR: John's a good name.

MRS. SWANSON: Thank you.

JANITOR: I guess they all are, when you think about it. *(A small sound from the baby.)* Hey, he's trying to talk. *(Last bit of janitorial work.)* Is the temperature all right in here?

MRS. SWANSON: Yes, thank you, it's fine.

JANITOR: Good. Okay, see you later. *(He exits.)*

MRS. SWANSON: Bye. *(To baby.)* Say bye. Say bye-bye.

> *A pause. Lights fade.*
>
> *END.*

COMPLETENESS

ITAMAR MOSES

Itamar Moses' play *Completeness* ran at Playwrights Horizons in Fall 2011, directed by Pam MacKinnon. Itamar is the author of the full-length plays *Outrage, Bach at Leipzig, Celebrity Row, The Four of Us, Yellowjackets,* and *Back Back Back,* a collection of short plays titled *Love/Stories (or But You Will Get Used To It),* and the musical *Nobody Loves You* (with composer Gaby Alter). He is presently adapting Jonathan Lethem's *The Fortress of Solitude* for the stage with composer Michael Friedman, and director Daniel Aukin. His work has appeared Off-Broadway and at regional theatres across the country; and in Canada, France and Brazil; and has been published by Faber & Faber, Heinemann Press, Playscripts, Inc., Samuel French and Vintage. He has received new play commissions from The McCarter Theater, Playwrights Horizons, Berkeley Repertory Theatre, The Wilma Theater, Manhattan Theatre Club, South Coast Repertory and Lincoln Center Theater, and the Goodman Theatre. Itamar holds an MFA in Dramatic Writing from NYU, and has taught playwriting at Yale and NYU. He is a member of the Dramatists Guild, MCC Playwrights Coalition, and is a New York Theatre Workshop Usual Suspect. He was a staff writer on Ray Romano and Mike Royce's *Men of a Certain Age* and on the second season of the acclaimed Martin Scorsese/HBO series *Boardwalk Empire.* He was born in Berkeley, CA, and now lives in Brooklyn, NY.

ITAMAR AND ME

Itamar Moses contacted me first; that much I remember for certain. I can't recall how he'd obtained my email address; the fault was probably my own. I suspect he was a young playwright I'd agreed to mentor and then promptly forgotten about (in my solipsistic haze) until his note popped up in my online mailbox.

I do, however, remember his sly pitch and I'll paraphrase it here: "Dear Mr. Wright: It seems that you and I might be living correlative lives. Like you, I did my undergraduate work at Yale. Like you I received my MFA in playwriting from NYU. I'd love to pick your brain about my own journey into this perilous profession we've chosen."

He knew just how to flatter me; here he was, an impressionable mind eager to be mentored by a veteran master like myself, a sponge ready to soak up my vast repository of knowledge; happy to endure the anecdotes about my early, crushing failures, my first juggernaut success, and how through it all I'd maintained my emotional equanimity and my aesthetic integrity, the highly burnished tales that wearied my friends and bored my family. Itamar was that most seductive and alluring of phenomena: a fresh audience! In short, I succumbed. I did something I never, ever do: I offered to read one of his plays.

A few days later it arrived via the digital ether. Its title alone further piqued my vanity: *Outrage*. Why, we shared the same muse! We both wrote from that inexhaustible well of fury so common to our tribe, the righteous sense of injustice and fury that comes from being a marginalized poet in a world filled with philistines. I'd barely cracked the first page and already I was smitten.

Fortunately, I remembered to temper my expectations before reading any further. He was, after all, a youngster, guaranteed to disappoint with a lack of craft, a paucity of stage-worthy ideas, and a fundamental misunderstanding of dramatic form. I readied myself with a legal pad and a pen. "Don't be too brutal," I cautioned myself. "Humble him you must, but you don't want to kill his spirit."

As I began to read, I felt a sick feeling in my stomach. Humility was the contagion, but it was mine, not his. This neophyte, this rube, had constructed a play of such ferocious intelligence, such formal daring that it left me almost speechless; he'd deftly woven characters as diverse and historic as Socrates, Galileo and Brecht into a fable about the very etymology of martyrdom. And it was funny.

Naturally I did what any self-respecting elder playwright would do in this situation to stave off the panic that inevitably attends the realization that an ambitious newcomer is nipping at your heels; I called the Wilma Theater in Philadelphia, the one company I felt could fully realize the shameless scope of Itamar's script, and promptly urged them to produce it. In doing so, I was able to recast myself from the role of the threatened has-been into that of the magnanimous elder statesman, eager to give a promising beginner a leg up; a tidy public relations trick and one practiced by many an artist to this day.

(Of course, Itamar had many champions in his early years, heavyweights like the Tom Stoppard among them; his writing was that good. So I've no definitive proof that my machinations lead directly to the subsequent production of *Outrage* in Philly. But by claiming it in this introduction, I hope to make it a central part of the lore of Itamar's now flourishing career.)

At some point along the way, I actually met Itamar in person. I found it no less traumatic than my first encounter with his work. He looked as young as he actually was, with a scruffy handsomeness that connoted "lady-killer" and a wit that came as readily to him in conversation as it did upon the page. He was every bit as charming as his incipient oeuvre; in one fell swoop, I wanted to kill, adopt and marry him.

When he wrote a second play, an uproarious and intelligent send-up of all things baroque entitled *Bach at Leipzig*, I promptly paved the way for its premiere at the New York Theater Workshop. (Okay, this is a bald-faced lie. The play had been produced previously and like many enterprising non-profit theaters in New York, the Workshop had been tracking Itamar's rise for some time. They pounced on the play of their own free will. But – once again – my claim, however fallacious, is going to appear in print, which gives it a distinct advantage over the truth.)

When the play opened, most of the critics agreed with me about Itamar's astonishing promise and a few did not. Nevertheless talent won out, and since that time he has been produced quite regularly in New York City and on stages across this great country of ours.

Itamar no longer sends me drafts of his plays. Like the great, unwashed public, I have to purchase tickets to see them. I am no longer the mentor I once claimed to be, because in the eyes of the tastemakers he and I are equals now and indeed we are: just two mid-career scribes who siphon a living in the more remunerative world of television and film but still return to our first cheeky mistress, the theater, who tempts far more than she rewards but who still gives us the satisfying sense that we are actually artists and not mere corporate functionaries.

No, I am something altogether new now: a fan. And like many of Itamar's fans, I've watched with admiration as his writing has become even more nuanced, acute and rich in feeling than in his early, panoramic works. His palette has become more refined, and his canvas smaller: he has supplanted the dozens of characters in *Outrage* for the two or three-person casts of *The Four of Us,* and *Back Back Back.* The plays are more achingly personal than they once were, and (no doubt) have been written with greater courage. Now Itamar draws not only on his prodigious intellect, but on the hidden depths of his subconscious as well. He's willing to risk personal disclosure to achieve lasting, universal truths, and that is the hallmark that separates the great writers from the amateurs.

This particular volume contains the play called *Completeness.* In it, two willfully idiosyncratic science geeks fall in love. It's a fitting entry to represent Itamar's canon because the journey of its characters mirrors his own as a playwright. Elliot and Molly must strive to integrate their over-active minds with their impetuous, unruly passions. Funnily enough, Itamar has done just that as he's morphed from a precocious tenderfoot into a mature writer. His work remains as smart as ever but now boasts a beating and vulnerable heart.

If Itamar ever needed me (a highly debatable premise, I admit), he certainly doesn't anymore. I say that wistfully, but even in my dotage I can still discern a silver lining. I look forward to the day when a publisher as august as Oberon consents to release one of my plays. Maybe – just maybe – I can convince Itamar to write the introduction.

Doug Wright, December 28, 2011

Playwrights Horizons produced the New York City Premiere of *Completeness* Off-Broadway in 2011.

Completeness by Itamar Moses. Artistic Director, Tim Sanford; Managing Director, Leslie Marcus; General Manager, Carol Fishman. Director: Pam MacKinnon. Scenic & Costume Design: David Zinn. Lighting Design: Russell H. Champa. Original Music & Sound Design: Bray Poor. Projection & Video Design: Rocco DiSanti. Casting: Alaine Alldaffer, CSA. Director of New Play Development: Adam Greenfield. Press Representative: The Publicity Office. Production Manager: Christopher Boll. Production Stage Manager: Charles M. Turner III.

Brian Avers	DON/CLARK/FRANKLIN
Aubrey Dollar	MOLLY
Meredith Forlenza	LAUREN/KATIE/NELL
Karl Miller	ELLIOT

Originally produced by South Coast Repertory. Artistic Director, Marc Masterson; Founding Directors, David Emmes & Martin Benson; Managing Director, Paula Tomei. Director: Pam MacKinnon. Scenic Design: Christopher Barreca. Costume Design: Sara Ryung Clement. Lighting Design: Russell H. Champa. Original Music & Sound Design: Bray Poor. Dramaturg: Kelly L. Miller. Production Manager: Jackie S. Hill. Stage Manager: Jennifer Ellen Butler.

Johnathan McClain	DON/CLARK/FRANKLIN
Mandy Siegfried	MOLLY
Brooke Bloom	LAUREN/KATIE/NELL
Karl Miller	ELLIOT

Originally commissioned by the Manhattan Theatre Club, Lynne Meadow, Artistic Director; Barry Grove, Executive Producer; Paige Evans, Director of New Play Development, with funds provided by the Alfred P. Sloan Foundation.

CHARACTERS

(2M, 2F with doubling)

    ELLIOT

    MOLLY

    DON/CLARK/FRANKLIN

    LAUREN/KATIE/NELL

1.

(The public computer cluster.)

(Rows of tables with computers, or at least the suggestion of this. Ugly fluorescent lighting. ELLIOT sits at a computer, working. He types for a while. Then clicks the mouse button to run something – a program of some kind? Then stares at the screen and waits.)

(He waits for a while. He shifts, annoyed. He clicks the mouse again. Then a few more times. Is the thing frozen? Frustrated, ELLIOT sighs. And restarts the computer. He gets up. He puts on his jacket, which is hanging on the back of the chair, picks up his backpack from where it is on the floor, and has just turned to go when…)

(…MOLLY enters and sits down at a different computer, nearby. ELLIOT hesitates. Then he pretends he has just arrived: puts his backpack down on the floor, puts his jacket over the back of the chair, sits at the computer, and pretends to start doing something, too.)

(ELLIOT and MOLLY both work in silence for a while. MOLLY is intent on her screen, reading, and then typing. ELLIOT is less intent on his screen and keeps sneaking glances at MOLLY. Then MOLLY sends an email. Her computer makes a "send" noise.)

ELLIOT: Email.

MOLLY: Excuse me?

ELLIOT: Sending, uhhh…

> *(Then, ELLIOT just looks down, lapsing back into awkward silence, and pretending to work some more. MOLLY rereads something on her screen and then sits back, annoyed.)*

MOLLY: *(Quietly.)* Not again.

ELLIOT: Is there a problem?

MOLLY: What?

ELLIOT: Is there a problem with the computer? Because I'm a C.A. I mean, I'm a grad student? In Computer Science? But I also work as a… So if there's –

MOLLY: There's no problem with the computer.

ELLIOT: Oh okay. *(Beat.)* I'm Elliot.

MOLLY: What?

ELLIOT: Sorry, just, I totally ambushed you without even… I'm Elliot?

MOLLY: There's not a problem with the computer, Elliot. Thanks.

ELLIOT: Okay.

MOLLY: Okay.

> *(A moment. MOLLY gets back to work. ELLIOT, internally kicking himself, starts to get back to pretend work, but then just shakes his head, gets up, grabs his jacket, and is reaching for his backpack, when:)*

MOLLY: I'm Molly.

ELLIOT: What? Oh –

MOLLY: Sorry, I can be… That was rude. I'm Molly.

ELLIOT: Oh, no. I mean: it's nice to meet you, Molly.

MOLLY: It's nice to meet you too, Elliot.

> *(A moment. MOLLY offers her hand for a handshake. ELLIOT shakes MOLLY's hand.)*

ELLIOT: All right. *(Beat.)* So, all right, um…

> *(A moment. ELLIOT walks away. A few moments pass. MOLLY types some more. ELLIOT comes back.)*

ELLIOT: I just… Forgot my…

> *(ELLIOT goes to get his backpack, which he left on the floor by his chair. Then he nods one more time, at nothing in particular, and has turned to go, when:)*

MOLLY: Hey, Elliot, let me ask you something.

ELLIOT: What? Yeah, okay.

MOLLY: Do you know what a two-hybrid screen is?

> *(Beat.)*

ELLIOT: Um –

MOLLY: Actually it doesn't matter.

ELLIOT: No, it's, you know, some kind of…method…whereby – ?

MOLLY: No that's not actually my question.

ELLIOT: Oh thank god.

MOLLY: Let's say you've accumulated a ton of data from an experiment. But the data is so sort of noisy and full of crap that it is very very difficult to know what it means. Don't you guys have ways of mitigating that?

ELLIOT: What guys? You mean in C.S.?

MOLLY: *(Overlapping.)* I, computer guys, yeah.

ELLIOT: Um, maybe. What's your project?

MOLLY: I work with yeast cultures, primarily? I –

ELLIOT: Yeast cultures? Seriously?

MOLLY: What.

ELLIOT: No, just, okay.

MOLLY: It's how we study protein-protein interactions. Which are responsible for more or less every process in your body.

ELLIOT: *(Catching up.)* This is Molecular Biology.

MOLLY: Yeah. Yeast is just a hospitable environment in which to perform screens. Of proteins we know against proteins we don't. Bait and prey.

ELLIOT: Huh. I like that. "Bait and pray." Kind of mystical for science, but –

MOLLY: No, prey. Like, prey. Like –

ELLIOT: *(Overlapping.)* Oh, oh, prey.

MOLLY: *(Miming one creature pouncing on another.)* Bait and prey.

ELLIOT: Gotcha.

MOLLY: Yeah. You use yeast as your host and plate a bunch of lines of a known protein, that's your bait, and then you criss-cross that with unknown protein strains, that's your prey, to make a grid. And then you add a reporter gene that causes a phenotype change? Only where the proteins bind. So at most of the intersections nothing happens, but… *(She beings rummaging in her bag.)* where two of the little guys do interact…when there's a pathway there…hold on… Ah.

ELLIOT: Ah!

> *(Because MOLLY has suddenly pulled a Petri dish out of her bag and, because ELLIOT was leaning in, she has held it up a little bit too near his face for comfort.)*

MOLLY: Oh god, sorry!

ELLIOT: Yeah, is that – ?

MOLLY: Yeah, no, don't worry, it's totally sterile, it's just… Here. Look.

> *(Tentatively, ELLIOT looks.)*

ELLIOT: It's blue.

MOLLY: Well it turns blue. Or it does whatever the reporter gene you chose tells it to do. I like blue.

ELLIOT: And then you know which proteins interact.

MOLLY: Well that's the problem because maybe not. My advisor keeps saying –

ELLIOT: Noisy and full of crap.

MOLLY: Exactly.

ELLIOT: Yeah. What you need is a data mining algorithm.

MOLLY: Okay. Say more.

ELLIOT: Where a computer looks at your data and then tells you the most likely interpretation of it.

MOLLY: I do need that. Thank you. *(Writing it down.)* "Data…mining… algorithm."

ELLIOT: *(Overlapping.)* I mean, I'd of course need actually to look at your data to figure out what specific kind you need, but, generally speaking –

MOLLY: What?

ELLIOT: Oh, well, just, I'd, um –

MOLLY: I, oh, no, sorry, I didn't, uh… (Beat.) I didn't mean you.

ELLIOT: Oh. *(Beat.)* Yeah, no, just, if –

MOLLY: Yeah I didn't mean you personally. Or, I mean, I should probably, like, go through the department, or –

ELLIOT: Oh, no, yeah.

MOLLY: Or through both of our departments in, like, some official way.

ELLIOT: Yeah, no, of course.

MOLLY: Yeah so… *(Beat.)* Why, would you do that for me?

ELLIOT: Uh, yeah. I mean, yeah, sure. If you want.

> *(Beat.)*

MOLLY: Okay.

ELLIOT: Okay, great, um, how can I get in touch with you?

MOLLY: What?

ELLIOT: What's the best way to get in touch with you?

MOLLY: I'm sitting right here. Like, now, in front of you, so –

ELLIOT: No, I know, I mean, later, to set up, like, a –

MOLLY: Oh, yeah, no, right, of course, here, let me… This is my cell.

> *(MOLLY tears off a corner of one page of her notebook and jots down her phone number. She slides it across the table to ELLIOT.)*

ELLIOT: Great. *(Beat.)* Actually could I have your email address?

> *(ELLIOT slides the paper back.)*

MOLLY: Oh. Um. Okay.

ELLIOT: Sorry, just, I'm more likely to actually… I'm a little more comfortable –

MOLLY: That's…fine. Here.

> *(MOLLY writes down her email address and slides the paper back.)*

ELLIOT: Great. Thanks.

> *(ELLIOT looks at the paper. Then he leans forward and types something into his computer. Then he clicks with the mouse and there is a "send"*

noise. A moment. ELLIOT nods and half-smiles awkwardly at MOLLY who half-smiles back perplexed. Then the email arrives at the computer in front of MOLLY with an "arrival" noise.)

MOLLY: Oh!

ELLIOT: Yeah, that's, um. That's me

(…transition…all the transitions cast the space into a dark blue light…)

2.

(ELLIOT's place.)

(The whole apartment is really one space: front door, kitchen area, sleeping area, work area with desk and computer. Another door presumably leads to the bathroom. Also, there is a white board on the wall with a to-do list written on it. LAUREN is in bed, in pajamas of some kind, working on her laptop. ELLIOT is at his desk, at the computer, in a t-shirt and boxers maybe, or otherwise dressed for bed. He is on his cell phone.)

ELLIOT: Uh-huh … Uh-huh … Well yeah I mean, nobody wants to feel that way…

(ELLIOT smiles at LAUREN, rolling his eyes. She smiles, understanding.)

ELLIOT: Uh-huh… Uh-huh. … Oh, I'm sure that's not true, I'm sure you both want it to work. I mean, you're not the easiest guy to… No, I know, I just mean she's been there, through all your… Uh-huh.

(ELLIOT shakes his head at LAUREN apologetically. She shrugs: "No problem.")

ELLIOT: Uh-huh. …. *(Then, a little exasperated.)* Well then why don't you guys just get divorced then? … *(Relenting.)* I, no, I didn't, I'm just… Uh-huh. … Uh-huh, I, oh, uh, Lauren just came over. …

(LAUREN smirks and nods: "Great. Use me." ELLIOT shrugs: "Sorry!")

ELLIOT: Yeah, so I should… Okay. … Okay. … I will. … Okay. … Bye.

(ELLIOT hangs up the phone. Then:)

ELLIOT: My Dad says hi.

(*LAUREN nods. Then:*)

LAUREN: Does it ever bother your Mom?

ELLIOT: What.

LAUREN: That he has these conversations with you.

ELLIOT: Should it?

LAUREN: It would bother me.

ELLIOT: Huh. (*Beat.*) Yeah I don't know.

(*ELLIOT gets back to work. LAUREN works. A silence. Then:*)

LAUREN: What are you working on?

ELLIOT: An algorithm.

LAUREN: For the TSP?

ELLIOT: No, not for me, it's a data mining algorithm. For an experiment.

LAUREN: What experiment?

ELLIOT: On yeast?

LAUREN: Yeast? Who's working on yeast?

ELLIOT: I know, right? Just some grad student, just this grad student, in bio.

LAUREN: Do I know him?

ELLIOT: Uhh… (*Beat.*) No, I don't think you do. (*Beat.*) I mean, it's pretty standard, pretty basic heuristics, so I can just…adapt existing code? But it's a nice change of pace, to, you know, work on something else.

LAUREN: And it might be good, for the department, which funds you, to see you branch out a little, yeah. (*Pause.*) Hey.

ELLIOT: What.

(*LAUREN closes her laptop and puts it away.*)

LAUREN: Come here.

(*ELLIOT looks over. LAUREN is looking at him suggestively.*)

ELLIOT: In, yeah, in just a second.

LAUREN: Uhh –

ELLIOT: No, I just, I'm almost… Hey, no…

> (Because LAUREN, feeling rejected, puts her laptop away, flicks off a light, and pretends to go to sleep, while in fact sulking. A moment.)

ELLIOT: Seriously. Just one second.

> (No answer. ELLIOT looks back at the computer. Then back at LAUREN. ELLIOT leaves the computer still working, crosses to the bed, and slips under the covers.)

ELLIOT: Hey.

LAUREN: (Muffled.) No.

ELLIOT: No? Just no?

LAUREN: No.

ELLIOT: "No" in reference to what, exactly?

LAUREN: No don't come over here.

> (A moment. ELLIOT gets out of bed and heads back to the computer.)

LAUREN: Oh my god! Elliot!

ELLIOT: What? You pushed me away!

LAUREN: So?

ELLIOT: So you're mad that I'm not in bed and then you're mad that I am in bed and now you're mad that I got out of bed?

LAUREN: No! I'm mad that you didn't stay in bed and try to make me feel better!

> (A moment. ELLIOT starts to move back towards the bed.)

LAUREN: Oh my god what's wrong with you?

ELLIOT: What? You just said – !

LAUREN: Yes so don't come back when I tell you to! Come back when you want to!

ELLIOT: But..! I…! (Pause.) I do want to.

LAUREN: No you don't.

ELLIOT: Okay so let me get this. Now that you've told me to come back to bed, my decision to return is thus rendered, a priori, meaningless.

LAUREN: Well –

ELLIOT: Because you do realize that, by that logic, once you've expressed a preference, I can never actually do what you prefer without my motives being suspect.

LAUREN: Well, okay, but –

ELLIOT: On top of which, the fact that my return to bed was preceded by you telling me you want me to does not necessarily mean that your telling me was the cause. Correlation is not causation.

LAUREN: I know that, Elliot. I'm just telling you how it feels.

ELLIOT: And, and! In any case: what's wrong with me just wanting to give you what you want? Don't you want me to...want to give you what you want?

LAUREN: I...guess, but –

ELLIOT: So okay then.

LAUREN: So, wait, so then which is it?

ELLIOT: Which is what.

LAUREN: Is it that you really want to come to bed or that you're trying to give me what I want by coming to bed?

        (Beat.)

ELLIOT: My point is that either way there's nothing for you to get upset about.

LAUREN: But I am upset.

ELLIOT: Okay.

LAUREN: Is the flaw in your theory.

ELLIOT: Well –

LAUREN: Because, you know what? Because it doesn't feel like you trying to do either of those things. It feels like you just trying to prevent me from getting mad.

ELLIOT: Well maybe that's because you're always on the brink of getting mad at me and so sometimes preventing that feels like the absolute best that I can do.

LAUREN: But it isn't! You can make me happy!

ELLIOT: How!?

LAUREN: I don't want to have to tell you!

ELLIOT: Right because you want me to just guess!

LAUREN: No. I want you. To just. Know.

> *(Pause.)*

ELLIOT: Well…

> *(A moment. ELLIOT shuts his eyes, rubs his forehead, something like that.)*

LAUREN: What. What is it.

ELLIOT: No, just… I feel a little nauseous.

LAUREN: Elliot. What is it.

> *(A moment. ELLIOT is not looking at LAUREN. Then his computer starts to make a little bit of noise, a gentle ticking, as though its hard drive is straining a little, or as though its a fan has turned on to cool it. Something like that. For a moment or two, ELLIOT, lost in thought, doesn't notice. But then it jars him out of his reverie. He hits whatever buttons are necessary to stop the computer from doing whatever it's doing, and, with that:)*

ELLIOT: All right, look. I've just, um. I've just been…thinking? About what kind of, like, situation, or relationship, you seem to want to be in.

LAUREN: What? What does that mean.

ELLIOT: Well, and, just that, if I don't know if that's the same kind of situation that I want to be in, necessarily, then it doesn't, like, seem exactly fair. To you. To not let you, like, go, and find that kind of relationship. Or situation.

LAUREN: Um –

ELLIOT: You know?

LAUREN: Well, not… I mean, look, Elliot, I don't know what you mean exactly, I mean, I don't have some, like, abstract kind of relationship that I wish to be in, if, you know, if something about the way… I want to, this is, so if, like, if the parameters… If something is making you uncomfortable then we can, you know, I can try to… Or, I mean, I'm sorry I, it's not a big deal, we don't have to even… I have this stupid cold that's been… Don't think you have to like set me free to find, like, some guy I haven't even met yet who'll, like, I don't even know what. *(Beat.)* What are you saying?

> *(Beat.)*

ELLIOT: What I'm saying is. I feel like if I don't know if I'm going to be a certain kind of guy for you. Like if I know that I'm not going to be that guy. It seems like I should say that. Like. As soon as possible.

LAUREN: *(Quietly.)* Yeah but what does that mean, though, "be that guy for me."

ELLIOT: Who'll want to turn this into…something permanent. (Beat.) Because, if –

LAUREN: Oh my god, what am I doing in your bed?

> *(LAUREN gets out of bed and moves as far away from ELLIOT as she can get.)*

ELLIOT: Hey –

LAUREN: Uh, no, I think I've, I think I got it, sorry, it took me –

ELLIOT: *(Moving toward her.)* No, listen to me.

LAUREN: Oh my god, get away from me.

> *(ELLIOT stops where he is.)*

LAUREN: What.

> *(Beat.)*

ELLIOT: You're amazing, okay? I think you're great.

LAUREN: Oh my god – !

ELLIOT: But, okay, but would you please just listen?

LAUREN: I…! Get away from me!

> *(Because ELLIOT is moving towards her again, so she shoves past him, and backs away to the other side of the room.)*

ELLIOT: Okay! Okay. I just, look, I just want to –

LAUREN: No! Don't tell me how great I am, okay? Don't do that.

ELLIOT: Okay.

LAUREN: Okay.

> *(Beat.)*

ELLIOT: Okay so then –

LAUREN: So wait so are you saying that you're not the kind of guy who will want something to be permanent, like, ever with anyone, like, that's just not something you're going to want to do, or are you saying it's not something you can see yourself doing with me because of something that you think isn't right for you about me.

> *(Beat.)*

ELLIOT: Well, that's, you know, that's not really a question that's possible to answer, is it.

LAUREN: It's not?

ELLIOT: Well, what, you want me to stand here and tell you that I will never want to stay with anyone, ever, because – ?

LAUREN: No, of course not –

ELLIOT: *(Overlapping.)* Because I mean, obviously, every relationship I've been in up to now has, you know, ended, I mean, manifestly, so –

LAUREN: *(Overlapping.)* Right, of course, but –

ELLIOT: But does that mean they all will, always, how should I know?

LAUREN: No, of course not, Elliot, I am not asking you to predict the future! I'm asking you if...! *(Pause. Maybe she starts to cry.)* What did I do wrong?

ELLIOT: You didn't do anything wrong.

LAUREN: No, I must have done something, I must have done something wrong, tell me what I did wrong.

ELLIOT: You didn't do anything wrong, it's, you know... Timing.

LAUREN: Timing?

ELLIOT: Yeah.

LAUREN: How is it timing?

ELLIOT: Well you knew that I was coming off a really bad break-up.

LAUREN: Right. I mean, so was I.

ELLIOT: And well right but –

LAUREN: I mean, we talked about it, we were like, hey, isn't it surprising and unexpected to be able to get into something with someone new, we talked about it –

ELLIOT: Yeah, it was, it is.

LAUREN: So, right, so then what the fuck is your point exactly?

ELLIOT: That maybe...

LAUREN: What.

ELLIOT: I mean don't you ever feel...

LAUREN: What. Tell me.

ELLIOT: Don't you ever feel like there are certain feelings inside you, that are curled up inside you, like a potential, and can stretch out and attach to another person. And when those feelings get bruised or hurt they curl back up again until they heal. And until that happens they aren't available. But maybe a different kind of feeling is, one that isn't bruised, and you attach in that way, but meanwhile, the other part of you, the bruised part, is healing, and then eventually, it's healed. And you feel that potential again.

(Beat.)

LAUREN: Oh my god –

ELLIOT: No, just, because, listen –

LAUREN: I'm, you're saying I'm, get away from me –

> *(ELLIOT reaches for LAUREN's hand but she pulls away and heads for the bathroom.)*

ELLIOT: But don't you feel that?

LAUREN: You're saying I'm a rebound?

ELLIOT: No, just, first of all, I don't really like that word?

LAUREN: Oh my god!

ELLIOT: I don't, I think that it's reductive!

LAUREN: Oh my god you fucking asshole!

> *(LAUREN disappears into the bathroom and slams the door. A moment.)*

ELLIOT: Come out of there. *(Pause.)* Hey. Hello? *(He knocks gently.)* Hey, come out of there and talk to me.

LAUREN: *(Off.)* I don't want to.

ELLIOT: You have to come out of there eventually.

LAUREN: *(Off.)* No I don't.

ELLIOT: You're going to live in my bathroom?

LAUREN: *(Off.)* I hate you.

ELLIOT: Okay. *(Pause.)* Or, look, you said it yourself. It was one of the first things you said to me, when we got together, that maybe we're too similar. We, you know, we do exactly the same thing, we're in the same department, we know all the same people –

> *(LAUREN opens the door.)*

LAUREN: Oh god, and I'm going to have to see you around the fucking department all the time, that's right, fuck!

> *(LAUREN slams the door again. A moment.)*

ELLIOT: And, so maybe it's too, you know... Maybe we'd each be better off with someone...complementary.

(A silence. LAUREN opens the door. A moment.)

ELLIOT: I mean, right?

LAUREN: Who is she?

(Beat.)

ELLIOT: What?

LAUREN: Who is she that's complementary that you feel that potential again with. It's that chick Nell, isn't it. That undergrad?

ELLIOT: I have no idea what you're talking about.

LAUREN: There isn't somebody else.

ELLIOT: No, Jesus, I would never...

LAUREN: Well then... Well then what if I hadn't gotten mad at you.

ELLIOT: What?

LAUREN: What if we hadn't had that stupid fight? Would we still be breaking up?

ELLIOT: I, what? I don't know –

LAUREN: What if instead I hadn't pushed you away before? Instead of breaking up, would we be having sex right now?

ELLIOT: I don't know. *(Beat.)* I guess. Probably.

LAUREN: Well then maybe we don't have to break up.

ELLIOT: Well, maybe we wouldn't have broken up tonight, but you were, I mean, you're right, you were mad at me because whatever I was or wasn't doing, you were sensing that underneath that I –

LAUREN: But, no, but listen, because it's, you feel these feelings that weren't available before because of your break-up with your ex-girlfriend from college have now healed and are available again.

ELLIOT: I guess.

LAUREN: And there isn't somebody else.

ELLIOT: No.

LAUREN: But so then… So then could they be available to me?

> (*LAUREN tries to take ELLIOT's hand but he pulls slightly away.*)

ELLIOT: I don't think that's how it works.

LAUREN: What?

ELLIOT: I don't think that that's how it works.

LAUREN: So there is someone else.

ELLIOT: No. What do you – ?

LAUREN: Well, there is or there will be, right? Maybe you know who it is already or maybe you don't but one way or another you're going to take all that potential that you built up while you were with me and you're going to give it to her, and that makes me sick, but you know what? It's not real. It's gonna feel real at first just because she'll be new but that will run out and you'll check out again, you'll check out again, inside, because that's what you do, and she'll feel it, and all this will just happen again.

> (*Beat.*)

ELLIOT: Well. If we're broken up. Then that really isn't any of your business. Is it.

> (*A moment. LAUREN goes back into the bathroom and slams the door. She can be heard sobbing, off. ELLIOT sighs, crosses to his computer, sits down. He starts to type, which itself perhaps almost seems to trigger the transition to…*)

3.

(*ELLIOT's place.*)

(*ELLIOT sits at his computer, as before. A cell phone rings somewhere in the room. ELLIOT looks around. It rings again. The bathroom door opens. MOLLY comes out.*)

MOLLY: Hey, sorry.

ELLIOT: It's fine, I think, um –

MOLLY: No, I totally didn't need to pee when I left my place, and then as soon as I got here I suddenly needed to…pee. Sorry, I'll stop talking about pee now.

ELLIOT: It's fine. I think your phone is ringing

MOLLY: What?

ELLIOT: Your phone.

MOLLY: Oh!

(*MOLLY heads for her bag, which is on the floor, behind something. She takes her phone, which is still ringing, out of her bag. Looks at it. Rejects the call.*)

ELLIOT: So –

MOLLY: Oh, I brought you something.

ELLIOT: What? Oh –

(*MOLLY puts the phone away and pulls a loaf of bread out of her bag.*)

MOLLY: As a thank you. For helping me with this. Um. Here.

ELLIOT: That's for me?

MOLLY: Yeah.

ELLIOT: That's, thanks, I really appreciate it. (Beat.) Is this a loaf of bread?

MOLLY: Yes, yeah. (*Beat.*) Oh I made it.

ELLIOT: Oh!

MOLLY: Yeah no because –

ELLIOT: That's really sweet.

MOLLY: No but it requires yeast. (Beat.) To rise, it –

ELLIOT: Oh!

MOLLY: Yeah it's a joke.

ELLIOT: Oh I get it.

MOLLY: Yeah. *(Beat.)* I mean you can also…eat it, I, it's good, I can –

ELLIOT: Yeah I, um, I will. *(Beat.)* Do you want me to show you how this works?

MOLLY: Please do yes.

> *(ELLIOT goes to his desk and sits at his computer awkwardly putting the bread down to one side. MOLLY follows him. During which:)*

ELLIOT: Just yell if it gets confusing.

MOLLY: That won't be a problem.

ELLIOT: So, basically, I designed a genetic algorithm, which, I know that you're not breeding anything, just, all that means is that it uses the principles of natural selection to arrive at better and better answers the same way that evolution gradually produces improvements in the species, or, you know, "so fashionable theory has it," uh, but, so, yeah, first the algorithm randomly generates interpretations of your data and treats each as a "parent" in an initial population. And then it computes a fitness value for each, based on…criteria that you can set yourself, I didn't know exactly –

MOLLY: Right.

ELLIOT: And, yeah, then it sort of…"mates" them, with, um, with of course only the "fittest" getting selected, and those produce…"offspring" interpretations, which are then assigned fitness values of their own, and so on, generation after generation, selection, mating, offspring, periodically introducing all-important random mutation, until, after many, many iterations, or, you know, about two hours, it will eventually plateau at the most likely interpretation of your data, so, here, if you were gonna… I just labeled your unknown protein "M"? For Molly?

MOLLY: Aw.

ELLIOT: And, yeah, based on whatever factors, it will tell you how much you can trust the bonds, or lack thereof, between Protein M and, for now, they're labeled A, B, C –

MOLLY: *(Starting to be really impressed.)* Yeah, okay.

ELLIOT: And you can just keep adding more, it's… When it runs out of letters it'll just go Double-A, Double-B, Double-C, or you could just put in the protein's real…names…

> *(Beat.)*

MOLLY: Thank you.

ELLIOT: It's no problem.

MOLLY: No, seriously, thank you, you're a lifesaver. Could I – ?

ELLIOT: Oh, of course.

> *(ELLIOT gets up. MOLLY sits at the computer to play with the algorithm. ELLIOT watches her work for a moment. Then he goes to his kitchen area.)*

ELLIOT: Do you want something to drink?

MOLLY: Like what.

ELLIOT: Uh. *(Beat.)* Like, tea, or –

MOLLY: Tea?

ELLIOT: Or…whisky?

MOLLY: Whisky.

> *(The phone in MOLLY's bag rings again.)*

ELLIOT: Great. *(Pause.)* I think your phone is –

MOLLY: Yeah.

> *(ELLIOT prepares two whiskies. MOLLY tries to ignore her phone and focus on the computer but then, after another ring, goes to her bag again, rejects the call again, and this time puts the phone in her pocket as she goes back to the computer. During which:)*

MOLLY: I like your place.

ELLIOT: Really? I don't.

MOLLY: What? Why not?

ELLIOT: I don't know, I kind of hate how it's set up, and, like –

MOLLY: How long have you had it like this?

ELLIOT: Basically since I started grad school.

MOLLY: And how long is that?

ELLIOT: Uh, longer than I care to think about?

MOLLY: And you hate it.

ELLIOT: Yeah what I like to do is get things a certain way that I don't actually like and, instead of fixing it, just complain about it forever. It's this trick I learned from my father.

MOLLY: Yeah? He should meet my mom.

ELLIOT: Oh, does she do that?

MOLLY: No she loves everything. For ten minutes. You should see the emails.

ELLIOT: What about you?

MOLLY: What about me what.

ELLIOT: How long have you been here?

MOLLY: Oh I just got here.

ELLIOT: Heh. No, I meant –

MOLLY: Oh, no, so did I. This is my first semester.

ELLIOT: Oh. I mean, yeah, that's what I figured.

MOLLY: What? Why?

ELLIOT: Oh just because I only recently…noticed…you, hey, cheers!

> (Because by now ELLIOT is standing by the desk with two glasses of whiskey.)

MOLLY: Cheers.

(*Clink. ELLIOT almost drinks. But instead of drinking MOLLY turns back to the computer and points at the screen, so ELLIOT holds off drinking as well.*)

MOLLY: Can I run it?

ELLIOT: Oh, yeah, sure, I… Here.

(*ELLIOT clicks the mouse button to run the algorithm. A few moments go by.*)

MOLLY: It's not doing anything.

ELLIOT: Oh, no, it is, it's just it… Here, if… You can watch the code run if you…

(*ELLIOT clicks his mouse again to open up the code and takes a step back. MOLLY watches the code run. Perhaps we see a different light playing across her face. ELLIOT watches MOLLY watch the code. A moment.*)

ELLIOT: Yeah it's a good way to make sure something's actually… happening…

(*A few moments. Then:*)

MOLLY: (*Reading what's on the screen.*) "Generating Init Pop. Init Pop Full."

ELLIOT: Yeah.

MOLLY: "If A greater than B then select dot crossover A else select dot crossover B. End If."

ELLIOT: Yeah it starts out slow but stick with it, it picks up.

MOLLY: I bet. Mm!

(*Because now MOLLY has tried her whiskey. So ELLIOT drinks his.*)

ELLIOT: Yeah, it's good, right?

MOLLY: Yeah, it's really good. (*Long pause.*) So.

ELLIOT: Yeah. What happens now?

MOLLY: Oh. Well now I take this data?

ELLIOT: *(This is not what he meant.)* Oh, um –

MOLLY: *(Continuous.)* And, well, I don't think you realize how helpful you just were because, this protein… I mean, you remember what proteins are, right? They're made up of amino acids, which are transcribed directly from our DNA – ?

ELLIOT: Uh, that all rings an incredibly vague bell, yeah.

MOLLY: Yeah, so they're really basic building blocks, only one level or so up from our genetic code, and they do everything, like, if DNA is like the architect? Proteins are the, like, little workers that actually have hammers and nails and saws and things, so when we find a new one, like this, which always happens accidentally, we'll be looking for something else and something we've never seen before will just pop up on a gel, when that happens, we try to determine what it's for, which, okay, enthralling, yes, I know –

ELLIOT: *(Trying to seem interested as possible in all this.)* I, no, it's –

MOLLY: But, okay: were you aware that if a three-year old child's finger is severed and you don't seal up the wound that the entire finger will grow back?

> *(Beat.)*

ELLIOT: What if my answer to that were "yes"? How creepy would that be?

MOLLY: Heh heh.

ELLIOT: "Of course! Did you not see my necklace made of child fingers?" No, I did not know that. Is that true?

MOLLY: If it's just the fingertip it can grow back on kids as old as ten.

ELLIOT: Really.

MOLLY: There's no fingerprint and the nail will for some reason be square but yes.

ELLIOT: How?

MOLLY: That is the wrong question. The right question is: why does it stop? Why does our capacity to regenerate diminish with age? And so that's what our lab is studying: tissue growth, wound healing, because once you understand how these things happen naturally, or don't, then the process can be synthesized to address damage that won't heal on its own, or, "so fashionable theory has it." New skin, or bones, or organs even, regrown with no scarring, no fibrosis, from inside yourself, from your own cells, so no chance of rejection, the…same way you grew them all in the first place. Which would obviously be great.

ELLIOT: I, yeah, that would.

MOLLY: But, and this is where the yeast two-hybrid screen comes in, proteins don't actually perform their functions on their own, they all have a place as part of a larger interaction network of other proteins, a, what we call an interactome, which, if you want to visualize it, *(Perhaps she draws this for him on a piece of paper.)* think of the proteins as nodes, and the interactions as lines, and it all makes one big 3D map, together, in which they perform all their various functions cooperatively, so you can only find out so much about a protein in isolation before you sort of have to take her on a fishing expedition, and see if she can lead you to her friends.

ELLIOT: Bait and prey.

MOLLY: Exactly. But the problem is these screens are kind of…error prone? In that they can create conditions that never actually occur in, like, actual nature, like, two proteins may bind but never really appear in the same cell, or only express at different times in the life cycle, and so the bonding is meaningless, or vice-versa, a failed bond that's actually just dependent on some external condition I excluded from the screen, or, you know, certain proteins might just behave differently in yeast than they do in us –

ELLIOT: False positives and false negatives.

MOLLY: Correct, but thanks to you, my friend, I can now filter out the garbage, know which bonds are for real, make some predictions about the network, and then test them, wet, in vivo, by engineering an organism designed to reveal as much as possible about the function, or functions, of Protein M. Which, again, adorable.

> *(Beat.)*

ELLIOT: *(Genuinely fascinated by now.)* And then what?

MOLLY: Um, then, depending on what I learn, I, probably give it a really literal minded-name based on its function, like integrin or versacan, and then go back, do more screens, get more data, make more predictions, do more experiments to test those, and so on, back and forth, like that, data, testing, data, testing, while other molecular biologists the world over do the same thing, gradually modeling the network more and more, until, I guess maybe, eventually, someday we'll have….mapped the whole damn thing.

ELLIOT: How close are we to that?

MOLLY: That depends on what you mean.

ELLIOT: By "close"?

MOLLY: By "that."

ELLIOT: Well how much of it have we mapped?

MOLLY: Less and less every day. I mean, not close, not the way you mean, because we keep discovering new corners we didn't even know about, so, if we're talking total human interactome? One or two percent completeness, maybe, tops? And every network is embedded hierarchically inside another, larger one, cellular, systemic, organismic, going from molecule to creature, as it were, so… I mean, that's why so many of the things our bodies do are still mysterious, because they're less functions than they are just emergent properties of this dynamic multi-layered fucking mess. So, even when the result is right in front of you, you're nowhere if you can't explain how it was reached. We grow and change and get sick and recover and age and die and by and large from our perspective these things just happen. Our bodies just know. So it'll be a long long time from now, if ever, before we can know with our brains all the things our bodies just already know.

(MOLLY is looking at ELLIOT. A moment.)

ELLIOT: What if I could help you more?

MOLLY: Oh, uhh –

ELLIOT: (Returning to his computer.) Or, I mean, what if I could write an algorithm that interpreted your data…better? Because this, all it will do is generate probable interpretations, highly probable, but, still, now that I know more what you… Before you rush off to test predictions based on this? What if I could write something that would give you... certainty, up front?

MOLLY: *(Now it was she who was expecting something else.)* Oh.

ELLIOT: I mean, I don't know exactly how it would work, but if you give me another few days, or more like a week? I could –

MOLLY: Right, but I'm already in your apartment. *(Beat.)* Right now, though. So...

ELLIOT: Oh. I mean, okay. *(Pause.)* Uhhh...

> *(MOLLY and ELLIOT start to make out. They make out for a little while. Then:)*

MOLLY: Okay, can I tell you something?

ELLIOT: Sure.

MOLLY: I wasn't sure that an algorithm would be useful to me? And actually I am pleasantly surprised by how incredibly useful it turns out in fact to be? But I sort of didn't care because I just wanted an excuse to hang out with you.

ELLIOT: Can I tell you something?

MOLLY: Please.

ELLIOT: When I said something came up this afternoon so we had to meet tonight, that was a total lie, and I figured either you'd say, oh, okay, then let's just meet up tomorrow, or you'd be like, okay, what time tonight? And you said the second one? And I was like, oh, okay. It's on.

> *(MOLLY and ELLIOT make out some more. Then:)*

MOLLY: That day, in the public cluster? I sat down at that computer because you were coming in.

ELLIOT: Actually I was leaving. I pretended to be coming in because you sat down.

> *(They make out some more. They move towards the bed. Then:)*

MOLLY: I bought this outfit on the way here.

ELLIOT: It's so nice.

MOLLY: Thank you.

ELLIOT: "Uh, but it would blah blah blah crumpled up on my floor."

MOLLY: Heh. Heh. Mm.

> *(MOLLY's phone rings again. This time she rejects the call without even looking at it.)*

ELLIOT: Seriously, if it's an emergency or something, you can go ahead and –

MOLLY: It's really not.

ELLIOT: Okay.

> *(They make out some more. Some clothes start to come off. Then she stops him.)*

MOLLY: I'm not staying over.

ELLIOT: Okay.

MOLLY: Just, I'm not going to stay over, or sleep here, or anything.

ELLIOT: Good. I'm glad.

> *(They make out some more. Then he stops her.)*

ELLIOT: But, wait, so you're not planning to leave until after the sex though, right?

> *(MOLLY just looks at ELLIOT, blinking. A moment.)*

ELLIOT: That looks like a yes.

> *(MOLLY rolls her eyes. Then ELLIOT touches her face. Her arms. Just touching her.)*

MOLLY: What are you doing?

ELLIOT: I don't know. I just love this moment when you're suddenly allowed to start…touching someone? Like, you've wanted to, but of course you can't just walk up to someone and touch them, but then, suddenly, you've passed through the membrane, and you can. Like. I'd been thinking about touching you? More or less since the first time I saw you?

MOLLY: Sure. I mean, I'd…seen you too.

ELLIOT: Well, right, but for all I knew that was imaginary? Like, the idea that they might be thinking the same thing about you, you don't even let yourself entertain that possibility? And but then you're actually here. Like. This person I can't even believe I'm lucky enough to get to touch and she's here, she's…letting me touch her.

(*Beat.*)

MOLLY: I have to teach in the morning?

ELLIOT: Okay.

MOLLY: I have teach in the morning, undergrads, so, I'm saying, if I do stay? I'd need to, like, set an alarm clock for pretty early, like six thirty – ?

ELLIOT: That is not a problem.

MOLLY: Really?

ELLIOT: I don't intend for us to sleep at all.

MOLLY: Heh.

ELLIOT: Oh not because we'll be fooling around. Just because after we're done I'll keep you awake with long boring stories about my family because physical intimacy will have created the illusion of emotional intimacy. Come here.

MOLLY: No really if you could set it now.

ELLIOT: Oh –

MOLLY: I just don't want us to forget.

ELLIOT: No, yeah, okay.

(*ELLIOT sets his alarm clock. During which:*)

MOLLY: Just, I co-teach, with this other grad student, and I'm chronically late, and it's important he not hate me, so –

ELLIOT: It's not a problem.

MOLLY: He gives genetic diseases to mice so there's no telling what he'd do to me.

ELLIOT: I teach in the morning too.

MOLLY: Oh okay.

ELLIOT: Yeah.

MOLLY: Kind of sucks, doesn't it.

> *(ELLIOT checks the alarm two or three more times before turning away from it.)*

ELLIOT: Uh, it can. When they're passive idiots. But once in a while... I've got this one incredibly sharp kid this semester, she –

MOLLY: Hey come here.

> *(ELLIOT goes there. More making out. Then ELLIOT struggles with whatever is keeping MOLLY's pants closed. He peers at her pants carefully.)*

ELLIOT: Huh.

MOLLY: It's, oh, you have to, if you... See?

ELLIOT: Oh yeah. It's, see real world objects... I can't...

> *(MOLLY does not struggle at all with ELLIOT's pants. Soon ELLIOT and MOLLY are both in their underwear. A moment.)*

ELLIOT: Hold on.

MOLLY: What.

> *(ELLIOT goes around and starts turning off the various lights.)*

MOLLY: You don't want to see me?

ELLIOT: Oh, no, just. Mood lighting.

MOLLY: I want to see you.

> *(The only light remaining is the lamp next to the bed, which ELLIOT was just reaching for. Instead, he leaves this on and reaches for MOLLY again.)*

MOLLY: I don't normally do this.

ELLIOT: Oh. Okay.

MOLLY: Just so you know.

ELLIOT: Okay. *(Beat.)* Why do girls always say that?

MOLLY: What?

ELLIOT: What.

MOLLY: "Girls"? "Always"?

ELLIOT: *(Overlapping.)* Oh, no, I just –

MOLLY: Cause invoking other girls right now isn't really, like…the best idea…

ELLIOT: *(Overlapping.)* No, please, I'm not, I don't mean… *(Beat.)* I just… Not that there have been… In my extremely limited experience. At a certain moment. Girls have a tendency to say. "I don't normally do this."

MOLLY: Okay.

ELLIOT: Which can only mean one of two things. That I'm just so appealing that I am an exception to the otherwise intractable courtship rules of the entire female population. Which let's table for the moment as unlikely. Or. They're lying. Which I would prefer also not to believe. So I was just wondering. As someone who has just now actually said it. If you had any insight into what it really means.

    (Beat.)

MOLLY: I think that you've failed to consider a third possibility.

ELLIOT: What's that.

MOLLY: That, because not only do they normally not sleep with someone right away, but, with most people, they don't do it ever, that it's not a lie. It's just that, with someone where they know they're going to want to? They figure that they might as well start, like, immediately. So it's not that you're in general so appealing either. It just looks that way from your perspective because your sampling size self-selects for people who have already decided to sleep, specifically, with you.

    (Beat.)

ELLIOT: You're right.

MOLLY: I know.

ELLIOT: I made a derivation error.

    (The phone rings in the pocket of MOLLY's discarded pants. A moment.)

MOLLY: If that's what it's…called… I'm going to turn that off. *(She goes to her phone and turns it off. Then:)* Hold on a second.

ELLIOT: What.

> *(MOLLY heads for the bathroom.)*

MOLLY: I, um. I have to pee again.

ELLIOT: It's the whisky.

MOLLY: No I think I'm just nervous.

> *(MOLLY exits. ELLIOT sits on the bed and waits. He grins and laughs slightly, basking in the awesomeness of this moment. Then he turns off the remaining light. Moves clothes off his bed. There is still light from his computer screen, so ELLIOT gets up and goes to turn it off. Light from the street through windows is all that's left. And ELLIOT is still in the middle of the room when MOLLY emerges from the bathroom, naked. Naked in streetlight and moonlight. A moment.)*

MOLLY: Hi.

ELLIOT: Hi.

MOLLY: Sorry, too much? Too soon?

ELLIOT: What? No. No no no. No, uh…

> *(ELLIOT removes his remaining clothing and tosses it aside. A moment.)*

MOLLY: I see what you mean.

ELLIOT: What.

MOLLY: About the light.

> *(They stand looking at each other, across the bed, for a moment. In the near dark, they look blue. Then they slip into the bed from opposite sides. ELLIOT moves to MOLLY but she stops him. She reaches down below the covers and peers after her hand. A moment.)*

ELLIOT: Uh, what are you doing?

MOLLY: Having sex without examining the genitals is like biting into a piece of fruit without looking at it. *(Pause.)* Okay.

ELLIOT: Okay?

MOLLY: Yeah. Just yell if it gets confusing.

(MOLLY and ELLIOT intertwine…transition…the sound of a ringing phone, as heard by the caller, takes us into…)

4.

(The front steps of a university housing building.)

(DON is here, holding a cell phone to his ear. He waits. Listens. Then, at last:)

DON: Hey I don't know where you are. *(Beat.)* Which is, that's fine, in… principle, I'm not, you are a free…person. Just. I'm worried about you. So call me. *(Beat.)* I mean maybe your phone is just off. But it seems like it's ringing and you're not… I mean, if you're angry at me, or, if I did something wrong, I'd rather you just talked to me or told me instead of disappearing, but, which, I mean if your phone is just off, then ignore that part, it's not a big deal, I just meant, mainly I'm worried. Because you're also not home either, so, or, if you are, just, okay, I'm on the street in front of your place right now? Not in a creepy way, I'm just…telling you where I am. Or, that's not, look, I know that I've been busy lately, okay? So I'm sorry if… *(Beat.)* You know what? Just ignore this entire message. And call me whenever. If you want. Or don't, I'll just…see you in the department. *(Beat.)* This is Don. *(Beat.)* Bye.

(DON hangs up. He does not feel good about how that went. Sits on the steps. Thinks. Shudders. Takes out the phone again. Scrolls through some numbers. Dials again. A phone rings.)

(Lights up on the Computer Science departmental office. The phone on the front desk is ringing, unattended. It rings again. LAUREN walks by the desk. Stops and turns back when she hears the phone ring. Looks around for anyone. It rings again.)

(DON is about to hang up. LAUREN answers the phone.)

LAUREN: Computer Science.

DON: Hi, this is Professor Davis, from Molecular Biology?

LAUREN: Okay.

(Beat.)

DON: Uh, yeah, one of my grad students, my, uh, my advisee, had a meeting scheduled this evening? With one of your grad students? And I was just wondering whether she was still there.

LAUREN: There's...no one here.

DON: Well could you maybe check?

> *(LAUREN looks around for a second, perfunctorily.)*

LAUREN: There's no one here.

DON: Well, if the departmental secretary is still there, then maybe –

LAUREN: Um, I'm not a secretary? I'm a graduate student.

DON: Well, whoever you are, you're there, so –

LAUREN: Yeah but no one else is here because it's night.

DON: Okay but could you please just actually – ?

LAUREN: MB and B is one floor down, why don't you just come up here yourself?

> *(Beat.)*

DON: I'm not there.

LAUREN: Yeah! No one is!

DON: Okay, okay, look, I'm sorry, just... Her name is Molly and she was supposedly meeting with this guy Elliot and I just want to know if they're still there. Please. *(Long pause.)* Hello?

LAUREN: Uh, no.

DON: What?

LAUREN: No. He's...not, there's... *(Beat.)* No one's here.

> *(LAUREN hangs up the phone. She sits down on the desk. She is shaking.)*

DON: Hello? *(Pause.)* Hello? *(Pause.)* Are you there?

> *(...transition...)*

5.

(ELLIOT's place.)

(Pre-dawn light through the window. MOLLY and ELLIOT are in bed together, after.)

ELLIOT: Well my Dad's a high school math teacher? So I guess it runs in the family, or it's what was, you know, modeled, or both.

MOLLY: That must be nice.

ELLIOT: What.

MOLLY: To have, like, an affinity, with your Dad –

ELLIOT: Yeah, you'd think. Or, I mean, it is. In a way. But he's also always giving me suggestions and advice about my work to which there's kind of no proper way to respond? Like, if I treat his ideas like they're coming from a peer, he gets offended by how gruff I am when I dismiss them? But if I treat them like they're coming from my father, and dismiss them gently, he feels condescended to, so –

MOLLY: What about when you don't dismiss his ideas?

ELLIOT: Heh. That's funny. *(Beat.)* Or, you're right, I mean, I think he wanted... But instead... *(Pause.)* What about you?

MOLLY: What about me what. Oh, I don't know, I mean, my mom's not, like, a biology teacher or anything. She's kind of a hippie, actually. Like, she and I moved a lot, and she's all about hiking and being in the woods and, like, the earth, and crystals and things? Which is not me. That's not me. But sometimes I think I'm, like, the science version of that? Like I sort of rejected what I saw as her, like, flakiness? But, like, secretly, even secretly from myself? I'm actually into exactly the same stuff as she is, just in the most, like, rigorous way possible.

ELLIOT: Heh. *(Beat.)* The last girl that I dated had this incredibly fraught relationship with her parents, like, they would talk on the phone every day, and she would always get off in tears, it was this, like, constant battle of justifying herself, everything she did, and this was not, by the way, a, like, wayward or unsuccessful person, but they somehow always made her cry about how she was disappointing them, or... And I'd just be like: maybe back off talking to them every single day. But she could not stop.

MOLLY: *(Not at all warily.)* Heh. When was that?

ELLIOT: Umm...

MOLLY: *(Somewhat warily.)* What, recently?

ELLIOT: Uhhh –

MOLLY: Hold on, did I, like, steal you from somebody, or – ?

ELLIOT: What? No! No, you... No.

MOLLY: Really?

ELLIOT: Or, so what if you did? Isn't that kind of awesome for you?

MOLLY: What? Ew! No!

ELLIOT: Huh. I find that fascinating. See, for me –

MOLLY: So I did steal you.

ELLIOT: No! No, it was... *(Beat.)* It was just this rebound that went on longer than it should have, it...needed to end.

MOLLY: And it was not because of me.

ELLIOT: No it was not because of you. *(Beat.)* Except for that it totally was insofar as you...opened my eyes to what else was out there, okay?

MOLLY: Okay. *(Long pause.)* So is there really a way to know, up front, for sure?

ELLIOT: What?

MOLLY: To fix the algorithm, like you said, to –

ELLIOT: Oh!

MOLLY: To interpret the data better.

ELLIOT: Yeah, no, I thought... *(Beat.)* Sorry, I thought we'd agreed that was a ruse upon which we'd mutually conspired to get each other into bed.

MOLLY: Well right but also you said that, given some more time –?

ELLIOT: Yeah, I, no, I may have said that? But, in the spirit of, um. post-coital honesty? It might not actually be what you'd call "possible." I mean, I could try, I could absolutely write something. But by the time it was done running we would both be dead and so would our children. *(Beat.)* I mean the children we might someday have. *(Beat.)* With anybody. Not necessarily with each other. *(Beat.)* I mean not with each other. *(Beat.)* What I'm saying is I think it might actually be an example of the TSP.

MOLLY: What's the TSP?

ELLIOT: Well, trying to produce a definitively correct interpretation of your data.

MOLLY: No, what do you mean "The TSP"?

ELLIOT: Oh! The Traveling Salesman Problem.

MOLLY: What's the Traveling Salesman Problem?

ELLIOT: Seriously?

MOLLY: Yeah. What.

ELLIOT: No, I'm just...so excited that I get to explain it, uh... Here. Okay. So. An algorithm is a set of instructions, right? A script, in code, like, "if this then choose that or else some other thing," which, when followed, will complete a task, in, given the computational speed of machines, much less time than it would take you or me, using only our pathetic brains. But. Some problems remain intractable. For instance: the Traveling Salesman Problem. Which goes like this: *(By now he is at his whiteboard, wearing only boxers and a t-shirt.)* Imagine you're a Traveling Salesman, from some hometown *(He writes "HOME" on the board.)* who needs to visit a certain number of cities, X, *(He writes "X =".)* and then return home, and you want to do this, naturally, while covering the shortest possible distance.

MOLLY: Okay...

       (Beat.)

ELLIOT: No, that's it, that's the problem.

MOLLY: *(Overlapping.)* Oh, that's it?

ELLIOT: Yeah.

MOLLY: But that's, but it's... I mean, do I fly, or – ?

ELLIOT: Doesn't matter. Assume straight lines.

MOLLY: Well then don't I just measure the distance between each city and add up the total distance for each route and then pick the lowest number?

ELLIOT: Yes. Or you could write an algorithm which could do that for you.

MOLLY: Okay so then –

ELLIOT: But. An algorithm that does that, that checks every possible option, or that, what we say is, produces the entire solution space and traverses it, that's called an exhaustive search or 'brute force' algorithm, and if the Salesman, let's say he's visiting three cities…

> (ELLIOT completes "X = " with "3" and then draws three dots, labeling them "A" "B" and "C".)

ELLIOT: …A, B, and C, it'll go *(He draws the paths quickly.)* ABC, ACB, CBA, it'll try all the routes, and the only actual math involved is, like you said, it's addition, and, sure, for three cities there's only six possible routes and the problem is trivial, but for four cities…there's twenty-four possible routes…and for five, there's a hundred and twenty, and, I mean you can begin to see how steep the curve is, it's a factorial, every time you add a city the number of possible routes goes up exponentially, so the real problem turns out to be the rate at which the complexity increases. Like, for eleven cities? Which is not that many cities? The number of possible routes is around forty million. For fourteen cities, which is still not that many cities? It's close to ninety billion. So for fifty, or a hundred, or a thousand cities – ?

MOLLY: Or protein pairs.

ELLIOT: – exactly? There aren't words for numbers that big. And, faced with that, a brute force algorithm will just freeze. It will just sit there and do nothing. And give you no answer at all. *(Beat.)* Or, okay, that's not accurate, that's not what's happening, what's really happening is it's not frozen? It's thinking. It's just that it will take so long to finish thinking, like, literally thousands of centuries, it might as well be frozen, from, like, the perspective of an actual human lifespan, so the problem is solvable, it's just not solvable in what we call polynomial time, in, like, a human scale of time, as opposed to exponential time, where some immortal being with infinite patience could be like, "What's the big deal? Just wait a hundred million years and the answer will pop right out." Or it could be solved by some kind of magical, nondeterministic computer, that at every crossroads makes an essentially random guess, but does this with perfect luck, like, hm, left turn, right turn, and every single choice is automatically correct, that would work too. But we're not immortal. And we can't make random guesses with perfect luck. And so there isn't, we can't, like… Do you, are you with me so far, or – ?

MOLLY: Yeah, yeah, no, keep going.

ELLIOT: Yeah but does this like actually interest you, or – ?

MOLLY: Yes very much.

ELLIOT: Really?

MOLLY: You listened to my whole thing about protein interaction networks.

ELLIOT: True but that was back before I knew if I was going to see you naked later.

MOLLY: And by the same token I am now trying to remain appealing after sex.

    (Beat.)

ELLIOT: Okay so obviously exhaustive search is pretty inelegant and clumsy, not to mention requires like a giant room full of enormous computers, so what you really do is you look at your underlying code and start to complicate it, you use pruning techniques, branch and bound techniques, ways of honing the algorithm, basically, so that it doesn't need to check every single possibility, like, it can dismiss obviously stupid ideas, going back and forth between cities that are really far apart for no reason, but even that won't work, not at high enough values of X. So you could also try a different category of algorithm all together, like the genetic algorithm I wrote for you, or some other kind of probabilistic or heuristic algorithm, because what they do is they optimize, they sort of say, "Hey, you know what? I don't need the best possible route. I just want a really really good one." But that method only gives you an answer in the sense that you changed the definition of what 'answer' is. You settled, in other words. So what's really required is an insight so profound into the deep structure of the problem that it gives rise to a new kind of algorithm, of unprecedented elegance, some, probably, some combination of brute force and heuristics, that searches and optimizes, embracing compromise en route to a kind of certainty, thereby unearthing a real genuine solution to this problem. Or for someone to prove, definitively? That no such algorithm exists. And in the fifty-odd years since the TSP was first described, no one, anywhere, has ever been able to do either of those things.

MOLLY: It's unsolved.

ELLIOT: It's the most important unsolved problem in all of Computer Science. It's one of the most important unsolved problems in all of mathematics. It has implications for, well, business, of course, it's a real world problem for, like, actual salesmen, on, like, an industrial scale, but it also turns out to be analogous to hundreds of other problems, in game theory, language theory, apparently in biology, to basically any problem of satisfiability, of exponentially branching choices that can be solved in our lifetimes seemingly only by random guesses made with perfect luck. Your nodes may be cities or proteins or…something else… but the problem remains the same. And because these NP problems, these Nondeterministic Polynomial Time problems, are all reducible to, or derivable from, one another? Because they're what we call NP-Complete? What this means is, if you solve any one of them? You'll actually have solved them all. And this is known as the Theory of NP-Completeness. And it's what I'm working on. Pretty much all the time.

（*Beat.*）

MOLLY: Have you done this before?

ELLIOT: What?

MOLLY: This little presentation.

ELLIOT: Well, yeah, of course, in class, or, I mean it's –

MOLLY: No have you done this before in more or less this context.

（*Beat.*）

ELLIOT: Um –

MOLLY: I knew it! This is your A material!

ELLIOT: No –

MOLLY: It totally is! You say this to all the girls!

ELLIOT: I, what, I talk about computational intractability?

MOLLY: I bet you do!

ELLIOT: And that gets everybody right into the sack.

MOLLY: I bet it does! I bet they're like, "Brute force? Oh, Elliot, tell me more."

ELLIOT: Look at it this way: would you rather be unworthy of my A material?

MOLLY: Oh I don't know. What does that look like?

ELLIOT: That's where, as soon as we're finished I just go, "So... How are you getting home?"

MOLLY: Heh heh heh.

ELLIOT: By the way, how are you getting home? Should I, like, call a car, or – ?

MOLLY: Shut the fuck up.

ELLIOT: I can walk you as far as the door.

MOLLY: And they say chivalry is dead.

(A moment. Then MOLLY starts to get out of bed.)

ELLIOT: Oh god, I was totally kidding, please stay.

MOLLY: No, I know.

ELLIOT: Yeah, no, I would never send you out there now. It's Winter.

MOLLY: No, I, haha, but, no, I just have to pee again. I don't know what's wrong with me.

ELLIOT: Maybe you're pregnant.

(Beat.)

MOLLY: That's not funny.

ELLIOT: It was a joke.

MOLLY: I know. But that joke's not funny.

ELLIOT: No, yeah, but: keep in mind that we had sex like an hour ago, so, even if you were pregnant, you wouldn't already be having, like, physiological –

MOLLY: Explaining it more does not help!

ELLIOT: Right, but the joke, I'm saying, was that –

MOLLY: Elliot. No woman. Anywhere. Ever. Since long before records of such things were kept. Has ever found that joke funny.

ELLIOT: Okay.

MOLLY: Okay.

> (*MOLLY turns away, as if to get up. But, then, instead she just sort of stares off into space for a second. Worried? Sad? Anyway, she doesn't stand. A silence.*)

ELLIOT: Yeah that was a really bad joke, I'm sorry –

MOLLY: Oh, no, it's totally not that, I just… I was just thinking.

ELLIOT: Oh. Well that doesn't sound like a good idea.

MOLLY: No, just… (*Beat. Then, quietly:*) I feel sort of like I tricked you.

ELLIOT: Oh. (*Beat.*) In, uhh… In what way.

MOLLY: Into thinking that I'm…happy. Or good. Or any fun to be around.

ELLIOT: Oh. (*Beat.*) Except. I am having fun. So…

> (*A moment. Then MOLLY gets up and moves towards the bathroom.*)

ELLIOT: But you aren't leaving, right?

MOLLY: What?

ELLIOT: You're gonna stay?

MOLLY: Yeah. I'm gonna stay.

> (*MOLLY exits to the bathroom. A moment. Then ELLIOT looks at his whiteboard, where, in the midst of all the lines and letters and numbers, is the word: "HOME." Intermission.*)

6.

(*MOLLY's lab.*)

(*MOLLY is standing here facing DON. She is holding the Petri dish she showed to Elliot in scene one. Other Petri dishes full of the results of various other hybrid screens, successful and unsuccessful, are all over the counter behind her. There is also a computer somewhere in the lab.*)

MOLLY: So you were right. I mean, you were right, to be worried, at first. Because, originally the...data was pretty messy, pretty difficult to read. But it turns out it's not a problem because this, I guess, algorithm? Once I worked out how to use it, could clean the data up enough that... I mean, not completely? That's impossible, apparently? For... very long and complex reasons? But enough to know where the real pathways likely are.

(*Beat.*)

DON: Sounds great.

MOLLY: Yeah and so I also wanted to just thank you for...pushing me to have such high standards. Because otherwise I might have stayed just, you know –

DON: (*Overlapping.*) You are very welcome.

MOLLY: Kind of stuck just where I was.

DON: Well that is my job.

MOLLY: Well, but, yeah, so... (*A moment. Then, glancing at the other Petri dishes:*) So what do we do with these now, do we wash them all, or – ?

DON: Oh, no no.

MOLLY: Well, but, for reuse.

DON: No, what do you – ? Molly, those will never be sterile again. We'll just order new ones.

MOLLY: Oh. Okay.

DON: Yeah, you're...not in college anymore.

MOLLY: Um. Okay. *(She puts the petri dish down among the others. A moment. Then she steels herself, and:)* So, okay, so I should tell you –

DON: That you're seeing this guy?

MOLLY: Um –

DON: This algorithm guy, this: Elliot? You're involved with him now, yeah?

MOLLY: I mean, I don't know if I'd say we're…involved, exac –

DON: No, it's, look, it's fine, I… Listen, this? You and me? This thing was bound to end, at some point, right? It was… I mean, it probably shouldn't have started in the first place, it's, you know, very… And so now that this happened, well, then, great, you know? It's probably for the best.

MOLLY: Oh. Um: okay.

DON: Yeah, so…do not worry about it.

MOLLY: Okay. Yeah. *(Beat.)* Except, in your voicemail? You seemed –

DON: Voicemail.

MOLLY: Yeah you left me, like, this message, where you sounded kind of – ?

DON: Huh.

MOLLY: Yeah.

DON: I do not remember that.

MOLLY: What? Really?

DON: I, yeah, no, I've been… You know what? I've been taking this, like, cold medication? And it makes me kind of… I mean that stuff's basically speed, so, who knows what I… I mean, haha, sorry about that. But no. Yeah. No.

MOLLY: Okay.

DON: Okay.

MOLLY: In that case can we talk about what's next?

DON: Of course!

(During the following, MOLLY heads over to the computer in the lab and brings up what are, presumably, the results of running ELLIOT's genetic algorithm.)

MOLLY: Well, because, according to this? Protein M binds to…: collagen, integrin, fibronectin, thrombospondin, myosin, perlacan, several growth factors –

DON: Wow, quite the molecular hussy.

MOLLY: 'Scuse me?

DON: And, I'm sorry: "Protein M?"

MOLLY: What? Oh –

DON: You named it after yourself?

MOLLY: No, I…didn't, he…

DON: Oh I see. Cute. Go on?

(Beat.)

MOLLY: I will rename it after its function with a nice vowel-n suffix like we do –

DON: I'm –

MOLLY: – once I know exactly what that function is.

DON: I am sure you will.

MOLLY: So! What I'd like to do is a straight knockout. In mice. I thought about RNA interference, but people are getting great results now by just injecting damaged genes directly into mouse gonads –

DON: I know what a straight knockout is.

MOLLY: – and, yeah, hoping for germ line transmission –

DON: I know how they work.

MOLLY: Well so then that's what I would like to do. (Beat.) Yeah, I'm sorry, what do you think?

DON: Well, first of all, I think, just slow down a second there, okay? Just slowww down.

MOLLY: Okay.

DON: Yeah. *(Beat.)* For one thing you can't really do knockouts in this area. The phenotypes are too severe. You'll kill the mice.

MOLLY: Well, but –

DON: Secondly. Mice are expensive. Like: an order of magnitude more expensive than drosophilae, elegans –

MOLLY: Franklin uses mice.

DON: Franklin's been here longer.

MOLLY: My results won't mean as much in anything but mice.

DON: Well, but, regardless, most importantly, um: what makes you so sure that this rather prodigious list of interaction partners is accurate?

MOLLY: Oh, well, because the algorithm –

DON: Heh, yeah, okay, um… *(Beat.)* Look, it's great you tried to mitigate false positives. That's great. And I know that these computational approaches can be very…flashy and impressive in the short term, that is, hey: that's why they're so fashionable right now, yeah? But, as the basis for devoting significant departmental resources, "because a computer said so" leaves, for me, something to be desired.

MOLLY: So…what are you saying?

DON: I'm saying either the band is on the gel, so to speak, or else it's not. I'm saying if you have to use statistical analysis to make your data say certain things then your data is itself unreliable. I'm saying that if you wish to move on to genetic perturbations of any kind, then you should go back, and do more screens, and get these results for real, because, in the end, in my experience, nothing takes the place of a person, in a room, just putting in the time, not even a big fancy algorithm, okay? Okay.

> *(DON crosses away. MOLLY is not looking at him. Then, as in scene two, the computer starts to get a tiny bit noisy, as though stuck, working hard on something. MOLLY immediately hits whatever buttons are necessary to stop it. She turns toward DON.)*

MOLLY: You told me I was brave.

DON: What?

MOLLY: It was one of the first things you said to me, when you took me on, you said that you thought I was brave, and –

DON: Yes, that's right.

MOLLY: And that that was important because the longer we do this kind of thing the harder it gets not to fall into certain patterns that can stunt our progress. That the cure for that is being brave.

DON: I remember saying those things, yes.

MOLLY: Okay, but in this case for some reason…?

   (Beat.)

DON: Molly, if there's something you'd like to say – ?

MOLLY: I, well, okay, I just question whether you're being impartial.

DON: Why, because of your personal life?

MOLLY: Because of your connection to my personal life, yes.

DON: Keep your voice down. *(Beat.)* I told you that's a non-issue.

MOLLY: What if I don't believe you?

DON: Oh because there couldn't possibly be problems with your work and so it has to be some kind of bias?

MOLLY: It's not what you're saying about my work, Don, it's how. It's the tone of condescension and barely concealed hostility which –

DON: Uh, well, maybe I sound that way because you're not being impartial.

MOLLY: What?

DON: That's right. Maybe the problem here is that you're so excited about your new boyfriend and –

MOLLY: I, he's not my…! Jesus…

DON: *(Continuous.)* – about how he has all the answers that your judgment as a scientist is clouded, because frankly, Molly, if I were you, I wouldn't be so quick to waste ten thousand dollars worth of grant money in your first semester here provided that your plan is to remain here very long.

MOLLY: Is that a threat?

DON: It is advice. In that you are my advisee.

MOLLY: I see. And do you think giving that sort of advice to your advisee right after she stops sleeping with you is really a recipe for career longevity yourself there, Don?

> *(Beat.)*

DON: You know what? Let's just slow this right back down a second here, okay? Let's just slowww down. *(Beat.)* Why don't we say this: write up what you'd like to do, as a proposal, and I will take it under –

MOLLY: *(Overlapping.)* No, I think under the circumstances? *(Beat.)* I think it would be best if I had a different faculty adviser from now on.

> *(Beat.)*

DON: That's not how it works.

MOLLY: What?

DON: There's an official… You have to go through the department and reque –

MOLLY: Well so I will do that then.

DON: If that's what you'd like to do.

MOLLY: It is.

DON: But what I think you'll find is that a similar philosophy to mine obtains more or less department wide.

> *(A moment. MOLLY is about to say something else when her phone rings. A moment. It rings again.)*

DON: Go ahead, don't keep him waiting.

MOLLY: It's, that's not funny, it's not even…

> *(MOLLY looks at her phone. Oh. It totally is ELLIOT calling. It rings again.)*

DON: It's all right, I'll go.

MOLLY: We're not finished.

DON: *(Already walking out.)* Yes we are.

MOLLY: Don –

DON: No, you should really call him back. I mean you don't want to burn that bridge too, do you? Not until you've worked out someplace else to go. Am I right? Molly? *(Beat.)* Good luck with your work.

> *(DON exits. MOLLY stands there for second. Then she realizes her phone has long since stopped ringing and puts it down. It instantly rings again. A beat. Then MOLLY answers.)*

MOLLY: Hello?

> *(ELLIOT enters the lab, phone to his ear. He looks extremely disheveled.)*

ELLIOT: Hi, sorry, it's just me, hi.

MOLLY: Oh. Hi.

ELLIOT: Is this a bad time?

MOLLY: Kind of, yeah.

ELLIOT: Oh. *(A beat. Then, lowering the phone:)* See this is why I hate the phone? You never know if people –

MOLLY: Elliot, what do you want?

ELLIOT: Um, well –

> *(An email arrives on the computer with an "arrival" noise. MOLLY goes to check it.)*

MOLLY: Hold on.

ELLIOT: That's from me.

MOLLY: What?

ELLIOT: I just sent that.

MOLLY: When?

ELLIOT: Just now, before I called you twice, and also ran downstairs.

> *(MOLLY has by now opened the email. She doesn't know what she's looking at.)*

MOLLY: Elliot, what is this?

ELLIOT: Well, it started… I was trying to help you. Not to…read your data better, I was still thinking that was impossible, but to, maybe, as you move forward to your next experiments? Might it not be helpful to have a computer model first, an…algorithmic simulation of the network that you're studying, with all the proteins you already understand doing their thing, and your unknown protein in the mix, so that you could make predictions and then test them I guess, dry, um, in silico, but then, I realized… Okay: when we think of the Traveling Salesman Problem what we always think about is one salesman, trying to choose a route. The nodes are destination points and the lines are paths he moves along. But what if… What if the nodes aren't points but more like bounded areas separated from the space around them by a sort of membrane. Like a cell. Each with its own ability to make choices as though there's a…salesman in every city, or like every city is a salesman, or… Sorry, I haven't left my office in almost four days? So I'm a little –

MOLLY: No it's fine.

ELLIOT: And what if you could then input, or, I guess, inject, something like the Traveling Salesman Problem, into each cell, as a propositional formula, a…question for it to answer, and what if those cells could then multiply, exponentially, to keep pace with exhaustive search, while also being probabilistic, because every cell is making its own random choices every time it runs, with each one finally, sort of, excreting its answer into the surrounding area, which, rather than there being set paths between them, would just be this, sort of, larger matrix they all share, in which all their answers are combined, and which is itself surrounded by another, larger membrane, which is itself just one cell among many, and so on, each level embedded hierarchically inside the next, such that their combined work gets passed up, and up, going from molecule to creature, as it were, until some outermost skin membrane, is reached, and one, sort of, ultimate answer is sent out, one collective answer, arrived at through a combination of brute force and heuristics, non-deterministically, but with perfect luck. What if the algorithm…is an organism?

MOLLY: You should try that.

ELLIOT: *(Pointing to the computer screen.)* I did. I did try it. And I think there's something wrong with it, because… Eventually, that answer does… It just…comes out! As an, I guess, emergent property of this dynamic multi-layered fucking mess. It just happens. The algorithm just…knows. (Beat.) And so there must be something wrong with it because if there's not, if I just built something that can solve an NP-

Complete problem like the TSP inside polynomial time, well, then that means…

MOLLY: That actually you've solved them all.

> (Beat.)

ELLIOT: Is…there a chair, anywhere – ?

MOLLY: I, can I see it?

ELLIOT: Uh, yeah, that's why I sent it to you. Here.

> (They go back over to the computer. ELLIOT opens something and
> MOLLY looks at it. Lights plays across their faces from the screen. It
> seems to be beautiful. Then:)

MOLLY: Oh.

ELLIOT: Right? I'd been working on this thing, non-stop, for years. And the right idea came as soon as I left it alone and worked on something else.

MOLLY: Isn't that just always how it goes.

> (They stare at the screen…ELLIOT takes MOLLY's hand…transition…
> during the transition, DON and LAUREN cross paths, in a hallway
> somewhere perhaps…LAUREN glances at DON as she passes him…DON
> looks back and checks out LAUREN…she continues off, oblivious…
> DON stops, turns, and follows LAUREN off…)

7.

> (MOLLY's place.)

> (One big space, desk, bed, kitchen, doors. A laptop computer on the
> desk. Afternoon light. ELLIOT and MOLLY are here, maybe both sitting
> on the bed, but in any case half-dressed, as though they had sex a little
> while ago and are in what they threw on after.)

ELLIOT: Well we all know what usually happens with something like this, right? We all know how it usually goes. For a while it seems like you got everything right, finally, like everything is perfect, and then suddenly some…unforeseen issue arises out of nowhere, and you're just like, oh god, no, not this again.

MOLLY: Right.

ELLIOT: And in this case I really do not want for that to happen.

MOLLY: Right, no. I mean, me either.

ELLIOT: Not with you and me.

MOLLY: Right, no.

> *(Beat.)*

ELLIOT: So then, okay, can I tell you something?

MOLLY: Sure.

ELLIOT: And allow me to preface this by saying that the reason I am telling
you this is, like I said, because I do not want for it to happen? But I
have had, historically? This…problem. Where as soon a, like, romantic
situation is established, like, officially? I start to get this….feeling, this,
like… persistent feeling, of, like, nagging discomfort, or, hm, like these
waves of…anxiety? Or paralysis? Or, just, obligation, just this feeling
of my whole life being circumscribed in this deadening way that fills
me with overwhelming dread, with this, just, sadness, this, just, heavy
choking sadness that turns me into this, like, shell of a person who is
not capable of joy, only suffering. *(Beat.)* And, you know, maybe I try to
sort of ride that feeling out, and see if it will go away, but it never does,
until, one way or another, the whole thing falls apart, about which I feel
secretly relieved.

MOLLY: Okay.

ELLIOT: And, again, I do not feel that happening here, like, it does not
seem to be happening in this case? But just to, like, preempt it or, I
guess, ward it off? I thought I'd put it out there.

MOLLY: Okay. *(Beat.)* I mean, yeah, let's keep on eye on all that, shall we?

ELLIOT: Um, okay, yeah.

MOLLY: I mean, my version of that is probably just…disappearing? Like,
I'll just be overtaken by this desire to get away from you as quickly
as possible and pretend the whole thing doesn't even exist and so,
suddenly, you will just never hear from me again, and you'll be like,
"What the fuck just happened? *(Then, quieter echoes:)* …happened…

happened…happened?" *(Beat.)* Those were the echoes of your question going unanswered –

ELLIOT: *(Overlapping.)* Yeah I got it.

MOLLY: I mean, I sort of…just did that to someone, actually.

ELLIOT: Oh.

MOLLY: Why, is that "awesome" for you?

ELLIOT: Kind of.

MOLLY: Gross.

ELLIOT: Probably.

MOLLY: Okay, well, the point is: that is what I do.

ELLIOT: Great. Let's keep an eye on that as well.

MOLLY: Yes, let's. *(Beat.)* So, wait, so what did we just decide?

ELLIOT: Umm… I don't know, what do you think we just decided?

MOLLY: I asked you first.

ELLIOT: Yes and my response was to ask you what you think we decided.

MOLLY: Hey, you started this!

ELLIOT: What? No I didn't.

MOLLY: Yes you did!

ELLIOT: Well, okay, I mean, I invited you over to my apartment, but then you were the one who was like, "Yes, but I'm already in your apartment, right now, though, so – "

MOLLY: No, Elliot, you started this conversation.

ELLIOT: Oh. Well –

MOLLY: No, never mind, forget it, I don't even want to know.

ELLIOT: Good. Me either.

MOLLY: Good. I'm glad. *(Beat.)* "How are you getting home?"

ELLIOT: Heh. Heh heh. Heh. *(Pause.)* Actually, I should probably be getting –

MOLLY: Oh, okay –

ELLIOT: No, just because… *(Beat.)* There's nothing more embarrassing than going public with something like this before you're sure, and so I don't want to get carried away. Before I do anything else I should really verify this thing. *(Beat.)* The algorithm.

MOLLY: Oh, right, no, of course.

ELLIOT: Yeah, as a wise woman once told me: even when the result is right in front of you, you're nowhere if can't explain how it was reached.

MOLLY: Right.

ELLIOT: In a way, I'm glad. That I still have more work to do on it, you know? Because once I know I've really done it? This thing that I've been, like, striving towards for…? Then, it'll just be like…

MOLLY: Yeah. What happens now? *(Pause.)* So, I guess we should –

ELLIOT: Yeah, let's…

> *(ELLIOT and MOLLY start to get dressed for real. This may involve just putting on the rest of their clothes, which are scattered around, or, for MOLLY, may involve getting new clothes entirely, this being her place, but regardless, they pick up their strewn clothing, and dress, in silence, for a little while. Then:)*

MOLLY: *(Indicating the bathroom.)* Do you need the…?

ELLIOT: No, it's all you.

MOLLY: Okay.

> *(MOLLY goes into the bathroom. ELLIOT finishes dressing, looks around at the things in Molly's room, really taking in the space. Maybe checks himself in a mirror. MOLLY emerges from the bathroom, maybe checks herself in the mirror, and then starts to make the bed. ELLIOT joins in, helps her finish making the bed. For instance. All in all, it's a nearly silent sequence about putting the space, and themselves, back together, during which, most importantly, a gradual shift in mood takes place, as though they both know, without speaking, that this very silence marks the end of the first, innocent phase of whatever is happening between them, and that they are now in an irrevocably new and more*

troubling place. Finally, ELLIOT has his bag on and looks ready to go, and MOLLY has settled in to work. He looks at her.)

ELLIOT: So…

MOLLY: So. *(Beat.)* Yeah, I'm just figured out how to branch out a little, cause there may be some problems with my…funding, so…

ELLIOT: Oh.

(A moment. They both know something is going unsaid. Then:)

MOLLY: So, okay. So I know that we sort of just… But, in the spirit of… *(Pause.)* Okay, when I came here… I mean, it was to go to school, of course it was, but it was also just to start over a little, to move on from… Just this guy, who sort of… Do you…? Just that first person with whom you can envision actually having, like, a Home.

(KATIE enters. She moves through the apartment engaging in various mundane activities as though it's her place. ELLIOT seems vaguely aware of her.)

ELLIOT: Her name was Katie.

MOLLY: His was Clark.

(CLARK enters, likewise. Likewise, MOLLY seems vaguely aware of him.)

ELLIOT: What happened?

MOLLY: It doesn't matter. Anyway, it's hard to explain. How you can feel like you let somebody down and like you're the one who got hurt.

(Perhaps, here, CLARK idly touches MOLLY and KATIE idly touches ELLIOT.)

ELLIOT: Yes.

MOLLY: The point is I couldn't stay in that same place, I had to leave, and I did.

(CLARK and KATIE exit and are gone.)

MOLLY: And it worked. In a way. Like, when things are pretty busy, and I'm preoccupied, or sometimes you just forget, I feel like I'm okay. But then also sometimes, when things get quiet enough, it feels like nothing else has happened to me since. Like nothing real has happened in my life since. Are you, does this make any sense, or – ?

ELLIOT: No, yeah. it does.

MOLLY: Yeah, but, is this, like, really boring to you, or – ?

ELLIOT: No, go on. Tell me.

MOLLY: Because this is what it's like. It's like you walk off down the road. And you think you're making all this progress. And then you stop, and look down, and you're like, oh: he is the road. And so then the question becomes: what am I supposed to do? Like, does that mean I shouldn't try again, or that I definitely should, like, right away? Like, is waiting the answer, or is it the problem because the answer is not waiting? And if I don't know then how am I supposed to tell somebody else I want to be with him and mean it? And, if I do like someone, and if that makes me forget my sadness for a while, then does that mean that that person make me happy? Or does that just mean that, once that fades, once he's not useful anymore, for like masking or replacing all my pain, then nothing will be left, except this guy who through no fault of his own will just be, like, repellent to me now, because he's just this other thing, with all of its own crap to deal with, just this extra burden on what I was carrying already? Or. If is this actually just unfixable now, if these feelings are just a part of me? Then is the right person someone who can just accept and live with them? And even if I find someone who can, what if I can't? Like, what if that's not how I want to live? Like. What if there's a place in you that's only really touched when you get hurt. And nothing else can touch you in that place. But certain things pretend they can, and so your choices are to believe until you can't anymore, and really hurt someone, and I've really hurt some people, or to keep believing, to make yourself believe, and then get hurt yourself, again, in that same place? Or does the fact that that's what all this taught me mean that I've been doing absolutely all of it in some way wrong, that there's some other, better, way to do it, and that, every time, there is at least the chance I'll finally figure out what other way that is? (Beat.) You know?

ELLIOT: Yeah.

MOLLY: Really?

ELLIOT: Yes. Why is the cure always the beginning of the next disease?

MOLLY: Yeah. *(Pause.)* So I guess you should probably –

ELLIOT: What if I worked here?

MOLLY: What?

ELLIOT: Well, I have my computer, so, what if I worked here, on my stuff, while you work on yours. Like we'd both be working, on different things, but in the same, shared –

MOLLY: No, I gotcha, yeah –

ELLIOT: Unless you don't want me to, or –

MOLLY: No, no, I think I'd really like that. *(A beat. Then, gesturing to her work, but in the same, raw tone as the above:)* See my plan was to make an organism that has my protein missing, because seeing what happens without it gives you clues to what it's for, and I wanted to do it in mice, because they're more like us than flies and worms and things, but, apparently, the result, in this case, would be too severe. It would kill the mice.

   (…transition…)

8.

(The Molecular Biology Departmental office.)

(MOLLY is here with FRANKLIN. He is looking at a computer printout.)

FRANKLIN: He said this wasn't accurate?

MOLLY: Yeah.

FRANKLIN: That's ridiculous.

MOLLY: Well –

FRANKLIN: You know what I think's going on?

MOLLY: What.

FRANKLIN: I think it's generational.

MOLLY: Oh –

FRANKLIN: I mean, whatever, I know Professor Davis is only six, seven years older than we are? But it makes a difference. To your comfort level with certain things, or what you're suspicious of, so when he hears these numbers came out of a computer you might as well be saying you waved a magic wand. He doesn't trust it.

MOLLY: Well, it's complicated.

FRANKLIN: Of course it's complicated but as someone whose responsibility is, in part, to remain up to date with advances in the field – ?

MOLLY: No, I –

FRANKLIN: And, yeah, he's your advisor, you're protective of him, I get it, all I'm saying? His reputation in the department?

MOLLY: Uh, what.

FRANKLIN: Just kind of hidebound, inflexible. All these guys, honestly.

MOLLY: Oh. *(Beat.)* Yeah he said that computational approaches were fashionable but unreliable.

FRANKLIN: Just like my ex-girlfriend. *(Beat.)* Sorry, other people's pain, nobody's interested. Point is, this old model? Of, oh, we're MB&B, over there's C.S., that's Chemistry, that's Physics, in ten years? Mark my words, all those barriers will be down, they will look laughable, this whole reductionist approach will be obsolete and Science, all of Science, will move inexorably toward integration, toward rigorous methods of integration that necessarily rely on interdisciplinary cooperation, and if you were at a different University? Where this culture had already taken hold? And there are some? None of this would have been a problem. In fact it's what would have been required of you.

MOLLY: Well, thanks, Franklin, I appreciate it.

FRANKLIN: Please, I was pissed, I mean, this has implications for us all, potentially.

MOLLY: Well I'm glad to hear you say that because, actually, I was wondering…

FRANKLIN: What.

MOLLY: I was wondering if I could use your mice.

FRANKLIN: What?

MOLLY: Oh not to take them, to breed them, you've... Since I can't get new mice right now, and since you have mice to which you have already given various genetic ailments, I'm thinking what if I just produce offspring from your mice, do a targeted insertion of Protein M, and see what preexisting conditions your mice already have get cured.

FRANKLIN: Ah. The ever-popular gene knock-in.

MOLLY: Yeah, which may take several generations, some mutation, but will, eventually, plateau at the most likely –

FRANKLIN: Yeah. I mean, you'd also need to add, like, a reporter gene that turns the affected mice a different color – ?

MOLLY: Oh, yeah, I –

FRANKLIN: I like blue.

MOLLY: Me too! *(Beat.)* So, wait, is that a yes?

FRANKLIN: I don't know. How specific can you get with your predictions?

MOLLY: Aha. What if I told you that I also have a computer model of my protein's interaction network in which I have already run, virtually, the experiment I just described?

FRANKLIN: Why, are you...about to tell me that?

MOLLY: Yes.

FRANKLIN: Seriously?

MOLLY: Yeah.

FRANKLIN: Did you...make that yourself, or – ?

MOLLY: Oh, no no, I –

FRANKLIN: See!? This is what I'm talking about! Cooperation! You went outside the department, right?

MOLLY: Yeah to this, uh...this other grad student, just this...grad student in C.S.

> *(MOLLY makes note of her own evasiveness as FRANKLIN goes on, heedlessly.)*

FRANKLIN: That is so fantastic. I have been trying to convince MB&B to look into computer modeling for, well, since I got here, so for longer than I care to... But that is great. I mean, I totally need one of those. Or, do you think it's adaptable, or, could I just look at it?

MOLLY: Yeah of course.

FRANKLIN: Great. Could, are you free right now, or – ?

MOLLY: We... Franklin, we have to teach in like five minutes.

FRANKLIN: Oh that's right. Fucking undergrads.

MOLLY: But, I mean, after class –

FRANKLIN: No, that's no good for me, um... Are you free tonight?

MOLLY: Oh, um... I mean, yeah, but –

FRANKLIN: Okay. Great. *(Beat.)* Or, I mean, I'm not asking you out or anything, I... Not that I'm not interested, I mean, you're very... Or, but, not that I'm assuming you'd be interested, just, it's more, as I just intimated, I am quite recently, uhhh... So I would probably not be good for anyone or anything right now except for, you know, something that's just really really... *(Beat.)* You did not need to know any of those things.

MOLLY: No, it's fine, I... *(Beat.)* Just let me make a quick...

> *(MOLLY takes out her phone and dials. Lights up on ELLIOT's office. A cell phone rings on the desk. NELL is here, sitting near, but not at, the desk. She looks over at the phone. Looks around. Should she answer it? She leans over towards the phone to see who's calling. MOLLY hangs up and the phone goes silent. NELL sits back. MOLLY turns to FRANKLIN who has been waiting patiently.)*

MOLLY: I actually always thought you hated me.

FRANKLIN: What? Why? What? No. Why would you...? No. Why?

MOLLY: Oh, just because, I'm always...late, and, like –

FRANKLIN: Oh, that's, no, hey, teaching sucks, I get it. No, no, I think... I think we're probably very similar, you and me.

> *(MOLLY and FRANKLIN exit together, as ELLIOT enters his office, to find NELL.)*

ELLIOT: Hey, sorry, I –

NELL: Your phone rang.

ELLIOT: What?

NELL: You missed a call. Your –

ELLIOT: *(Going to check his phone.)* Oh, okay. Umm…

NELL: Am I in trouble?

ELLIOT: What?

NELL: Well, I know that my heuristics problem set was late, and that my
brute force problem set was very late, in that I've not yet turned it in?
But I've been going through something of a personal crisis, which, okay,
I know –

ELLIOT: Nell.

NELL: I know is not a legitimate excuse, like, scholastically, but as a, like,
mitigating circumstance – ?

ELLIOT: *(Overlapping.)* Nell. Nell.

NELL: What.

ELLIOT: Relax. I just need your help with something.

NELL: Oh.

ELLIOT: Yeah. Here.

> *(ELLIOT tosses NELL a very large computer printout.)*

NELL: Ah! What's this?

> *(Beat.)*

ELLIOT: Do you know what a two-hybrid screen is?

NELL: Um, no, look, like I said, I haven't really been so good lately about –

ELLIOT: It's, no, we didn't cover it in class. This is molecular biology.

NELL: Oh.

ELLIOT: Yeah, okay, here's what's happening: I have designed an algorithm
that produces answers to NP-Complete problems inside polynomial
time but the only way to know for sure that an answer it's producing

is actually correct would be to already have the answer in hand to compare that answer to which is something of a vicious cycle as you can I am sure see so what I actually need is: a problem that's NP-Complete when you try to tackle it all at once but which has already been solved, piecemeal, in some other way.

(Beat.)

NELL: You designed what?

ELLIOT: I have designed an algorithm –

NELL: Oh no I heard you. Is this it?

ELLIOT: Ah. No. That is the most complete map, to date, of the protein interaction network, or, um, interactome, of Mus Musculus, the mouse.

NELL: Okay.

ELLIOT: Yes. Through painstaking research the world over molecular biologists have successfully identified many, though not near all, of the protein-protein interactions that take place inside the various cells and matrices of the common or "house" mouse, which, given how many proteins that is, represents an exponentially large number of potential pairings. A two-hybrid screen is a wet experiment which, by recreating the binding or the failure to bind of these proteins, in yeast cultures, like so…? (He pulls Molly's original Petri dish out of his back pocket.) Can be used either to confirm or to explode predictions regarding the network, with me so far?

NELL: Yeast cultures, seriously?

ELLIOT: *(Already opening up the simulation on his computer.)* I have arranged my algorithm to mimic a massive yeast two-hybrid screen, like that Petri dish but much much larger, capable of checking every known mouse protein against every other known mouse protein and telling us what interacts, and, since we have the answers, we will know whether our simulation gets it right. So. I am going to run this and monitor its progress. You are going to check the results against the pre-existing data. Ready?

NELL: Are we…doing this right now?

ELLIOT: Do you have time? This could take a while.

NELL: I, yeah, I have… Sure.

> (ELLIOT glances at his phone again.)

ELLIOT: Great. Um, actually, just let me make a quick –

NELL   Oh, yeah, of course.

> (NELL retreats to a slight distance. ELLIOT opens his phone. Then changes his mind, puts the phone away, and starts to type an email on his laptop. Then, NELL, having let everything sink in:)

NELL: Uhhh… Why me?

ELLIOT: Oh, umm… (He sends his email with a "send" noise.) Well, this is not the kind of thing I want to bring up with my professors and turn out to be wrong about. And as for my direct peers, if I tell them I have a solution to a major problem they'd certainly be eager to poke holes in it, but maybe not in the most unbiased, scientific way, so –

NELL: What about your girlfriend?

ELLIOT: What?

NELL: That chick Lauren? In C.S.? She was my T.A. last semester and she talked about you a lot. A lot, she –

ELLIOT: Yeah, umm… That is not an option anymore.

NELL: Oh. Okay.

ELLIOT: Yeah. Which, um, which leaves undergraduates.

NELL: I see. So you settled, in other words.

ELLIOT: I, heh, no I, um… (Beat.) I think that you're brave. (Beat.) Or, I mean, it is traditional to be assisted in one's work by one's students, and you seem, more than your classmates, to have an essential quality that will prevent you from falling into certain, um… (Beat.) I chose you specifically, okay?

> (Beat.)

NELL: Okay.

ELLIOT: Okay. Here goes.

(ELLIOT turns back to his computer clicks his mouse. At this, a line of computer code prints, unobtrusively, across an upper corner of a back wall of the space, say. Perhaps we don't even notice it at first. But it says:)

Generating Init.Pop...

(Also, at the same time, MOLLY and FRANKLIN return, now in yet another space: MOLLY's apartment. MOLLY heads straight for her computer.)

FRANKLIN: I like your place.

MOLLY: Thanks. Me too. I, here, I have it on my… And, actually, you can open up the underlying code, to see what it's doing while it…

(MOLLY has opened up the simulation on her laptop and clicks to run it and to open up the code. Thus, again, elsewhere:)

Generating Init.Pop...

ELLIOT: This first part is random but soon it will start matching proteins in a systematic way, and then we can…

MOLLY: *(Overlapping on "start.")* Right now it's of course set to simulate the ECM of mouse cartilage but it can probably mimic anything, so…

(During this, first one line of code, and then the other, are replaced:)

Init.Pop Full

(Meanwhile, NELL looks at ELLIOT and FRANKLIN puts a hand on MOLLY's back.)

NELL: Hey.

MOLLY: What.

(NELL kisses ELLIOT. FRANKLIN kisses MOLLY. MOLLY and ELLIOT kiss them back. Then MOLLY and ELLIOT both break away. A moment. Then an email arrives on Molly's computer with an "arrival" noise.)

FRANKLIN: *(Pointing.)* Email.

(And, with that, lines of code start to run down the walls, onto the floors, looking something like this:)

```
IF (E > F)
THEN
{SELECT.CROSSOVER(E)}
ELSE
{SELECT.CROSSOVER(F)}
END IF
IF (F > G)
THEN
{SELECT.CROSSOVER(F)}
ELSE
{SELECT.CROSSOVER(G)
END IF
IF (G > H)
THEN
{SELECT.CROSSOVER(G)}
ELSE
{SELECT.CROSSOVER(H)}
END IF
IF (H > I)
THEN
{SELECT.CROSSOVER(H)}
IF (I > J)
THEN
{SELECT.CROSSOVER(I)}
IF (J > K)
IF (K > L)
IF (L > M)

IF (M > N)
THEN
{SELECT.CROSSOVER(M)}
ELSE
{SELECT.CROSSOVER(N)}
END IF
IF (N > O)
THEN
{SELECT.CROSSOVER(N)}
ELSE
{SELECT.CROSSOVER(O)}
END IF
IF (O > P)
THEN
{SELECT.CROSSOVER(O)}
ELSE
{SELECT.CROSSOVER(P)}
END IF
IF (P > Q)
THEN
{SELECT.CROSSOVER(P)}
IF (Q > R)
THEN
{SELECT.CROSSOVER(Q)}
IF (R > S)
IF (S > T)
IF (T > U)
```

(…and so on, through the alphabet, faster and faster. Along with this, a sound we now recognize, of a hard drive straining and trying to cool itself, begins, and swells, this time not localized to a particular computer on the set, but rather coming from everywhere. A transition begins. FRANKLIN and NELL exit. ELLIOT and MOLLY attempt to follow, but then, suddenly, as the technical spectacle around them reaches its peak, the sound cuts out, the code vanishes, and the lights freeze in a strange, mostly dark, intermediate cue. ELLIOT and MOLLY, still on stage, are caught awkwardly in mid-exit. Perhaps they glance at one another. Then they scurry off. MOLLY quietly mutters, "Not again." Then, for a few moments, the stage is empty, in this odd cue, the only sound the faint, gentle tick of a computer, somewhere, still working. Then from backstage, someone calls: "Can we get more light?" The work lights come on. Then, after another moment, the actors playing FRANKLIN and NELL emerge. There is a loose, improvisatory energy to what follows.)

FRANKLIN: *(To the audience.)* Hey, sorry about that –

NELL: *(Overlapping.)* Yeah, sorry.

FRANKLIN: This, uhhhhh… This has been happening? On occasion? When –

NELL: Yeah, at this point in the show –

FRANKLIN: Yeah, presumably because of the intensity of the whole technical sequence just there, which –

NELL: *Yeah apparently what can happen here is that the whole board just… freezes?*

FRANKLIN: *No. Sort of. Not really.*

NELL: *Or, okay, I guess that's not technically precisely exactly what's happening? But the point is, what we've learned is that rather than resetting? That the best thing to do is to wait for it to…unfreeze.*

FRANKLIN: *And so what has been, um, decided is that, if this happens, rather than there being some impersonal announcement from the stage manager, while all of just disappear, and let you sit here in the dark wondering what the hell is happening, that we, _____[1] and I –*

NELL: Hello.

---

1   Here he says the actual name of the actor playing Nell.

FRANKLIN: – since we do not appear for the remainder of the play –

NELL: _____ [2] –

FRANKLIN   That we will come out, and tell you what is actually
   going on. On the theory that it's better…if you know something's
   actually… happening…

        (Beat.)

NELL: *This should be over very soon.*

FRANKLIN: *Yes.*

NELL: *It never takes very long.*

FRANKLIN: *And, but, you know what? If it turns out we can't fix it, that's okay,
   too, because, regardless, our stalwart fellow cast members, _____* [3]
   and _____ [4], will come back out, and complete the play for you
   in any case. Which, in my experience, is all that this stuff really needs,
   just…people. In a room. And time.

        (*Then, FRANKLIN and NELL just stand there, looking out at the
        audience. Being with them. Silence. Stillness. This is at first probably
        awkward. Then, perhaps, truly connected. Until finally the silence
        feels full. Throbbing. Mystical. At which point, perhaps FRANKLIN
        glances towards the back of the house, to the booth…the transition
        picks up from where it left off, FRANKLIN and NELL exit…and we
        land at last in…*)

9.

        (*The public computer cluster.*)

        (*MOLLY enters, puts her jacket over the back of a chair, and sits at
        one of the computers. She types for a while. Then ELLIOT enters. A
        moment. She turns and sees him.*)

ELLIOT: Hey.

---

2   Here she says the actual name of the actor playing Franklin.
3   Here she says the actual name of the actor playing Molly.
4   Here she says the actual name of the actor playing Elliot.

MOLLY: Hey. *(Then, pretending she was just leaving, putting on her jacket:)* I was actually just...

ELLIOT: Oh, okay.

MOLLY: Yeah, so –

ELLIOT: Or, could I maybe talk to you for a second?

MOLLY: Oh, uhhh... *(Beat.)* Yeah, okay.

ELLIOT: Okay. *(Pause.)* How've you been?

MOLLY: Good. You?

ELLIOT: Good, yeah, good. Good. *(Pause.)* I, um, I have something for you.

MOLLY: What?

ELLIOT: Yeah, it's... I got it for you back when we were... But I haven't seen you in a while, so I've been carrying around in my bag for weeks like and idiot, I... Here...

> *(ELLIOT has been rummaging in his bag and now pulls out a bottle of whiskey.)*

MOLLY: Is that whiskey?

ELLIOT: Yeah, it's...

MOLLY: You know, I'm not, like, a lush or anything.

ELLIOT: No, I know, I just... I don't know for sure anything else you like? Except for sex, and I already...got you that, like, a bunch of times, so –

MOLLY: *(Taking the bottle.)* Thank you.

ELLIOT: You're welcome. Also for the whiskey.

MOLLY: Uh-huh.

> *(Beat.)*

ELLIOT: So –

MOLLY: Listen, Elliot, I get it.

ELLIOT: What do you get.

MOLLY: What it's like when... It's amazing. And I'm sure it's going to change your life, and, so, you don't have to explain, I –

ELLIOT: It doesn't work.

MOLLY: What?

ELLIOT: The algorithm. It doesn't work. Or, I mean, it works, it applies… biological rules to mathematical propositions and produces answers but the problem is: actual living things, in the, like, real world? Are affected by it. By the world. So no matter how many levels of complexity you add to the simulation all you're getting are more and more refined answers generated from the inside, out, you're missing the…other half, the, everything that runs from outside, in, so you don't just need an exponentially increasing number of membranes in the simulation itself, you would need an exponentially increasing number of other independent simulations sending answers to one another, to be taken in, again, and then sent back out, and so on, and, without that, the versions of these problems that it's solving are not, in fact, analogous to one another, at all, and so cannot be considered NP-Complete, and so it is, in the end, useless, except as applied, one at a time, to every single hyper-specific case.

MOLLY: You made a derivation error.

ELLIOT: That is what it's called.

MOLLY: When did you figure that out?

ELLIOT: It was, um…pointed out to me?

MOLLY: When though.

ELLIOT: Um, recently.

MOLLY: Ah.

ELLIOT: What.

MOLLY: Let's just say your sudden desire to talk to me is starting to make sense.

ELLIOT: Oh come on.

MOLLY: What, I haven't heard from you in weeks, so –

ELLIOT: I, okay, may I point out that I also haven't heard from you in weeks?

MOLLY: Well right but that's because I wasn't hearing from you.

ELLIOT: Except I'm pretty sure the last communiqué came from me.

MOLLY: I, okay, I suppose that technically that's true? But it was I think you'll admit relatively spare and remote and came only after I reached out to you a couple of times and so I got the message and backed off a little myself and then I didn't hear from you again.

ELLIOT: I wasn't hearing from you!

MOLLY: What did I just explain?

ELLIOT: Well…! *(Beat.)* I'm here now.

MOLLY: Yeah. Who's Nell?

ELLIOT: What?

MOLLY: No, just, who's this girl "Nell", I'm – ?

ELLIOT: I, she's…! Why, who's "Franklin"?

MOLLY: Oh so we're going to do this now.

ELLIOT: What? You started it!

MOLLY: No. You did.

ELLIOT: I did not!

MOLLY: Yes! You did! By claiming to be "here" now!

ELLIOT: But…I am!

MOLLY: If you say so, Elliot, but it doesn't really matter cause I'm leaving.

ELLIOT: Okay. Where are you going? I'll come with you.

MOLLY: No. No, I'm…*(Beat.)* I'm leaving town.

ELLIOT: What? When?

MOLLY: At the end of the semester, I'm…transferring.

ELLIOT: Transferring.

MOLLY: Yeah.

ELLIOT: As in: "to a different graduate school" transferring?

MOLLY: Uh, yeah.

ELLIOT: Where?

MOLLY: I don't know. I mean, not yet, first I'm...just going home, to... regroup, see Mom, and then...yeah, onto the next place. I heard about some programs where there's more of a culture of like, cooperative...? So I applied to a bunch of those and I should know exactly where I'll land by Spring.

ELLIOT: When were you going to tell me?

MOLLY: What do you mean?

ELLIOT: Well, so, if I hadn't happened into this room today I'd just have heard that you were gone?

MOLLY: Hey, if I hadn't "happened into this room" that other day you'd never have had to know that I was even here in the first place.

ELLIOT: I...! What? That's...! So?

MOLLY: Well...!

ELLIOT: I just... *(Beat.)* I mean, is this because of funding, or – ?

MOLLY: Oh, no, I sort of...worked that out? But I still just... I don't know. I guess it just felt like...time.

ELLIOT: Oh. So...that's you then.

MOLLY: Yeah. That's me.

(Long pause. Perhaps we think the play might be ending. But then:)

ELLIOT: Want to hear a joke? *(Beat.)* Guy walking down the street at night sees a scientist under a streetlamp looking for something in the gutter. Says, "Hey, is there a problem?" Scientist says, "Yes, actually, I dropped my car keys, and I can't seem to find them." Guy says, "I'll help you look." But after a while of searching and searching and not finding anything the guy looks up and says, "Are you sure that this is where you dropped your keys?" Scientist says, "No, actually, I dropped them over there." And he points to a dark alley about halfway down the block. And the guy says, "Then what the hell are we looking here for then?" And the Scientist says, "This is where the light is." *(Pause.)* You know, I've been...coming to this computer cluster, a lot, lately, just at random, different times of day, just... Even though it's not remotely convenient for me, or on my way anywhere, but just because I've been I guess... hoping... And I know that I probably could have written to you, or... called, I guess, but for some reason I felt like I was supposed to just... *(Beat.)* Molly, I really like you?

MOLLY: That's fantastic, Elliot.

ELLIOT: No, like, really a lot, and I'm attracted to you, and you're really smart, and we're interested in a lot of the same things, and I look forward to seeing you, and I think about you when you're not around, and so if I seem spare, or remote, well, then, I'm sorry that I seem that way, but I promise it has nothing to with not wanting to be close to you, or...wanting to be with other people, or, okay, I mean, it does, of course it does, a little, I mean, sure, I want to sleep with every attractive woman I meet, or pass on the street, or am told about second hand, I mean, you people don't know what it's like, you think you do, and maybe you kind of do, in your way, but you don't, not really, you do not... Not that I actually want to go out and actually sleep with lots of people, that's an awful lot of work, and it usually turns out to be more trouble than it's worth, and, I'm getting off topic? What it is is: the fear that actually knowing everything about each other will eliminate the wanting. And so maybe what I was hoping was that, this time, if I could hold something just close enough to keep it from disappearing, but just far away enough to maintain how I felt about it, which was good, by the way, this felt really really good, then maybe I could draw this first part out a little, because, I don't know about you? But I don't have any compelling evidence that something better after this? Even exists. That it ever gets any better than still wanting to be with you, and still knowing that I can, or...could, because this obviously doesn't work either, does it, so... Maybe, what's req... *(Beat.)* I'm so tired. Of going back and forth. Between failing at this and wondering why I failed. *(Beat.)* I want us to know everything about each other. I want us to know so much it turns out we know less and less every day. *(Beat.)* Sorry. Too much? Too soon?

MOLLY: No. *(Beat.)* You know, it's not...totally useless.

ELLIOT: What?

MOLLY: The algorithm.

ELLIOT: Oh.

MOLLY: I mean, I used it. Just, for what it was originally intended: to make a prediction about the function of an unknown protein, and then test it, live. Turns out it does good things for mice with damage in a particular area, though, in fact, a couple other proteins do more or less the same thing, and so it could be it's a redundancy, or possibly even something we found already and mistook for something new, but until proven otherwise we're treating it as a unique molecule, and have even, provisionally at least, named it. For it's particular usefulness in aiding cell migration.

ELLIOT: Yeah? What'd you call it?

MOLLY: Travelin. *(Beat.)* Anyway, now I have a little more information to go back and do my next screen.

ELLIOT: Bait and Prey. *(Beat.)* Are you gonna say anything about what I just said?

MOLLY: What do you want me to say, Elliot? I... *(Beat.)* I mean, thank you. For saying all of that. But this is still probably not a very good time for me to... For either of us, really, for something like this... For, just, you know what? This is just a terrible time in all our lives. And a terrible terrible generation to be a part of. To know just enough to know that this stuff never works but not enough to know what the fuck we're supposed to do about it. *(Beat.)* I will never be a clean slate. I will never be a clean slate. Again. So...

> *(A moment. MOLLY turns to walk away.)*

ELLIOT: Whoa, where are you going?

MOLLY: I just have to go.

ELLIOT: Right now? Really?

MOLLY: Yes. Or, no, I just, I... *(Beat. Then, quietly.)* I just really really have to pee.

ELLIOT: Oh. *(Then, proudly.)* Still got it

MOLLY: Shut up, it's not you, it... That was an extremely long speech. And I appreciate it. And I have to go.

> *(MOLLY turns to go again.)*

ELLIOT: Can I come with you?

MOLLY: What?

ELLIOT: Can I come with you.

MOLLY: To…pee?

ELLIOT: No, when you go, when you –

MOLLY: You want to come with me?

ELLIOT: Yeah. *(Beat.)* Why, how are you getting there, did you already by a plane ticket, or are you driving or – ?

MOLLY: I, that's not, who cares! Elliot!

ELLIOT: What.

MOLLY: You can't come with me, that's insane!

ELLIOT: Why?

MOLLY: Because…! It's…! *(Beat.)* I mean what if I said yes?

ELLIOT: What?

MOLLY: What if I said, yeah, sure, pack your things, come with me, let's just see where this goes. What then?

ELLIOT: Well… *(Beat.)* I mean is that what you're saying?

MOLLY: What if it is?

ELLIOT: Is it, though?

MOLLY: What if it is?

ELLIOT: Yeah but is it?

MOLLY: What if it is?

ELLIOT: I don't know! I just…! *(Beat.)* I mean now I'm a little nauseous.

MOLLY: Maybe you're pregnant.

ELLIOT: You're right, that joke's not funny.

> *(A long silence. There is just the ambient sound of all the computers. Then, at last MOLLY offers her hand. For a handshake. A moment. ELLIOT shakes MOLLY's hand. The handshake complete, MOLLY tries*

to pull her hand away. But she can't. Because ELLIOT is gently holding on. The handshake thus morphs into them holding hands.)

ELLIOT: So…

MOLLY: So…?

ELLIOT: How are you getting home?

(Lights fade…first to blue…then to black…)

END OF PLAY.

GOD'S EAR

JENNY SCHWARTZ

Jenny Schwartz's plays include *God's Ear*, *Somewhere Fun*, and *Cause For Alarm*. She received the Frederick Loewe Award for Musical Theatre for the development of her new musical *Iowa*, which she is writing with composer Todd Almond. Jenny has also received the American Academy of Arts and Letters' Benjamin H. Danks Award in Drama, a Kesselring honor, a Susan Smith Blackburn special commendation, and two grants from Lincoln Center's Lecomte du Nuoy Foundation. Additionally, she was selected as the inaugural recipient of Soho Rep's Dorothy Streslin Playwriting Fellowship. She chairs the Soho Rep Writer Director Lab and is a member of New Dramatists. Jenny received an MFA in Theatre Directing from Columbia University and graduated from Juilliard's playwriting program. She is currently under commission from South Coast Rep. Jenny is honored to be included, in such great company, in this anthology. She thanks Mark Subias and Edward Albee from the bottom of (what used to be) her heart.

THE WRITER'S EAR

Whenever somebody tells me that there is an extraordinary new play being performed and I should see it, I make plans to do so – but only after having obtained a copy of the play so that I can read it before I see it, and certainly before I read reviews of it.

My reasoning is simple: I would rather form my judgment of the play's worth before I am subjected to the secondhand of a director's interpretation, and certainly before my objectivity is clouded by a critic's opinion. In other words, I want to experience the piece as the author intended, and take my chances.

This usually works out just fine. I have seen so many splendid plays damaged by misunderstanding productions – commercializations, say, or willful distortions brought about by the assumption that a director's vision of a text must be clearer than the instigators'. And, conversely, I have seen not a few mediocre (or worse!) scripts jazzed by a skillful director to give the illusion of a quality unsupported by text. I make the assumption that firsthand experience is firsthand and all else is not.

(I am so envious at a concert when I see people reading the score during performance of a piece; they are able to experience the intention *and its variants simultaneously.*)

*   *   *

Now and again, however, my way is not the best way to first experience a play, and this is the case with *God's Ear* by Jenny Schwartz.

Now, *God's Ear* is a very fine play; it is fully three-dimensional; it is fully informative and both moving and deeply funny, and its comedic and tragic values nudge each other so positively that they create a reality not always present in constructed fictions.

I saw *God's Ear* before I read it, however, as no script was available and the play's run was short. My experience with the play was all that I have mentioned – plus beautifully acted and directed so well you were not aware of either acting or directing. What I felt seeing the play – and I saw it twice in the same production – was that I was in the presence of something amazingly real. We all know, of course – or should! – that a play on the stage is as artificial as anything could be: the actors are not the characters; they are playing the characters; the settings are artificial – there is nobody really living there; and all the speeches are by neither the actors nor the characters they are portraying; they are by yet someone else: the author.

Of course, that is what all art is about: the suspension of disbelief. Art is all representation.

When I thought about the play after I saw it I was fully convinced that I had experienced Ms. Schwartz's play precisely as she had written it. Nothing so perfect comes about by accident. And I remain convinced that this is the case here, even though, as those of you who have just read it (never having seen it) will attest, there is very little evidence in the printed text to support the theory – any theory. For Ms. Schwartz does not share with us a text in any way concerned with physical action or intention.

For example: you seldom know where a scene is taking place; you seldom know how many people are in a scene for they often appear and disappear without any expectation; you don't always know when one scene has become another one. Frequently, the author puts down what (and who) she hears without bothering to fill us in on what we would have noticed had we been there with her – had we been seeing the scene.

I spoke with *God's Ear*'s very fine director, Anne Kauffman, about this and she explained to me that Ms. Schwartz does not always bother to put down visually in the text what she has seen, because, for her, what she has heard takes care of it all, for what she has heard is also what she has seen, and, if she has, why can we not?

So, in a case like this the director's job is not to guess what was going on, but to have the author specify who was who and what was what so that we – seeing the play – could participate as the author had so clearly participated in writing it.

I grant you this can make a director's job tedious and for a tough reading, at least until you have read the text two or three times, by which point the inevitabilities become clear and we are able to hear and see what we are supposed to even without the help of a normally composed text.

The director did not invent and guess; the director ferreted out what was clear to the author, and gave us the breathtaking play that was there all along.

I recommend you read the text of the play aloud as it "sounds" to you, as a kind of stream of consciousness. Read it a couple of times this way and you will begin to "see" and "hear" what was always there, however it was cleverly disguised from those who were not fortunate enough to have written it.

Among other things, you will understand that what Anne Kauffman did with Jenny Schwartz's play was more translation than interpretation. It was faithful and clear – once the language was fully understood.

For *God's Ear* is a truly wonderful play, one of the finest I have experienced in the last five years or so.

Edward Albee, New York City, 2012

God's Ear was developed at the Juilliard School and the Vineyard Theatre, New York City.

God's Ear had its world premiere in a New Georges (Susan Bernfield, Artistic Director; Sarah Cameron Sunde, Associate Director) production at the East Thirteenth Street Theatre in New York City on May 2, 2007. Director: Anne Kauffman. Songs by Michael Friedman with additional lyrics by Jenny Schwartz. Dramaturg: Sarah Stern. Set Designer: Kris Stone. Lighting Designer: Tyler Micoleau. Sound Designer: Leah Gelpe. Costume Designer: Olivera Gajic. Casting: Paul Davis/ Calleri Casting. Assistant Director: Maryna Harrison. Production Stage Manager: Megan Schwarz. Assistant Stage Manager: Danielle Teague-Daniels. Production Management: Samuel C. Tresler, Hilary McHone.

MEL	*Christina Kirk*
TED	*Gibson Frazier*
LANIE	*Monique Vukovic*
THE TOOTH FAIRY	*Judith Greentree*
LENORA	*Annie McNamara*
FLIGHT ATTENDANT / GI JOE	*Matthew Montelongo*
GUY	*Raymond McAnally*

God's Ear was subsequently produced by the Vineyard Theatre, in association with New Georges, in New York City and opened on April 17, 2008. Vineyard Theatre: Douglas Aibel, Artistic Director; Jennifer Garvey-Blackwell, Executive Director; Sarah Stern, Associate Artistic Director; Reed Ridgley, General Manager; Benn Morris, Production Manager. The creative team and the cast remained the same except for the role of Lenora, which was played by Rebecca Wisocky.

CHARACTERS
(in order of appearance)

MEL
TED   Mel's husband
LANIE   Mel and Ted's six-year-old daughter
TOOTH FAIRY
LENORA   a lady at a lounge
FLIGHT ATTENDANT
GUY   a guy at a bar
GI JOE

* GI JOE and FLIGHT ATTENDANT are played by the same actor.

PROLOGUE – MEL AND TED

A hospital.

MEL:
He's in a coma.
He's hooked up to a respirator.
He has a pulse.
He has brain damage.
Due to lack of…
Extensive brain damage.
Due to lack of…

His pupils are unreactive,
they said.
He doesn't withdraw from pain,
they said.
The next twenty-four hours are critical.

Or was it crucial?
Or was it critical?
Or was it crucial?

He's in critical condition,
they said.
Survival.
They said.
His chances of survival.
They said,
low.

They said,
the next twenty-four hours are crucial to his chances of
survival,
they said,
lost.

They said,
his reflexes are –
lost.

What do you mean he has a pulse?
I said.
Of course he has a pulse,
I said.

They're doing all they can,
they said.
Helping him to breathe.
Providing him with –

TED: Oxygen?

MEL: Fluids.
Electrolytes.
Nutrients.
They said.

Most children,
they said,
most children who do survive this extent of a near –
drowning, extent of a,
most children,
they said,
are unable to walk and unable to talk,
and most children –

TED: Our son isn't like most children.

MEL: That's what I told them.
That's exactly what I told them.
I told them our son isn't like most children.

He's not.
Is he?

TED: I don't think so.

MEL: I don't think so either.

Unlikely,
they said,
recovery is unlikely.
They said,

poor.
They said.
Prognosis is —
poor.

TED: Did you tell them to go to hell?
I would have told them to go to hell.

MEL: I told them,
take my reflexes,
I told them,
give him my reflexes,
I told them.

TED: They didn't say anything about miracles, did they?

MEL: Miracles?
No.
Not that I recall.

TED: Hope?

MEL: What about hope?

TED: Did they happen to mention hope?

MEL: They asked us to consider organ donation.

Gentle,
they were,
gentle,
with a,
hand on my shoulder,
they were,
gentle.

What's the definition of prognosis?
Exactly.
I know, but I don't know.

TED: I *don't* know, but I know.

MEL: I told them,
take my brain stem,

I told them,
give him my brain stem,
I told them.

TED: I'm here.

MEL: No,
                but thank you,
                I told them.
                I do not deserve gentle.
                I told them.

        LANIE sings a song

LANIE: *(Singing.)*

                You can't see the cars on the street today.
                Only mounds of snow.

                No cars.
                No cars.
                Today.
                Only snow.

                You don't see people at all.
                Today.
                You don't see any people at all.

                Sometimes in the winter, you will catch yourself in the mirror,
                and you will know what you will look like when you are old.
                When you are old.

                You can't go anywhere at all.
                Because all the cars are buried.

                Pretend all the cars are buried.
                Pretend all the cars in the world are buried.

ACT 1

SCENE 1 – MEL AND TED, TOOTH FAIRY, LANIE

Late at night. MEL and TED are husband and wife. LANIE is their daughter.
MEL is at home, in bed. LANIE is also at home, in bed. TED comes and goes.

MEL: Are you my husband?
        I can't tell.
        It's dark in here.
        And I'm floating around.
        And my mind is empty.
        And my body is empty.
        And my soul…
        Do I *have* a soul?
        How was your flight?

TED: Fine.
        I slept.

MEL: Did you sleep?

TED: Off and on.

MEL: The whole time?

TED: Almost.

MEL: Good.
        You needed it.
        Did you take a pill?

TED: I did.

MEL: One or two?

TED: Just one.

MEL: One and a half?

TED: Just one.

MEL: Three?

TED:	One.
MEL:	Good.
TED:	Three are two too many.
MEL:	I know. Are you mocking me? You're mocking me. Did you eat?
TED:	A little.
MEL:	Are you hungry?
TED:	Starving.
MEL:	Don't say starving. I'm trying to get Lanie to stop saying she's starving. She's not starving. She gets a hundred percent of her daily everything. Should I fix you something when you get home? I could make my famous omelet. Although I'd rather not break any legs.
TED:	Eggs?
MEL:	Danger: salmonella. Let me know what you decide.
TED:	How is Lanie?
MEL:	Fine, she's fine. She wants to be Helen Keller when she grows up. I don't know what to tell her.
TED:	And you?
MEL:	I'd like to own my own shop. Flowers. Maybe. No…convenience. No…concessions. Ted?
TED:	Yes?

MEL: Remember that pillbox?
       The one I got you?
       The organizer?
       With the days of the week?
       I looked for it.
       I couldn't find it.
       Will you look for it?
       For me?
       Please?
       When you get home?
       I went to the doctor.
       He says I'm deficient.
       I have deficiencies.
       He gave me a list.
       A list of vitamins.
       Have you heard of boron?
       Selenium?
       Vitamin B12?
       Vitamin C-3PO?
       I went to the drugstore.
       I bought some for you, too.
       Men's vitamins.
       You'll find them in the kitchen, on the counter, next to the
       tea.
       I moved the tea.
       I took the tea bags out of their boxes and put them in
       jars, glass jars, in the kitchen, on the counter, next to the
       vitamins.
       I cleaned out the medicine cabinet.
       I cleaned it up.
       I cleaned it out and up.
       There was a bottle of cough medicine stuck to the shelf.
       I couldn't get it off.
       I chipped away at it.
       With a knife.
       Finally, it gave.
       But then, it slipped and shattered, and I must have
       screamed, because Lanie came running, and she was

screaming too, and I said, "Don't come in here, Lanie, not with bare feet."

And she said, "What about the dog?"

And I said, "What about the cat?"

And she said, "What about the bunny?"

And I said, "We don't have a bunny."

And she said, "Please can we get a bunny, please please please?"

And I said, "Bunnies aren't domestic."

And she said, "Neither are you."

And I said, "Some things are better left outside."

But then, it wasn't blood at all.

Only cough medicine.

From 1903.

Oh and Ted, the closet in the hallway, with the full-length mirror, I went to open the door, and the doorknob came out. There I was with a doorknob in my hand.

There I was with a doorknob in my hand.

There's an echo.

Do you hear it?

There's an echo.

Do you hear it?

I tried to shove it back in, but it wouldn't catch.

Would you mind prying it open for me, please, the closet door, when you get home, if you don't mind?

Thanks.

Or else I'll have to go out and buy all new everything.

And I don't want to do that.

I'm ill-equipped.

TED: How are you otherwise?

MEL: The same.
        Pretty much.

TED: More or less?

MEL: More.

TED: Give or take?

MEL: Take.

TED: Damn it!
I cut my ear.
Earlier.
I was shaving.

MEL: I bit my lip.
Before.
I also burned my tongue.
And my urine, Ted, it's blue, baby blue.
Not to worry, though, I called the doctor, and it's normal to
be deficient.
How was your flight?

TED: Pain in the neck.
The woman sitting next to me on the plane, she looked so
familiar.

MEL: Was she an actress?

TED: I don't think so.

MEL: A movie star?

TED: I don't know.

MEL: Next time have her sign something.
Have her sign your ticket.
Was she a news anchor?

TED: She asked me what I did to my ear.

MEL: Why do they call themselves anchors?

TED: I told her I cut it shaving.
She ordered five vodkas.
I said, "Who orders five vodkas?"
She said, "Who shaves their ear?"
Anyway, we got to talking, and what do you know…

MEL: Why is it that everyone you talk to has a dead son?

TED: Small world?

MEL: Tiny.

TED: Life is short?

MEL: Life is a shrimp.

TED: He was ten, she said.
        He drowned.
        She was looking the other way.

MEL: On the plane?

TED: Never mind.

MEL: At the lake?

TED: What lake?

MEL: And my feet are pale.
        And I've lost my slippers.
        And the cat has chlamydia.
        Again.

TED: Not again.

MEL: And the dog bit the electrician.
        His upper, inner thigh.
        It's too bad because I liked the electrician.
        Ruddy cheeks.
        He was Irish.
        He was here every day for seven days, and on the seventh
        day, she bit him.
        And now he's gone, and look at me, I can't see a thing.
        Where are you now?

TED: Baggage claim.

MEL: What are you doing?

TED: Waiting for my bag.

MEL: I thought you hate checking bags.
        I thought as long as you live, you'll never check another
        one.

TED: I was early.
        I had time to kill.
        I didn't want to lug it around.

MEL: Did you go to duty free?

	Did you buy me my perfume?
	I'm out.
	I'm almost out.
TED:	I did.
	I tried.
	There was a line.
MEL:	Did you forget?
TED:	I never forget.
MEL:	You were early.
	You could have waited.
TED:	I was starving. I had to eat.
MEL:	Don't say starving.
	I'm trying to get Lanie to stop saying she's starving.
	She's not starving.
	She gets a hundred percent of her daily everything.
	Should I fix you something when you get home?
	I could make my famous omelet.
	Although I'd rather not break any legs.
TED:	Eggs?
MEL:	Danger: salmonella.
	Let me know what you decide.
TED:	How is Lanie?
MEL:	Fine, she's fine.
	You'll never guess…
	She lost a tooth.
TED:	Which one?
MEL:	The loose one.
TED:	Which one?
MEL:	This one.
	Here.
	She was eating popcorn.
	Unpopped.

Just the kernels.
I have the tooth fairy here.
We're waiting for you.
Are you almost home?
Or should we go ahead without you?

TED: I'm on the bridge.

MEL: You should avoid the bridge.

Tooth Fairy enters.

Remember when I looked in the mirror and caught your eye, and all of a sudden, we were together again?
And then you went away.
And I was somewhere else.
We'd call and check in.
At first, every day.
Then, less so, over time.
I wrote you a letter.
Did you get it?
Did I mail it?
Dear Ted,
Are you my husband?
I can't tell.
You have the silhouette of my husband.
But silhouettes can be deceiving.
Are you coming home for dinner?
Christmas?
Easter?
Nor'eaaster?

TED: Maybe.
Maybe not.

MEL: Which is it?
Maybe?
Or maybe not?
Is my guess as good as yours?
Oh and Ted, your sister called.

TED:	Which one?
MEL:	The loose one.
TED:	Which one?
MEL:	That one. There. I told her you were out. Exploring other options. Signed, M. As in empty. Smiley face. P.S. Send this letter to twenty-five people in twenty-five minutes and get rich quick. Otherwise…

(Makes throat-slitting gesture and sound.)

	You're soaking wet.
TED:	It's raining.
MEL:	Do you want a towel? I'll get you a towel.
TED:	I'm sorry.
MEL:	Don't be sorry.
TED:	I'm sorry.
MEL:	You should be.
TED:	I'm sorry.
MEL:	You always say that and you always lie.
TED:	I'm somewhat sorry. Does that count? I lost my umbrella.
MEL:	You could have bought a new one.
TED:	I wanted to get home.
MEL:	I'm glad you're home.

TED:	I'm glad I'm home, too.
	I missed you.
MEL:	I missed you, too.
TED:	No, but I really missed you.
	Those are just words to you, but I mean it.
MEL:	I mean it, too.
TED:	Then, tell me again.
MEL:	I mean it, too.
TED:	Damn it!
MEL:	You did cut your ear.
TED:	Look at you.
MEL:	Don't look at my feet.
	Take off your clothes.
	You're going to catch cold.
	Tomorrow, you'll call in sick.
	I'll take care of you.
	I don't know how, but I'm sure I'll think of something.
	I'll make you chicken soup.
	And cinnamon toast.
	You can blow your nose in my sleeve.
	Remember I used to roll up my sleeve, and you'd tickle my arm?
	At the movies?
	Under the table?
	And now, I'd rather cut off my arm than have you tickle it.
	Don't go.
	Stay.
	You're always running off.
	How was your flight?
TED:	What do you care?
MEL:	Come back.
TED:	And then what?

MEL:	And then you'll say, "Why? Why are you always so mean?"
TED:	You used to be so sweet. You used to say 'Gesundheit' to the dog.
MEL:	And then we'll kiss. And then I'll scratch your back.

Higher.
A little higher.
There.
Right there.

And then you'll hold me.
And protect me.
And I'll forgive you.
And you'll understand me.

And I'll never stop loving you.
And you won't ever think of leaving me.
And I'll laugh at all your jokes.
And you'll never disappoint me.

And you'll swoop down and save the day.
And I'll bend over backwards and light up the room.

And we'll thank God.
And God will bless America.
And with God as our witness, we'll never be starving again.

And the fog will lift.
And we'll see eye to eye.
And the cows will come home.
And we'll dance cheek to cheek.

And we'll face the music.
And smell the coffee.
And know where to turn.
And which end is up.

And the dogs will stop biting.
And the bees will stop stinging.
And this too shall pass.
And all good things.

And we'll make love.
The old-fashioned way.
Blind-folded.
With one hand tied behind our back.

And Hell will be freezing.
And pigs will be flying.
And Rome will be built.
And water will be wine.

And truth will be told.
And needs will be met.
And boys will be boys.
And enough will be enough.

And we'll cross that bridge.
And bridge that gap.
And bear that cross.
And cross that 't'.

And part that sea.
And act that part.
And turn that leaf.
And turn that cheek.

And speak our minds.
And mind our manners.
And clear our heads.
And right our wrongs.

And count our blessings.
And count our chickens.
And pick our battles.
And eat our words.

And take it slow.
And make it last.
And have it made.
And make it fast.

And take it back.
And see it through.
And see the light.
And raise the roof.

And make the most.
And make the best.
And work it out.
And mend the fence.

And wait it out.
And play it down.
And live it up.
And paint the town.

And take care.
And eat right.
And sleep well.
And stay calm.

And have fun.
And have faith.
And face facts.
And move on.

And own up.
And come clean.
And start fresh.
And take charge.

And stand tall.
And save face.
And steer clear.
And live large.

And then we'll kick up our heels.
And have it both ways.
And take a deep breath.
And take it like men.

And sit back.
Relax.

And ride off into the horse-shit.

For richer, for poorer.
In sickness and in health.
And the fat lady will sing.
With bells on.

The Tooth Fairy sings a song.

TOOTH FAIRY: *(Singing.)*

The sun is rising on the sea.
My bowl is full of cherries.
The best things in life all are free,
And we believe in fairies.

My life is like Act Five, Scene Three,
Where everybody marries.
And if misery loves company,
Why am I standing here all alone?

There are rings and rings around the moon.
The clouds have silver linings.
I gather all the teeth at noon,
And take them to book signings.
I'm whistling a happy tune,
And drinking tea from Twinings.

And if nothing interesting happens soon,
I'm gonna –

(Makes throat-slitting gesture and sound.)

She finishes her song and takes a bow.

You have no idea what it means to be a public figure.

I'm not usually this heavy.
But I recently had a baby.
Unfortunately –

TED: Did he die?

TOOTH FAIRY: He did.

TED: Anything I can do?

TOOTH FAIRY: You can hand me a tissue.
With aloe.
Aloe is nature's way of saying I'm sorry.

TED: Sorry?

TOOTH FAIRY: Nothing.

TED: What?

TOOTH FAIRY: Forget it.

TED: Sorry?

TOOTH FAIRY: Nothing.

TED: What?

MEL: Ow!
Paper cut.
I'm bleeding.

TED: Are you bleeding?

MEL: It's deep.

TED: Is it deep?

MEL: Quiet.
It's healing.
A scab.

TED: Don't pick it.

MEL: I'll pick it if I want to.
It's my scab, isn't it?

TED:	I paid for it, didn't I?
MEL:	I took a bath, then cleaned the tub, then took a bath, then cleaned the tub. I made a list, then ripped it up, then made a list, then ripped it up. I bought a new fish for the fishtank. But it killed all the other fish, and then it killed itself.
TED:	How are you otherwise?
MEL:	I'm not all I'm cracked up to be.
TED:	I don't know what that means.
MEL:	Don't sell yourself short.
TED:	I brought you something.
MEL:	You shouldn't have.
TED:	I wanted to.
MEL:	Why?
TED:	No reason.
MEL:	You know I hate surprises.
TED:	Why?
MEL:	No reason.
TED:	Now, close your eyes.
MEL:	For what?
TED:	For fun. Now, open your eyes.
MEL:	For what?
TED:	For fun.

He gives her the gift.

MEL:	Oh Ted, they're…
TED:	Slippers.
MEL:	Do they keep on giving?

TED: What do you think?

MEL: I love them, I think.
       But I don't like them, I don't think.
       I like the idea of them, I think.
       But I don't like the expression of the idea of them, I don't
       think.

TED: I saw them in the store window, and I thought of you.
       I thought they looked like you.
       Like the way you used to look.
       Before you bit your tongue.

MEL: Lip.

TED: Before you burned your tongue.
       I can't talk.
       I'm in a room full of people.
       It's hot.
       We're sweating through our suits.

MEL: And the women?

TED: There are no women.

MEL: And the hotel?

TED: It's all right.

MEL: How's your room?

TED: I suppose.

MEL: Wait.

TED: What?

MEL: Shh…
       I'm trying to imagine the rest of my life without you…

       Ted?

TED: Yes?

MEL: What's that around your ankle?
       Is that a thong?
       Is that a thong around your ankle?

	Why is there a thong around your ankle?

Why is there a thong around your ankle?
Who does it belong to?
No don't tell me please don't tell me no don't tell me I don't want to know.

TED: Amanda.
It belongs to Amanda.

MEL: Does Amanda have a name?

TED: Tina.

MEL: Does Bridget have a name?

TED: Marie.

MEL: Does Chloe have a name?

TED: Sonya.

MEL: Does Hilary have a name?

TED: Gail.

MEL: Does Ellen have a name?

TED: Nancy.

MEL: Does Barbara have a name?

TED: Lourdes.

MEL: Does Ingrid have a name?

TED: Lenora.

MEL: I only know one Lenora.
The electrician, this morning, he gave the dog the finger.
There's a child in this house, I said.
We don't use that finger.

TED: How is the dog?

MEL: Ask her yourself.

TED: How is the dog?

MEL: She doesn't exist as far as the cat's concerned.

TED: How is the dog?

MEL:	Needy.
	She thinks I'm going to leave her.
	I can't imagine why.
TED:	How is the dog?
MEL:	Clever.
	She thinks you get Lyme disease from limes.
TED:	How is the dog?
MEL:	Bloated.
	She thinks food is love and love is food and love is food and food is love.
TED:	How is the dog?
MEL:	She has a feeling we're not in Kansas anymore.
TED:	How is the dog?
MEL:	Pissy.
	She's given up caffeine.
	She's gone cold turkey.
TED:	And you?
MEL:	I turned on the TV and lit a cigarette.
TED:	Just one?
MEL:	Yes.
TED:	Two?
MEL:	Yes.
TED:	Six?
MEL:	Yes.
TED:	Ten?
MEL:	Did you go to duty free?
	Did you buy cigarettes?
TED:	I did.
	I tried.
	There was a line.

MEL:	Did you forget?
TED:	I never forget.
MEL:	You were early. You could have waited.
TED:	I was starving –
MEL:	GO AHEAD! STARVE! SEE IF I CARE! SEE IF I NOTICE THAT YOU'RE GONE! SEE IF I WONDER IF YOU'RE EVER COMING BACK! ARE YOU EVER COMING BACK? SEE IF I CARE! SEE IF I NOTICE THAT YOU'RE GONE! There's an echo. Do you hear it? There's an echo. Do you hear it? SEE IF I CARE! SEE IF I NOTICE THAT YOU'RE GONE!

He kisses her.

TED:	I kissed you this morning, but you didn't wake up. Like that. But with more tenderness. If you can imagine more tenderness.
MEL:	Was I dreaming?
TED:	I don't know.
MEL:	I must have been dreaming.
TED:	I don't know.
MEL:	Did you ever have that dream? Where you're falling? And your organs are suspended? And there's nowhere to go but down?
TED:	You're cold.

MEL: Let's go inside.
I'm cold.

TED: We are inside.

MEL: What about the dog?

TED: What about the cat?

MEL: Danger: chlamydia.
Again.

TED: Not again.

MEL: What about the bunny?

TED: We don't have a bunny.

MEL: Did you ever have that dream?

TED: I'm having it now.
Oh well.

MEL: Oh well what?

TED: I'll call you when I land.

MEL: The man in the shop, he sold me a killer fish.
I still haven't cleaned out the tank.
I can't.
I won't do it.
If it's the last thing I don't do.

TED: I brought you something.

MEL: You shouldn't have.

TED: I wanted to.

MEL: Why?

TED: No reason.

MEL: You know I hate surprises.

TED: Why?

MEL: No reason.

TED: Now, close your eyes.

MEL:	For what?
TED:	For fun. Now, open your eyes.
MEL:	For what?
TED:	For fun.

He gives her the gift.

MEL:	Oh Ted, they're…
TED:	Milk Duds.
MEL:	Do they keep on giving?
TED:	In case you forgot the day I fell in love with you.
MEL:	You know I have a weakness for anything sweet… Lenora from high school. She was the star of all the plays. Is your Lenora the star of all the plays?

LANIE sits up in bed.

LANIE:	Look Ma! No hands!
TED:	*(To MEL.)* Sit down.
MEL:	*(To TED.)* Tell me.
TED:	Sit down.
MEL:	Tell me.

LENORA sings a song.

LENORA:	*(Singing.)* *At the airport,* *At the airport last week,* *At the airport the other day, I saw a man I thought I knew,* *I thought that I'd been introduced to at a party.* *I was about to say, "Hello.* *Aren't you someone I know?"*

But I couldn't remember if his name was Stan or Sid or Marty.
And I thought he might not remember me at all.
I think he'd said that he was going to call.
I haven't seen him since.
This is the first day of the rest of my diet.
It's nice.
It's nice.
And quiet.
Here.

End of song.

TED: I came all the way back here and I'll be damned if I can remember why.

SCENE 2 – MEL AND LANIE

LANIE sits up in bed.

LANIE: Who's that?

MEL: That's Dad.

LANIE: Where?

MEL: Right there.

LANIE: Whose voice is that?

MEL: That's Dad's voice.

LANIE: Which voice?

MEL: Speaking.

LANIE: That's not Dad's voice.

MEL: Shh.
            In the morning.

LANIE: That's not my dad's voice.

MEL: We'll talk in the morning.

LANIE: That's not my dad.

MEL: We'll talk loud in the morning.
            We'll sing our songs.

LANIE: Where's my Dad?

MEL: Stop it.
            Go back to bed.

LANIE: Where?

MEL: Go back to bed for Sam.

LANIE: Where is he?

MEL: Go back to bed for Dad.

LANIE: Where's Dad?

MEL: Go back to bed, and Dad will come home.

LANIE:	Is there God?
MEL:	Hold my hand. Squeeze my fingers.
LANIE:	Is there heaven?
MEL:	I don't know.
LANIE:	What will we do when Dad comes home?
MEL:	I don't know.
LANIE:	What will we do?
MEL:	I don't know.
LANIE:	Who's sadder? You or Dad?
MEL:	Shh.
LANIE:	Who's sadder? Me or you?
MEL:	Shh.
LANIE:	Who's sadder? Me or Dad?
MEL:	Shh.
LANIE:	Who's sadder? Me, you, or Dad?
MEL:	Shh. I don't know. We'll do lots of things. When Dad comes home. We'll do lots of things.
LANIE:	Like what?
MEL:	Like sledding.
LANIE:	What does Sam look like?
MEL:	Sam is buried.

LANIE:	In the ground?
MEL:	That's right.
LANIE:	Sam is in the ground?
MEL:	That's right.
LANIE:	What does Sam look like?
MEL:	Shh. In the morning.
LANIE:	No, now please.
MEL:	Shh.
LANIE:	No, now please, right this second or I'll forget.
MEL:	When Dad comes home, we'll go sledding in the backyard. I'll bring the camera. Dad will pull you around and around and around, and I'll take pictures. We'll stay outside for hours and hours, but we won't feel the cold. And then, when we're tired and hungry, we'll go inside and I'll make dinner. We'll turn on the TV and watch the news. You'll sit on your stool and be my helper.
LANIE:	What will we sing?
MEL:	You'll chop vegetables, but you won't chop your fingers. You'll be very, very careful not to chop your fingers.
LANIE:	In the kitchen, what will we sing?
MEL:	Promise you'll be careful?
LANIE:	Will we sing from Oklahoma?
MEL:	Promise?
LANIE:	Will we sing "Oh, What A Beautiful Morning"?
MEL:	I don't know. I don't know anything. I don't know anything more than you do.

I know less today than I did yesterday, and tomorrow I'll
know even less.
Shh.
Sam was beautiful, and Dad's sad, so sad.
Dad misses Sam just like we do.
We miss Sam so much, don't we?

LANIE: And Dad?

MEL: We miss Dad, too.

LANIE: And Dad's beautiful?

MEL: And Dad's beautiful, too.

LANIE: And me?

MEL: And you're beautiful, too.
My beautiful, beautiful girl.
On the night you were born, it was snowing and raining at
the exact same time.
And it looked the lake was boiling.

LANIE: Boiling…

MEL: And the fog was thick.
Like soup.
And it took forever to get to the hospital.
And then I pushed and pushed, but you were stuck.
And then you were in distress.
And then it was the longest minute of my life.
And then the doctor said, "Here comes the baby, and it's a
girl."
The end.

LANIE: You're the saddest, then me, then Dad.

MEL: No.

LANIE: I won't chop my fingers.

MEL: No.

LANIE: You have the prettiest voice in the world.

MEL: No.

LANIE:	I'm fair.
	Like my father.
	That's what everyone always says.
	Why?
TOOTH FAIRY:	Luck of the draw.
LANIE:	Are you fair?
TOOTH FAIRY:	Do I look fair?
LANIE:	Open up.
	Say ah.
TOOTH FAIRY:	*(Opening her mouth.)*
	Ah.
LANIE:	Fair enough.

SCENE 3 – TED AND FLIGHT ATTENDANT, LANIE AND MEL

An airplane. TED waits for take off. He talks to MEL on the phone.

TED:
> *(To MEL.)*
> I have to go.
> I have to go now.
> Because I do.
> I just do.
> Because it's time.
> Because they made an announcement.
> Because there's a transvestite stewardess with a gun to my head, and she wants me to hang up the phone.

FLIGHT ATTENDANT enters and puts a gun to TED's head.

> Because I know.
> I just know.
> Because you can tell.
> You just can.
> No, I don't think it's sad, not really, no, I don't, not at all.
> Because she looks happy, that's why.
> She looks content.
> She looks like she likes what she does, and how many people can you say *that* about?
> Right, right, right, right?
> Count 'em on one –
> I don't know.
> How should I know?
> Do you want me to ask her?
> Alright.
> I'll ask her.
> Excuse me, but my wife, she wants to know, what's your favorite part of your job?

FLIGHT ATTENDANT:
> Demonstrations.

TED: *(To MEL.)*
                        Did you hear that?

FLIGHT ATTENDANT:
                        I like demonstrations.
                        And also –

TED: *(To MEL.)*
                        Did you hear that?

FLIGHT ATTENDANT:
                        I like answering questions.
                        I like my uniform.
                        I like my hips in my uniform.
                        I like my teeth, in the mirror, in the lavatory.
                        I don't mind lipstick on my teeth.
                        I don't mind turbulence.
                        I like children, babies, even when they scream.
                        I welcome turbulence, flatulence, pestilence, arrogance, war –

TED: *(To MEL.)*
                        Did you hear that?

FLIGHT ATTENDANT:
                        Famine –

TED: *(To MEL.)*
                        Did you hear that?

FLIGHT ATTENDANT:
                        Denial, anger, bargaining, depression, acceptance.

TED: *(To MEL.)*
                        Did you hear that?

FLIGHT ATTENDANT:
                        Passion.
                        All in a day's work.

TED: *(To FLIGHT ATTENDANT.)*
                        My wife says lucky you.

FLIGHT ATTENDANT:
                        Your wife doesn't know dick about dick.

FLIGHT ATTENDANT pistol-whips TED. He collapses.

MEL: *(Stepping on an action figure.)*
                        Ow.

LANIE: *(To MEL.)*
                        What's wrong?

FLIGHT ATTENDANT: *(To TED.)*
                        Sorry.
                        I don't make the rules.

MEL: *(To LANIE.)*
                        I stepped on an action figure.
                        I stepped on another.
                        They're everywhere.
                        Underfoot.
                        I'm going to take them outside and bury them.

LANIE: *(To MEL.)*
                        Can I help?

MEL: Help me.

LANIE: Can I help?

MEL: Help me help myself.

TED: *(To FLIGHT ATTENDANT.)*
                        Am I dead?

FLIGHT ATTENDANT:
                        (To TED.)
                        Stunned.
                        How do you feel?

TED: I don't.

FLIGHT ATTENDANT:
                        If you did?

TED: Stunned.

FLIGHT ATTENDANT:
                        If you did?

TED: Nostalgic.

FLIGHT ATTENDANT:
                If you did?

TED: Like a shadow of my former self.
                Future self.
                Former self.
                Future self.

FLIGHT ATTENDANT:
                Don't worry.
                You'll be home soon.

TED: I'm not going home.

FLIGHT ATTENDANT:
                Don't worry.
                You'll be home sooner or later.

TED: I'm never going home.
                Am I dead?

FLIGHT ATTENDANT:
                Stunned.
                Is there anything you want?
                Pillow?
                Blanket?
                Headset?

TED: What happens now?

FLIGHT ATTENDANT:
                Soda?
                Diet soda?
                V8?

TED: What happens now?

FLIGHT ATTENDANT:
                Peanuts?

TED: What happens now?

FLIGHT ATTENDANT:
        Pretzels?

TED: What happens now?

FLIGHT ATTENDANT:
        There's no need to panic, but you certainly shouldn't relax.

LANIE: Why?

MEL: Bundle up.

LANIE: Why?

MEL: You'll get frostbite.

LANIE: Why?

MEL: Because I said.

LANIE: Why?

MEL: Ask your father.
        Call him up and ask him.

LANIE: I bet he's on the plane.

MEL: I bet he's on the prowl.

FLIGHT ATTENDANT:
        Sorry.
        I don't make the rules.

TED: Isn't it a rule that you can never go home again?

FLIGHT ATTENDANT:
        Don't worry.
        You'll be home soon.

TED: Isn't it a rule that home is where the heart is?

FLIGHT ATTENDANT:
        Don't worry.
        You'll be home sooner or later.

TED: Isn't it a rule that everything we want we already have?

FLIGHT ATTENDANT:
        Is there anything you want?

TED: I want to watch my son grow up and get married.
                        Or grow up and not get married.
                        I don't care if my son gets married.
                        I just want my son to grow up and be happy.
                        I just want my son to grow old and be safe.
                        I just want my son to outlive me by a million and one years.
                        By a million and two years.
                        I just want my son to outlive me by a million and three
                        years.
                        I just want my tears to roll up my face instead of down my
                        face.
                        I just want my tears to defy the laws of gravity.
                        I just want my son to defy the laws of nature.
                        I just want a drink.

FLIGHT ATTENDANT:
                        Alcoholic beverages are four dollars.

TED: I just want another drink.

FLIGHT ATTENDANT:
                        Alcoholic beverages are three euros.

TED: One night, I don't know when, last year sometime, I got
                        home from work, and I was tired, and I changed out of my
                        clothes, and I went in to watch TV.
                        A few minutes later, my son came in, and he had this
                        enormous grin on his face.
                        He had snuck into my room and put on the clothes that I
                        had just taken off.
                        My jacket, my tie, my shoes, everything.
                        And he was so proud.
                        And I was so tired.
                        And I screamed at him.
                        At the top of my lungs.
                        I screamed at him.
                        "LOOK AT YOU.
                        YOU'RE RUINING EVERYTHING."
                        Why?

FLIGHT ATTENDANT:

       I don't know.

TED: What for?

FLIGHT ATTENDANT:

       I can't say.

TED: And he cried.

FLIGHT ATTENDANT:

       Of course.

TED: And he went away.

FLIGHT ATTENDANT:

       Of course.

TED: I just want to take it back.

FLIGHT ATTENDANT:

       Alcoholic beverages are forty-four pesos.

TED: I just want to buy my son every action figure in the history of action figures.

FLIGHT ATTENDANT:

       Alcoholic beverages are four hundred rubles.

TED: He wouldn't have to share them.

       I just want to watch my son outgrow his action figures.

FLIGHT ATTENDANT:

       Had I the lips, the tongue, the mouth, the song of Orpheus, I'd go beneath the earth and bring him back, and sing him back, I'd sing him back.

TED: I just want to bring him back.

FLIGHT ATTENDANT:

       Alcoholic beverages are one hundred yen.

TED: I have a question.

FLIGHT ATTENDANT:

       I have an answer.

LANIE: Are snowmen always men?

TED: Am I dead?

FLIGHT ATTENDANT:
                Stunned.

TED: I have a question.

FLIGHT ATTENDANT:
                I have an answer.

MEL: Are call girls always girls?

TED: Am I dead?

FLIGHT ATTENDANT:
                Stunned.

TED: I have a question.

FLIGHT ATTENDANT:
                I have an answer.

LANIE: What's a call girl?

MEL: Ask your father.
                Call him up and ask him.

TED: Am I dead?

FLIGHT ATTENDANT:
                What part of *stunned* don't you understand?

LANIE: I bet he's asleep.

MEL: I bet he's with a call girl.

TED: I wish I were dead.

LANIE: I wish I were Helen Keller.

FLIGHT ATTENDANT:
                How do you feel?

TED: Like a recent college grad.
                I feel like a need a new wardrobe.

FLIGHT ATTENDANT:
There's no need to panic, but you certainly shouldn't relax.

MEL: Ow.

LANIE: What's frostbite?
Does it have to do with teeth?

MEL: Ow.

LANIE: Is my guess as good as yours?

MEL: Ow.
I stepped on an action figure.
I stepped on another.
They're everywhere.
Underfoot.
I'm going to take them outside and bury them.

LANIE: Can I help?

MEL: Help me.

LANIE: Can I help?

MEL: Help me help myself.

GUY and LENORA sing a song.

An airport lounge.

GUY and LENORA: *(Singing.)*
Here in the underworld.
Here in the underworld.
Here in the underworld.
I'm sitting.

GUY: *And watching.*   LENORA: *I'm waiting.*
UNC lose to   *For Bombay Sapphire*
Tennessee   *Or Ketel One*
And Texas A&M   *Or Belvedere*

GUY:	*Up by nine*	LENORA:	*Or Tanqueray*
	And Pebble Beach		*Or Belvedere*
	And Notre Dame		*Or Tanqueray*
	And even tennis		*Or even Gordon's*
	And even bowling		*Or even Smirnoff*
	And waiting.		*And waiting.*

GUY and LENORA: *(cont'd.)*

       It was never my intention to give so much attention

LENORA: *To drinks*

GUY: *To sports*
              To golf links

LENORA: *To airports*

GUY: *To tomato juice*

LENORA: *To married men*
              To Grey Goose

GUY and LENORA: To CNN.

       Here in the underworld.
       It makes me feel
       It makes me feel as if
       It makes me feel as if
       I could call someone back from the dead.

   End of song.

SCENE 4 – TED AND GUY

A bar. TED is drinking beer and watching the game. So is some guy named GUY.

GUY: Is your wife a wife-wife?
Or is she one a those take-charge, split-your-lip, bust-your-balls, pull-your-chain, cook-your-goose, get-your-goat, rip-you-to-shreds, kick-you-when-you're-*down*...types a gals?

TED: Somethin' like that.

GUY: Best a both, huh?
Lucky guy.
Lucky guy.
Lucky guy.

TED: You want her?
Take her.
She's yours.

GUY: Free a charge?

TED: Small fee.

GUY: Thanks.
Thanks, man.
Generous offer.
You got yourself a generous spirit.
And that's a rare thing to come by in this day and age.
Trust me on that.
Take it from me.
Trust me on that.
Take it from me.
But I got my own little lady back home to contend with,
if you know what I mean.
You know what I mean.
How much we talkin'?

TED: Zero down.

GUY: Money-back guarantee?

TED: No questions asked.

GUY: You got a recent photo or what?

TED hands GUY a photo.

TED: Her name's Mel.
                Short for Melanoma.
                But you can change it.

GUY: Say, not bad.
                Those your kids?

TED: Those?
                No.
                No.
                Those are…
                No.
                I should warn you, though, because you can't really tell in
                the picture:
                Her vagina is green and her urine is blue.

GUY: Green, huh?
                What, you mean, like, fertile ground?
                Or, like, green with envy?
                Or, like, cold… hard… cash?

TED: Somethin' like that.

GUY: And is it a green-green or, like, more like a pastel?

TED: Actually, it's –
                Well, I don't want to say lime, but –

GUY: And is this a permanent situation or –

TED: Let me put it this way:
                If she's wearing, say, a green camisole or a green bustier or
                a green negligé or what-have-you, it might bring out the
                green in her vagina.
                Or it might not.
                Vaginas are…
                What's the word?

GUY: Mercurial.

TED:	Mercurial.
	But it's really only a slight hue.
	I just thought I should mention it because of…
GUY:	Company policy.
TED:	Company policy.
	So what do you think?
	Take her out for a test drive?
	Little spin around the block?
	One-time offer.
	Won't last.
	Vaginas sell themselves.
GUY:	Does she need a lot of light?
TED:	A little.
GUY:	Water?
TED:	The usual.
GUY:	Wish I could.
	Wish I could.
	Wish I could.
	But like I said, I got my own little lady back home to contend with, if you know what I mean.
	You know what I mean.
	How 'bout we do a trade?
	My little lady for your little lady?
TED:	For keeps?
GUY:	Trial basis.
	And if we're not completely satisfied, then no big deal, no harm done, no big whoop, no sweat.
	I think I got a recent photo here someplace.

GUY hands TED a photo.

	Her name's Meg.
	Short for Smegma.
	But you can change it.
TED:	That your daughter?

GUY:	Sure is.
TED:	That your son?
GUY:	Sure was.
TED:	Huh… *(Looking at the photo.)* I thought you said your little lady was a little lady.
GUY:	Did I? No kidding.
TED:	Don't kid a kidder.
GUY:	Did I? No shit.
TED:	Don't shit a shitter.
GUY:	Now, don't get me wrong. I love her to death and all. She's the mother of my kid and crap. But between you, me, and the lamppost, my little lady is not the little lady I married. How 'bout Melanoma?
TED:	Can I have my recent photo back?
GUY:	Is she the little lady *you* married?
TED:	Gimme my recent photo back.
GUY:	Gimme gimme never gets. Crybaby.
TED:	Who you calling crybaby?
GUY:	Wuss.
TED:	Who you calling wimp?
GUY:	Creep.
TED:	Who you calling loser?
GUY:	Moron.
TED:	Who you calling reject?

GUY:	Lame brain.
TED:	Who you calling jerk off?
GUY:	Jackass.
TED:	Who you calling candy ass?
GUY:	Limp dick.
TED:	Who you calling pecker head?
GUY:	Pansy.
TED:	GIMME MY FREAKIN' PHOTO!
GUY:	TAKE YOUR FREAKIN' PHOTO!
TED:	YOUR WIFE DOESN'T KNOW DICK ABOUT DICK!

GUY gives TED back his photo.

What's your favorite part of your job?

GUY:	I'm a people person.
TED:	I like numbers.
GUY:	It's not that I *don't* like numbers…
TED:	*(Telling a joke.)* What's the difference between your wife and your job?
GUY:	What?
TED:	After twenty years, your job still sucks.
GUY:	Beauty is in the eye of the beer holder.
TED:	Good one.
GUY:	Beauty is in the eye of the beer holder.
TED:	Good one.
GUY:	Beauty is in the eye of the beer holder.
TED:	Good one.

They laugh.

GUY:	I feel for you.

	Is all I'm sayin'.
	I feel for you.
TED:	I don't know you from a hole in the wall.
GUY:	I don't know you from Adam.
TED:	I don't know you from Adam's house cat.
GUY:	Beat it.
TED:	Can it.
GUY:	Shove it.
TED:	Save it.
GUY:	*(Giving him the finger.)*
	Save this!
	I don't know you from a hole in the ground.
	But I feel for you.
	Man.
TED:	Hey man, don't call me "man".
GUY:	Sorry, man.
TED:	*(Giving him the finger.)*
	Feel this!

SCENE 5 – MEL AND LANIE

MEL and LANIE are outside burying action figures in the snow.

MEL: A call girl is a girl that you call.

LANIE: Why?

MEL: Because you're lonely.

LANIE: Why?

MEL: Because you're bored.

LANIE: Why?

MEL: Because you're weak.

LANIE: Why?

MEL: Because you're pathetic.

LANIE: I want a call girl for Christmas.

MEL: Christmas is over.

LANIE: I want a call girl for next Christmas.

MEL: Christmas is never coming back.

LANIE: I want a call girl now.

MEL: You can't have one now.

LANIE: Why?

MEL: Because call girls are for grown men.

LANIE: Why?

MEL: Because you're a little girl.

LANIE: Why?

MEL: Because that's the way God made you.

LANIE: Why?

MEL: Because God has a master plan.

LANIE: He does?

MEL:	Maybe.
LANIE:	He does?
MEL:	Maybe not.
LANIE:	I want a master plan for my birthday.
MEL:	Your birthday is over.
LANIE:	I want a master plan for my next birthday.
MEL:	Your birthday is never coming back.
LANIE:	I want a master plan now.
MEL:	You can't have one now.
LANIE:	Why?
MEL:	Because master plans are overrated.
LANIE:	Why?
MEL:	Because master plans are overpriced.
LANIE:	Why?
MEL:	Because master plans are underfunded.
LANIE:	Why?
MEL:	Because master plans are all sold out.
LANIE:	I want to be a grown man.
MEL:	Don't be silly. You want to be Helen Keller.
LANIE:	I want God to make me into a grown man.
MEL:	Don't be silly. You want God to make you into Helen Keller.
LANIE:	Grown men are the luckiest.
MEL:	Helen Keller was lucky.
LANIE:	Helen Keller wasn't lucky.
MEL:	Helen Keller was very lucky.

LANIE:	Why?
MEL:	Because Helen Keller endured the unendurable.
LANIE:	Why?
MEL:	Because Helen Keller achieved the unachievable.
LANIE:	Why?
MEL:	Because Helen Keller the surpassed the unsurpassable.
LANIE:	Why?
MEL:	Because Helen Keller stood the test of time.
LANIE:	I want to stand the test of time.
MEL:	Don't be silly. You have to be dead to stand the test of time.
LANIE:	Oh.
MEL:	You have to be a dead grown man to stand the test of time.
LANIE:	Oh. Helen Keller wasn't a dead grown man.
MEL:	Helen Keller was an exception to the rule.
LANIE:	I want to be an exception to the rule for Halloween.
MEL:	Halloween is over.
LANIE:	I want to be an exception to the rule for next Halloween.
MEL:	Halloween is never coming back.
LANIE:	I want to be an exception to the rule now.
MEL:	You can't be one now.
LANIE:	Why?
MEL:	Because you have to be foreign to be an exception to the rule.
LANIE:	Why?
MEL:	Because you have to be weird to be an exception to the rule.
LANIE:	Why?

MEL:	Because you have to be eight to be an exception to the rule.
LANIE:	Why?
MEL:	Because "i before e except after c."
LANIE:	I want to be eight.
MEL:	You will. If you're lucky.
LANIE:	I want to be lucky.
MEL:	You will. If you're weird.
LANIE:	I want to be weird.
MEL:	You will. If you're foreign.
LANIE:	I don't get it.
MEL:	Don't be silly. There's nothing to get.
LANIE:	I want to be a dead grown man.
MEL:	I'll see what I can do.
LANIE:	I want to be a dead grown man who stood the test of time.
MEL:	I'll see what I can do.
LANIE:	I want to be a dead grown man who stood the test of time with a master plan.
MEL:	I'll see what I can do.
TOOTH FAIRY:	The apple doesn't fall far from the tree.
MEL:	The tooth fairy says the apple doesn't fall far from the tree.
LANIE:	Did you know that razor blades hide in apples, and when you bite into them, they slice up your mouth and cut up your throat, and you can't scream for help because your tongue is missing and your vocal chords are gone?
MEL:	The tooth fairy says you're going to follow in my footsteps.

LANIE:	But what if I hate you?
	But what if I hate your fat footsteps?
TOOTH FAIRY:	Hate is a form of love.
MEL:	Good news.
	Hate is a form of love.
LANIE:	Not in my book.
MEL:	You don't have a book.
LANIE:	Not in my book, it isn't.
MEL:	You're too young to have a book.
	On the night you were born, it was snowing and raining at the exact same time.
	And it looked like the lake was boiling.
LANIE:	Boiling…
MEL:	And the fog was thick.
	Like soup.
	And it took forever to get to the hospital.
	And then, I pushed and pushed, but you were stuck.
	And then, you were in distress.
	And then, it was the longest minute of my life.
	Except for this one.
LANIE:	And then what?
MEL:	The end.
LANIE:	Hey, you skipped my favorite part where I was a girl.
MEL:	Don't play favorites.
LANIE:	Takes one to know one.
MEL:	I know you are, but what am I?
LANIE:	Let that be a lesson to you.
MEL:	You started it.
LANIE:	Serves you right.
	Let's play house.

MEL: Don't be silly.
                 There's no one to play with.

LANIE: Let's play hide-and-seek.

MEL: Don't be silly.
                 There's no place to hide.

LANIE: Let's play tag.

TOOTH FAIRY: You can run, but you just can't hide.

MEL: Bad news.
                 You can run, but you just can't hide.

        GUY sings a SONG

GUY: *(Singing.)*
                 These are a few things you cannot sell on eBay:
                 Alcohol.
                 Pets.
                 Babies.
                 Drugs.
                 Even prescription drugs.
                 Credit cards.
                 Encouragement of illegal activity.
                 Fire arms and knives.
                 Chemicals and combustibles.
                 Intellectual property.
                 Livestock.
                 Lottery tickets.
                 Stolen stuff.
                 Human body parts or remains.
                 Used cosmetics.
                 These are a few things you cannot sell on eBay.

        End of song.

SCENE 6 – TED AND LENORA

A lounge. TED and some lady named LENORA are at a table with drinks.

TED: My daughter's six and my son is dead.
                Ted.
                Ten.
                You'll have to forgive me.
                I'm not usually this –

LENORA: I am!

TED: – drunk.

LENORA: Ask anyone!

TED: Let me start over.

LENORA: You should see my liver, later, liver, later, liver, later.

TED: I'm Ted and my son is –

LENORA: Pleased to meet you!

TED: – ten.

LENORA: Likewise I'm sure!
                Help me with your name.

TED: We almost lost him though.
                One summer.
                He swallowed a box of –

LENORA: Ow!

TED: Pushpins.

LENORA: Wow!

TED: You're tellin' me.
                But we pumped his stomach, so...

LENORA: Where I come from, they're called thumbtacks, pushpins,
                thumbtacks, pushpins.

TED: I'm kidding.

LENORA: I'm not.

TED:	He swallowed a box of Wheat Thins.
LENORA:	You must be very proud.
TED:	We am. I. Were. We was.
LENORA:	Pushpins, Wheat Thins, thumbtacks, Cracker Jacks. You're dead and your son's Fred and he swallowed a box of –
TED:	Correct!
LENORA:	But you punched his stomach, so –
TED:	Correct!
LENORA:	May both of you rest in –
TED:	Death is a fact of –
LENORA:	Life is short!
TED:	Life is a shrimp!
LENORA:	Life is a shrimp and then you die!
TED:	I'll drink to that!
LENORA:	Hear hear!

They kiss.

	Mmm. Martini. Where were we? Shrimp. Sucks to be a shrimp. Crustaceans have no bones.
TED:	I like your bones.
LENORA:	All of them?
TED:	I like your bone structure. I want to suck on your bones.
LENORA:	All of them?

TED: I want to suck on your bone structure.

LENORA: Do you have a problem with condoms?
            Just so you know, I'm disease free, and I fully intend to –

            (Handing him a note.)

            See.

TED: What's this?

LENORA: A note from my doctor.
            It's laminated.
            Are *you*?

TED: Disease free?

LENORA: Laminated?

TED: I think so.

LENORA: I thought so.

TED: The last time I –

LENORA: Let me check –

            She brings her fingers to his throat.

TED: I like it when you check my pulse.

LENORA: I like it too.

TED: I like it when you like it too.
            It's better that way.

LENORA: You can tell a lot about a man by his pulse.
            My ex, for instance, you can tell by his pulse, that a) he's
            dehydrated, and b) he's sick and twisted and c) he doesn't
            want to be tied down.
            And I'm like, "No problem. Neither do I."
            And so I buy him a watch.
            Gold plated.
            And I get it engraved.
            Genuine leather.
            And he's like, "Is it waterproof?"
            And I'm like, "It's engraved."

And he's like, "Is it waterproof?"
And I'm like, "It's engraved."
And he's like, "Is it waterproof?"
And I'm like, "It's engraved."
And he's like, "A figure eight?"
And I'm like, "An infinity sign."
And he's like, "A figure eight?"
And I'm like, "An infinity sign."
And he's like, "A figure eight?"
And I'm like, "An infinity sign."
And he's like, "Because time is infinite?"
And I'm like, "Because love is infinite."
And he's like, "I told you from the start…"
And I'm like, "Who is that in the background?"
And he's like, "Francine."
And I'm like, "My cousin?"
And he's like, "She's hot."
And I'm like, "I'm pregnant."
And he's like, "Get rid of it."
And I'm like, "I'm 35."
And he's like, "You're 39."
And I'm like, "I'm 35."
And he's like, "You're 39."
And I'm like, "I'm 35."
And he's like, "You're a train wreck."
And I'm like, "I need you in my life."
And he's like, "You're damaged goods.
And I'm like, "I need you in my life."
And he's like, "You wanna have a three –way?"
And I'm like, "Isn't that incest?"
And he's like, "Forget it."
And so I go over.
And I ring the bell.
And I know they're in there.
And I bang on the door.
And I guess I pass out.
And the next thing I know, there's a foot in my face.

And I'm like, "Where are you going?"
And they're like, "Starbucks."
And I'm like, "Wait up."
And they're like, "Go home."
And I'm like, "Francine, how can you do this to me, Francine?"
And he's like, "Francine can't help it if she's hot. Can you, Francine?"
And she's like, "No, not really, no."
And I'm like, "Haven't you ever heard of loyalty?"
And they're like, "Haven't you ever heard of fetal alcohol syndrome?"
And I'm like, "I'm not even going to dignify that with a response."

TED: Am I dehydrated?

LENORA: *(Feeding him an ice cube.)*
Have an ice cube.

TED: Am I sick and twisted?

LENORA: You're fair and square.
Are you a politician?
You look like a politician.
Didn't I see you on C-SPAN?

TED: I like it when you feed me.

LENORA: I like it when you chew me up and spit me out and spit me up and chew me out and hang me out to dry.

TED: I like it when you need me in your life.

LENORA: I need you in my life like I need another foot in my face.

TED: I like it when you need another foot in your face.

LENORA: I do need another foot in my face.
Bad.
I need it bad.
And while you're at it, stick another fork in my eye.

TED: I like it when you need it bad.

LENORA:	I'll take what I can get, if you know what I mean.
TED:	I know what you mean.
LENORA:	I know what I mean too.
TED:	I like it when you know what I mean too.
LENORA:	And then he takes off the watch and throws it at me and I'm thinking, you know what I'm thinking, "Catch it or move or blink, Lenora. Catch it or move or blink."
TED:	And then what happens?
LENORA:	Three guesses.
TED:	You blink?
LENORA:	I barf.
TED:	I like it when I look like a politician.
LENORA:	Hey, wait a minute here, you're not gonna get all kinky on me, are you? Because contrary to popular, because contrary to popular, because contrary to popular, because contrary to popular, I'm not that kind of a – Who am I kidding? Kinky's my middle name. You name it, I invented it. Basically. Do you have a middle name, Fred?
TED:	Ted.
LENORA:	Did we just have our first fight, Fred?
TED:	Ted.
LENORA:	Tell me, Fred-Ted, do you know any tricks?
TED:	I don't think so.
LENORA:	Jokes?
TED:	I don't know. I can whistle.

LENORA:	Can you wrestle?
TED:	I can parallel park.
LENORA:	Well, aren't you a regular Houdini.

They kiss.

Whodunit.

They kiss.

Houdini.

They kiss.

TED:	Why was Helen Keller's leg yellow?
LENORA:	Why?
TED:	Because her dog was blind too.
LENORA:	Huh?
TED:	Because her dog was blind too.
LENORA:	Huh?
TED:	Because her dog –
LENORA:	Oh! Oh! Because her dog… So he peed… So her leg… That's crazy! That's insane! That's the craziest thing I ever heard! Oh my God! Will you look at me! I'm crying! I'm totally crying! Look at me! Will you look at me? Oh my God! I'm totally dying!

He was blind!
Helen Keller!
Oh my God!
Her dog was blind!
I love you, Fred-Ted!
I love everything about you!
Were your parents poets?

TED: I should tell you –

LENORA: I appreciate your honesty.

TED: I'm a married man.

LENORA: Aren't we all?
In some ways?
Poets?
My point being that as an independent woman of what used to be the nineties, I love you from the bottom of what used to be my heart.

TED: Thanks.

LENORA: Sure.

TED: You mean it?

LENORA: Would I lie?

TED: It's been so long since I've been on the receiving end of a compliment.

They kiss.

LENORA: Did she really have a dog?
Helen Keller?

TED: She may have had.

LENORA: But was he blind?
Pets are therapeutic.
So they say.
I wouldn't know.
I'm allergic.
To everything.

To anything organic.
I'm having an allergic reaction right now.
Are you organic?

TED: I think so.

LENORA: I thought so.

They kiss.

Mmm.
Martini.
Where were we?
Houdini.
I love olives.
I love pimentos.
I love cocktail onions.
I love cocktail napkins.
I love lemon wedges.
I love lime wedges.
I love mini paper umbrellas.
I love mini plastic swords.
I just have so much love and nowhere to put it.

TED: I'll take it.

LENORA: You want it?

TED: Gladly.

LENORA: Great.

They kiss.

TED: Why can't Helen Keller drive?

They kiss.

LENORA: Why?

They kiss.

TED: Because she's a woman.

They kiss.

Why can't Helen Keller drive?

They kiss.

LENORA: Why?

            They kiss.

TED: Because she's dead.

LENORA: I have a mute half sister.
            Last I heard, she lived in Tucson.
            I haven't ever met her, but I know she's out there.
            Staring.
            You been to Tucson?

TED: We flew to Sante Fe.
            And then we drove to Albuquerque.
            And then to the Four Corners.
            And then to the Grand Canyon.
            And then we drove to Phoenix.
            And then we flew home.
            My kids, the whole time, they were fighting over the arm-
            rest.
            They liked the Four Corners, though.
            Hopping back and forth.
            We skipped Tucson.

LENORA: I don't blame you.

TED: Can you blame us?

LENORA: I'd be scared too.
            That the car would drive off and leave me with my sister.
            The mutant.

TED: There's a town in Utah called American Fork.
            We didn't make it up there, but we saw it on the map.
            We circled it.

LENORA: Someday I'm gonna find her.
            Bring her a cat.
            Call it Puss.
            After Oedipus.
            From the Bible.
            She'd like that, I think.

Get a kick out of it, I think.
Pets are therapeutic.
So they say.
I wouldn't know.
I'm allergic.
To everything.
To anything organic.
I'm having an allergic reaction right now.
Are you organic?

TED: I think so.

LENORA: I thought so.

They kiss.

TED: I've never done this before.
Lately, I have.
Thought about it.
Looked around.
Sometimes, I take off my ring.
In my head, I'm a widower.

LENORA: Why not a bachelor?

TED: I have to account for the loss on my face.

LENORA: You do have loss on your face.
I was pretending not to notice.
Do I?

TED: Maybe a little.
In your teeth.

LENORA: Where?

TED: Up here.

LENORA: Hang on.

TED: By all means.

LENORA: Are you sure it's not spinach?

TED: Spinach is green.

LENORA:	I used to be a drunk.
	Ask anyone.
	You should have seen my liver.
	But now, I wake up in the morning, and I take a look around, and I see the world exactly as it is.
	No better.
	No worse.
	And I take pride in everything I do.
	My friends are like, "What's up with *you?*"
	And I'm like, "I've found love in the twenty-first century.
	It's about space and choice and a terrific sense of freedom."
	And they're like, "Who is this guy?
	Does he have a brother or what?"
	And I'm like, "He's a politician.
	You've probably seen him on C-SPAN.
	It's great because he's out all day…saving schools…waging wars…
	And at night, he comes home, and he cries on my shoulder, and I tell him, everything's gonna be okay."
	And he's like, "How do you know?"
	And I'm like, "I just know."
	And he's like, "How do you know?"
	And I'm like, "I just know."
	And he's like, "How do you know?"
	And I'm like, "Trust me."
	And he's like, "I trust you."
	And I'm like, "Trust is my favorite foundation."
	And he's like, "Loyalty, thy name is Lenora."
TED:	Let's go.
	Right now.
	You and me.
	Against the world.
	We'll drive cross country.
	I'll parallel park.
LENORA:	Naked?
TED:	Absolutely.

LENORA:	With the top down?
TED:	Why not?
LENORA:	To American Fork!
TED:	To American Fork!
LENORA:	To American Fork-in-the-eye!
TED:	To American Fork-in-the-eye!

They kiss.

LENORA:	In the land of the blind, the one-eyed man is king…
TED:	Huh?… He who's most dangerous sleeps with his eyes open…
LENORA:	Huh?…
TED:	Where are you from, anyway?
LENORA:	Originally? All over. You?
TED:	Me too.
LENORA:	Do you think we know any of the same people?
TED:	We both know our waitress.
LENORA:	That's true. We both know Sharon.
TED:	But Sharon doesn't know us.
LENORA:	No.
TED:	So Sharon doesn't count. Are you involved?
LENORA:	With a man? Maybe.
TED:	With a woman?
LENORA:	Why do you ask? Do I have lesbian in my eye?

TED: I thought so for a second.
                        But now I can see it's just…
                        Sex.

LENORA: I don't like you.
                        But I like your type.
                        Do you have any friends you could set me up with?

TED: *(Looking at her birthmark.)*
                        I have a friend who has the exact same birthmark.
                        Where did you say you were born?

LENORA: Do you live around here?
                        Or work around here?
                        Or both?

TED: Neither.

LENORA: Likewise.
                        I'm rarely in this part of town.

            They kiss.

                        Tell me something, stranger to stranger: Am I a train wreck?
            They kiss.

                        Tell me something, stranger to stranger: Am I damaged good
            They kiss.

            The FLIGHT ATTENDANT sings a song.

FLIGHT ATTENDANT:
                        (Singing.)
                        Ladies and Gentleman,
                        The captain has turned on the fasten seat belt sign.
                        Please remain in your seats.

                        In case of emergency,
                        Please remain calm.

                        If the oxygen masks descend,
                        Place your mask over your face,
                        Before placing your child's mask over his or her face.
                        Please remain calm.

If the plane should suddenly descend.
Or the wings should fall off.
Please remain calm.

If fire should engulf the cabin.
Or other passengers are raptured.
Or we land in choppy waters.
Please remain calm.

If you are uncomfortable sitting in an exit row,
Please contact your flight attendant.
Please remain calm.
Please remain calm.

    End of song.

TED: Ma'am?

FLIGHT ATTENDANT:
          You rang?

TED: I'm uncomfortable sitting in an exit row.

FLIGHT ATTENDANT:
          Right this way.
          Sir.

ACT 2

LANIE: *(To TED.)*
Dad!

TED: *(To LANIE.)*
Lanie!

LANIE: Is there a McDonald's around here?

TED: If I believe in God, and I do believe in God, I'd have to say
there's a McDonald's around here someplace.
One McTickle coming right up…

MEL: *(To TED, as if on the phone.)*
What are you doing?

TED: *(As if on the phone, watching TV.)*
Nothing.
I don't know.
What's it called.

MEL: Me too.

TED: With the cop and the cop and the lawyer and the judge.
It's an old one.
About a suitcase.
And a kid inside.
And they find him, but…
No dice.
Huh…

MEL: Who's winning?

TED: Hard to say.

MEL: Take a stab.

TED: The other guys.

LANIE: Tell me all about childbirth.

MEL: Well, first of all, there are lots of things that no one tells you.
And then, you give birth to the placenta.

LANIE:	I get it.
	Does it hurt?
	Childbirth?
MEL:	You can't remember pain.
LANIE:	I remember when I pencil-sharpened my pinky.
MEL:	I suppose I remember my paper cut.
	Ow.
	When I was pregnant with Sam, the dog got sick.
	I went to give her a pill, and I don't know what came over me, but I took it myself.
	I just popped it in my mouth and swallowed it down.
	A big, green pill with a big glass of water.
	I was seven months pregnant.
	I wasn't thinking.
	I don't know what I was thinking.
	After about ten minutes, I realized what I had done.
	God, I was worried.
	I was so worried.
	My baby…
	What have I done to my baby?
	I tried to throw it up, but it wouldn't come out.
	It was somewhere inside me.
	Dissolving.
	But then, Sam was fine, and I was fine, and the dog was fine, and three years later, you were born, and you were fine too, and for a fraction of a second, we were, all of us together, fine, just fine, no…happy.
	Terribly.
	Oh…
	Oh God…
	Why was I always worried about the wrong things?
LANIE:	What's a fraction?
MEL:	A fraction is a piece of pie.
	A call girl is a piece of ass.
TOOTH FAIRY:	Happiness is fleeting.

MEL: The tooth fairy says happiness is fleeting.

GI JOE enters.

GI JOE: GI Joe says, "Knowing is half the battle."

MEL: But we buried you.

GI JOE: I escaped.

MEL: Didn't we bury you?

GI JOE: I escaped.

MEL: *(Introducing them.)*
                GI Joe, Tooth Fairy.
                Tooth Fairy, GI Joe.

GI JOE: We've met.

TOOTH FAIRY: We have a history.

GI JOE: We have a history.

TOOTH FAIRY: We've met.

TED appears.

TED: Hi.

MEL: It's me.

TED: I know.

MEL: Hi.

TED: What are you doing?

MEL: Living and learning.

TED: Anything going on?

MEL: We have new neighbors.
                As of last week.
                As of the week before.
                They're quiet as mice, but I know what they're up to. Eating.
                Sleeping.
                Having sex.
                We have new neighbors.

As of the week before, the week before, the week before.
I haven't yet met them, but I'm planning on it.
When the time is right.
Pop on over in my Sunday best.
Smile and say, "Can I pretty please borrow some legs?"

TED: Eggs?

MEL: *(To the TOOTH FAIRY.)*
My son, his teeth, I need them.
Do you have them?
I'd like to make a necklace.
I used to be crafty.
In the best sense of the word.

TOOTH FAIRY: I don't keep the teeth.
I give them back.

MEL: Back?

TOOTH FAIRY: Back to God.

MEL: Why to God?
What does he want with them?

TOOTH FAIRY: Well, for starters, he's not a *he*, now is he, now?

MEL: The tooth fairy hates me.

TOOTH FAIRY: You shouldn't say "hates".
It's a five-letter word.

GI JOE: You know what they say about God?

MEL: What?

GI JOE: He helps those who help themselves.
You're in the driver's seat.
It's your finger on the trigger.
Mind over matter.
What's the matter?
Your mind.
To be all that you can be.
Or not to be all that you can be.
That is the question.

	Now, drop and give me twenty.
MEL:	But we buried you.
GI JOE:	I escaped.
MEL:	Didn't we bury you?
GI JOE:	I escaped.
TED:	Hi.
MEL:	It's me.
TED:	I know.
MEL:	Hi.
TED:	What are you doing?
MEL:	Sitting and spinning.
TED:	Anything going on?
MEL:	I got my period.
	This morning.
	In the mail.
	In a big pink box.
	With a big pink bow.
	It looks so pretty.
	The packaging.
	I hate to open it.
	So I'm sending it back.
	Unless you want it.
TED:	Thanks.
MEL:	No backsies.
TED:	My day was long and grueling, too.
	Not that you asked.
MEL:	How was your day?
TED:	Same old same old.
	Mind your own business.
	Cut the crap.
	Do you know how little affection I feel from you?

	From you, I said.
	Not *for* you.
	From you, I said.
	Not *for* you.
	What are you doing?
MEL:	Cutting the crap.
TED:	Say something nice.
MEL:	Something nice.
TED:	What's up?
MEL:	*(To the TOOTH FAIRY and GI JOE.)* I'd like to run away. Disappear. Change my name.
TOOTH FAIRY:	What's the use? You'd still have lower-back pain.
GI JOE:	You'd still be frightened of the chiropractor.
TOOTH FAIRY:	It's the way she was raised.
GI JOE:	Her parents, they were frightened of everything. Of anything tactile.
TOOTH FAIRY:	Tangible.
GI JOE:	Corporeal.
TOOTH FAIRY:	Material.
GI JOE:	Maternal?
TOOTH FAIRY:	I think so.
GI JOE:	I thought so.

GI JOE exits.

| MEL: | *(To TED.)*
What are you doing?
Let me guess.
Nothing.
What are you watching? |

Let me guess.
Porn.
I'm not a prude.
I'm hardly a prude.
I watch porn.
Myself.
On occasion.
To digest.
After lunch.
With the vacuum cleaner.
No, I mean, no, I mean-not what you're thinking.
You're disgusting.
Your mind.
Where it goes.
It's disgusting.
You should be ashamed.
I hope you're ashamed.
You should be put away.
I hope you're put away.
IF YOU WANT TO WATCH PORN, WATCH PORN!
Let's have phone sex.

TED: I'm exhausted.
            My head is pounding.

MEL: I'm exhilarated.
            My vagina is glowing.
            Like kryptonite.
            Like a phosphorescent lake.

TED: You have no idea what I do all day.

MEL: You have no idea what I'm wearing.
            I bought a new –
            What's it called?
            Nightie.
            Silk.
            Sea-foam green.
            It clings to my body like that stuff in the kitchen.
            Saran Wrap.

Touch me.
Hold me.
Feel me.
Bitch-slap me.
Finger my phosphorescent lake.

TED: Are you peeing?

MEL: I'm chitchatting.
              Excuse me while I pee.

          LENORA enters.

LENORA: You know what I could live on is finger food.
              I like crudité.
              I like canapé.
              You know what I could live on is nachos.
              I like french fries.
              I like cheese fries.
              You know what I could live on is baby quiches.
              You know what I could live on is baby lamb chops.
              You know what I could live on is babies.
              You just wanna eat 'em.
              Don't you just want to eat 'em?
              You just wanna eat 'em.
              Don't you just wanna eat 'em?

TED: Let's order.

LENORA: Should we order?

TED: Should we order?

LENORA: Let's order.

TED: I'm trying to decide between something and nothing.

LENORA: I'm trying to decide between nothing and something.
              I'm not usually this heavy, but I recently had a baby.
              Unfortunately –

TED: Did he die?

LENORA: He did.

TED: Anything I can do?

LENORA: Finger my phosphorescent lake.

TED: I just had a déjà vu.
                    And you were in it.

          Beat.

MEL: *(To TED.)*
                    Thanks, by the way, for my slippers.

TED: You like them?

MEL: I'm going to keep them.

LANIE: *(Referring to TED and LENORA.)*
                    What are they doing?

MEL: He's sucking on her bone structure.

LANIE: Why?

MEL: It tastes good.

LANIE: What's bone structure?

MEL: I've heard it tastes good.

          GUY enters.

GUY: Who are you rootin' for?

TED: Neither.
                    They both suck.

GUY: Suck this!

          FLIGHT ATTENDANT enters.

FLIGHT ATTENDANT:
                    I also like the call bell.
                    Situated above your head.
                    Go ahead.
                    Push it.
                    I'm more than happy to assist you.

TED: What's more than happy?

FLIGHT ATTENDANT:
                    I'm more than happy to assist you.

TED: What's more than happy?

FLIGHT ATTENDANT:
                    I'm more than happy to assist you.

LANIE: Does it hurt?
                    Childbirth?

MEL: You can't remember pain.

LANIE: I remember when I threw up a thumbtack.

MEL: I suppose I remember my funny bone.

LENORA, GUY, FLIGHT ATTENDANT, TOOTH FAIRY:
                    Ha!

            The following jokes are told to MEL.

GUY: Why did God invent alcohol?

MEL: I give up.

GUY: So fat women could get laid too.

TOOTH FAIRY: What's funnier than a dead baby?

MEL: I give up.

TOOTH FAIRY: A dead baby in a clown costume.

FLIGHT ATTENDANT:
                    What do you call a transvestite cow?

MEL: I give up.

FLIGHT ATTENDANT:
                    A dairy queen.

LENORA: What was Helen Keller's favorite color?

MEL: I give up.

LENORA: Corduroy.

GUY: How can you tell if your wife is dead?

MEL: I give up.

GUY: The sex is the same, but the dishes pile up.

TOOTH FAIRY: Why did the baby cross the road?

MEL: I give up.

TOOTH FAIRY: It was stapled to the chicken.

FLIGHT ATTENDANT:
                        What did the transvestite do for fun?

MEL: I give up.

FLIGHT ATTENDANT:
                        Eat, drink, and be Mary.

LENORA: What did Helen Keller do when she fell down the well?

MEL: I give up.

LENORA: She screamed her hands off.

LANIE: Look, Ma!
                        No hands!

TED: *(To MEL.)*
                        Sit down.

MEL: *(To TED.)*
                        Tell me.

TED: Sit down.

MEL: Tell me.

GUY: Your wife's so fat, she used a mattress as a tampon.

TED: Your wife's so dumb, she tried to drown a fish.

GUY: Your wife's so fat, she has her own area code.

TED: Your wife's so nasty, she could make an onion cry.

LANIE: I'm crying.

LENORA, GUY, TOOTH FAIRY, FLIGHT ATTENDANT:
                        Smile!
                        You're on Candid Camera!
                        Ha!

LANIE: Did you know that the tongue is a muscle?
          Did you know that the dandelion is a weed?
          Did you know that the sun is a star?
          Did you know that the coconut is a seed?

          Did you know that spiders are helpful?
          Did you know that the earth is a magnet?
          Did you know that tomatoes are fruit?
          Did you know that whiskey is a spirit?

          Did you know that hamsters eat their young?
          Did you know that you can't lick your elbow?
          Did you know that snails have sex with themselves?
          Did you know that the bald eagle is a cymbal?

          Did you know that one year for me is seven years for
          Snoopy? Did you know that Snoopy is a beagle?
          Did you know that Walt Disney is cryogenically frozen?
          Did you know that suicide is illegal?

          Did you know that avocados are the good kind of fat?
          Did you know that our relatives are monkeys?
          Did you know that we grow and grow until we're twenty-
          six, and then we start to atrophy?

          Did you know that peanut-butter and jelly are inextricably
          linked?
          Did you know that Eskimos live in igloos?
          Did you know that men are from Mars and women are
          from Venus? Did you know that no news is good news?

          Did you know that Peter Pan won't grow up?
          Did you know that Jesus wept?
          Did you know that George Washington cannot tell a lie?
          Did you know that Latin died?

          Did you know that Shakespeare was more than one person?
          Did you know that bad things happen in threes?
          Did you know that God is nondenominational?
          Did you know that Grandma had two left feet?

Did you know that good things happen to bad people,
and bad things happen to good people,
and bad things happen to bad people,
and good things happen to good people?

Did you know that you can't get a sunburn through the
window, but you can get cancer?

Did you know that kisses and hugs are better than drugs?

Did you know that you can pick your friends and you can
pick your nose, but you just can't pick your friend's nose?

Did you know that our hearts are the same size as our fists?

But what if you have no hands?
What then?
But what if you have no hands?
What then?

TED:	Hi.
MEL:	It's me.
TED:	I know.
MEL:	Hi.
TED:	What are you doing?
MEL:	Reading and weeping.
TED:	Anything going on?
MEL:	I over-watered a plant.
TED:	It happens.
MEL:	No, it doesn't.
TED:	These things happen.
MEL:	No, they don't.
TED:	I'm sorry.
MEL:	I was going to say it's not your fault, but then I couldn't.

TED: What's up?

MEL: I should go.
                  Probably.
                  I should let you go.
                  Probably.
                  Bye.

TED: Why?

MEL: I said bye.

TED: I said why.

MEL: It's 10 p.m.
                  Do you know where your children are?

TED: Our children.

MEL: Our children.

TED: What do you want to do?

MEL: The tooth fairy suggests meditation.

TOOTH FAIRY: She coulda shoulda woulda made an excellent mother.

GI JOE: He coulda shoulda woulda made an excellent father.

LENORA: *(To GUY.)*
                  Have you ever meant nothing to someone?
                  Something to no one?

GUY: *(To LENORA.)*
                  I don't know.

LENORA: I don't know either.
                  I just have so much love and nowhere to put it.

GUY: I'll take it.

LENORA: You want it?

GUY: Gladly.

LENORA: Great.
                  I used to be secretly in love with you.

          They kiss.

But now it's more out in the open.

They kiss.

GUY: Tell me something no one knows about you.

They kiss.

                  Except for maybe someone who forgot.

They kiss.

LENORA: Come home with me.
                  I'll show you my thread count.

GUY: I want to grab your pony tail.
                  And hang on for dear life.

LENORA: I want to finish your –

GUY: – sentences.

LENORA: Me –

GUY: – too.

LANIE: What are they doing?

MEL: Where?

LANIE: Right there.

MEL: Oh, they're riding off into the horseshit.
                  Ha!

LANIE: You shouldn't say shit in front of the D.O.G.

MEL: The D.O.G. hates me.

GI JOE enters.

GI JOE: How is the dog?

MEL: She has a lump in her throat.

GI JOE: How is the dog?

MEL: She wishes she had something to suck on.

GI JOE: How is the dog?

MEL:	She's working on her upper-body strength every day, starting today.
GI JOE:	How is the dog?
MEL:	Easily, she bruises.
TED:	Hi.
MEL:	It's me.
TED:	I know.
MEL:	Hi.
TED:	What are you doing?
MEL:	Trying and failing.
TED:	Anything going on?
MEL:	There's a new sheriff in town. And he's stalwart. But I can't say I trust him. I swear he keeps checking out my eggs.
TED:	Legs?
GI JOE:	How is the dog?
MEL:	She's constantly on the verge of tears, but she just can't cry.
LANIE:	I'm crying.
MEL:	Bundle up! You're on Candid Camera!
LANIE:	*(To the TOOTH FAIRY.)* On the night I was born, it was snowing and raining at the exact same time. And the fog was thick. Like soup. And it took forever to get to the hospital. And then, she pushed and pushed, but I was stuck. And then, I was in distress. And then, it was the longest minute of her life. Except for this one.

	And then, the doctor said, "Here comes the baby, and it's a girl."
	The end.
	Oh and also, the lake was boiling.
MEL:	Excuse me, but the lake wasn't boiling.
LANIE:	Yes, it was.
MEL:	No, it wasn't.
LANIE:	The end.
MEL:	The lake looked like it was boiling, but it wasn't really boiling.
LANIE:	Yes, it was.
MEL:	No, it wasn't.
LANIE:	The end.
MEL:	Lakes don't boil.
	Not in real life.
LANIE:	That's not what I heard.
	The end.
	I guess it was the weatherman told my brother, and my brother told me, and now, I'm telling the tooth fairy.
MEL:	Liar!
	There is no such thing as the Tooth Fairy.
LANIE:	I heard it was boiling.
	The end.
MEL:	This morning, I woke up, and for a fraction of a second, I didn't know which one of you was dead.
	And which one of you was alive.
	And then, I remembered.
	And then, I sat up.
	And then, I looked life in the eye, and I winked.
LANIE:	A fraction is a piece of pie.
	A call girl is a piece of ass.

MEL:	*(To the TOOTH FAIRY.)* My son, his teeth. I want them back.
TOOTH FAIRY:	No backsies.
MEL:	I'd like to make a necklace. I used to be crafty.
GI JOE:	Crafty, my ass. You're all thumbs. Butterfingers.
MEL:	But we buried you.
GI JOE:	I escaped.
MEL:	Didn't we bury you?
GI JOE:	I escaped.
LANIE:	*(To GI JOE.)* Sir?
GI JOE:	Present.
LANIE:	Excuse me. But I need to find my dad.
GI JOE:	Hmmm… Does he have a long face?
LANIE:	I think I've got a recent photo here someplace.

She shows him a photo.

GI JOE:	Right this way. Miss.

GI JOE leads LANIE to TED.

MEL and TED face each other. Slow. Lots of air.

TED:	Hold on.
MEL:	Sure.
TED:	Hold on a second.

MEL:	Fine.
TED:	Okay, I'm back.
	I said I'm back.
	Hello hello?
MEL:	Sorry, wrong number.
TED:	I'm back.
MEL:	I said, "No backsies."
TED:	Hello hello hello hello hello hello? I'm back.

LANIE approaches TED. Slow. Even more air.

LANIE:	You look different.
TED:	I do?
LANIE:	Yes. Did you grow?
TED:	I don't think so.
LANIE:	Did you shrink?
TED:	Could be.
LANIE:	That's silly.
TED:	You're silly.
LANIE:	What happened to your hair?
TED:	Oh. Right. Well… It turned gray. A little. Didn't it?
LANIE:	Yes. On the sides.
TED:	I know.

LANIE:	Why?
TED:	Why?
	Because of age…
	I suppose…
	And…genetics…
	And also…probably because of…
LANIE:	Sam?
TED:	I was going to say *stress*.
	Do you know how smart you are?
	Do you know how very, very special?
	Sometimes, I look at you, and I…
LANIE:	Dad.
TED:	Lanie.
LANIE:	Can I see it?
TED:	What?
	You mean…?
LANIE:	Your hair.
TED:	Of course.

He bends down. She looks at his gray hair.

LANIE:	Oh.
	Wow.
	I like it.
TED:	You do?
LANIE:	Yes.
TED:	Really?
LANIE:	Yes.
	A lot.
TED:	Thank you.
	I –
	I can't even begin to tell you…
LANIE:	Tell me what?

You're welcome.
What's wrong?
I like your beard.

TED: I have to shave.

LANIE: I lost a tooth.

He is crying.

They hold each other.

Shhh.
Oh.
You did shrink.

TED: You grew.

MEL speaks back and forth to the TOOTH FAIRY and GI JOE.

MEL: When my son was in the lake, I was putting sunblock on
                my daughter.
                Or at least I was trying.
                She was stubborn and difficult.
                You know how she gets.
                "Enough already all right already enough already all right
                already."
                But I wanted to be firm.
                For once.
                I wanted to stand my ground.
                For once.

                They asked us to consider organ donation.

                They did.
                They were gentle.

TOOTH FAIRY: And what did you tell them?

MEL: They were ever so gentle.

GI JOE: And what did you say?

MEL: I said,
                "You have very fair skin, and it's my job to protect it."

I said,
"Hold still.
I'm just doing my job."
But she was crazed.
Hysterical.
Screaming her head off.
Thrashing around.
You would have thought I was trying to hurt her.
My child.
You would have thought I was causing her pain.
My child.
"You win,"
I said,
"I quit,"
I said,
"Go be someone else's daughter...
Get yourself another mother...
I don't want you anymore..."
And so she gave up.
Because she had no choice.
And she sat still.
Because she didn't have a choice.
I was meticulous.
Rapt.
I didn't miss a spot.
And when I finished,
When I finally, finally finished,
I stood up,
Pleased,
And I looked around,
Proud,
And he was...

TED: Sit down.

MEL: Tell me.

TED: Sit down.

MEL: Tell me.

TED: He's gone.

The TOOTH FAIRY and GI JOE speak very simply and sweetly to and about MEL.

TOOTH FAIRY: *(To MEL.)*
When your son was a baby, you would hold him in your arms for hours.
And you would just say hi.
"Hi hi hi hi."
For hours.
And then one day, when he was five months old, he said it back.
Crystal clear.
You were sitting in the chair by the window.
And you couldn't believe your ears.
"Ted,"
you said,
"Come quick,"
you said,
"He said hi.
He said hi.
He said hi."

GI JOE: *(To MEL.)*
Your daughter's first word was "Dada".
When she was seven months old.
And then "duck".
And then "book".
She refused to say "Mama" for over a year.

TOOTH FAIRY: Hard consonants are easier for babies.
Apparently.

GI JOE: "Not Daddy,"
She would call you,
"Not Daddy."

TOOTH FAIRY: You bought your son a bike for his second birthday.
But he couldn't reach the pedals until his third birthday.

GI JOE:	You bought your daughter a bike when she was 22 months old.
	But she wouldn't go near it until she was 32 months old.
	Then, after five weeks of practice, she could pedal down the street.
	With her brother.
TOOTH FAIRY:	"Look, Ma!"
	No hands!"
GI JOE:	"Look, Ma!
	No hands!"
TOOTH FAIRY:	You bought your kids bike helmets.
	And they wore them all the time.
	In the house.
	In the car.
	In the grocery store.
	They pretended to be astronauts.
	Or pumpkins.
GI JOE:	*(To TOOTH FAIRY.)*
	Pumpkins were their favorite.
TOOTH FAIRY:	*(To GI JOE.)*
	They loved to count backwards.
GI JOE:	*(To TOOTH FAIRY.)*
	They loved to catch crickets.
	And let them go.
TOOTH FAIRY:	*(To GI JOE.)*
	They loved to sing.
GI JOE:	*(To MEL.)*
	Your son stuck an action figure behind the wheel of your car. In the driveway.
	You ran it over.
	Backing up.
TOOTH FAIRY:	*(To MEL)*
	When your daughter was a baby, your son would peer into her crib.

On his tippy-toes.
And watch her sleep.
Early one morning, you helped him climb into the crib and lie beside her.
You took a picture.

GI JOE: *(To TOOTH FAIRY.)*
                   She was always taking pictures.

TOOTH FAIRY: *(To GI JOE.)*
                   Always taking in strays.

GI JOE: *(To TOOTH FAIRY.)*
                   Always taking little trips.
                   And excursions.

TOOTH FAIRY: *(To GI JOE.)*
                   She loved to watch the leaves turn orange and red.

GI JOE: *(To TOOTH FAIRY.)*
                   Her kids would make piles of leaves and jump in them.

TOOTH FAIRY: *(To MEL.)*
                   Your daughter's fair.
                   Like her father.
                   That's what everyone always says.
                   She has his eyes.
                   His skin tone.
                   And his hair.
                   And his mild-to-moderate eczema.
                   And his build.
                   And his deep disdain for government.
                   And his spine.

GI JOE: *(To MEL.)*
                   Your son looked like you.
                   That's what everyone always said.
                   You couldn't see it at first.
                   But then, you could.

TOOTH FAIRY: How could you not?

GI JOE: He had your eyes.

Your skin tone.
And your hair.
And your slight lactose intolerance.
And your smile.
And your minor aversion to minivans.
And your guts.

TOOTH FAIRY: She has his spine.

GI JOE: He had your guts.

LANIE sings a song.

LANIE: *(Singing.)*
                  The cat isn't coming back.
                  Again.
                  She isn't coming back.

                  The cat isn't coming back.
                  Again.
                  She isn't coming back.

                  Soon, the snow will be melted.
                  But we won't find anything.
                  There's nothing under the snow.

                  The cat isn't coming back.
                  Again.
                  She's never coming back.

                  I love the whole world.
                  I love the whole world.
                  I love the whole world.

End of song.

MEL is alone. TED enters.

Very slow. Full of air.

TED: Did I scare you?

MEL: No.

TED: You jumped.

MEL:	Did I?
	When?
TED:	Just now.
	When I walked in.
MEL:	I did?
	That's funny.
	I don't remember jumping.
	Are you sure I didn't flinch?
TED:	You may have.
MEL:	Did I shudder?
TED:	You cringed.
MEL:	Did I cringe?
TED:	You grimaced.
MEL:	Did I gasp?
TED:	You winced.
MEL:	That's funny.
	I don't remember wincing.
	Was I startled?
TED:	You were awake.
MEL:	Was I in shock?
TED:	You were in pain.
MEL:	Was I in physical pain or emotional pain?
TED:	Both.
MEL:	Shut up.
TED:	You asked.
MEL:	Shut up.
TED:	You asked.
MEL:	Shut up.
TED:	You asked.

MEL: That's funny.
        I don't remember asking.
        Was I like this?

She wails. Long and loud.

TED: Hardly.

MEL: Like this?

She wails again. Long and loud.

TED: Not at all.
        It was nothing.
        It was subtle.
        Just a flash of pain.
        Panic.
        A pang of grief.
        Anguish.
        A twinge of agony.
        Despair.
        And then…

MEL: And then?

TED: A glimmer of hope.

MEL: A glimmer of what?

TED: And then…

MEL: And then?

TED: Normal.

MEL: Are you there?

TED: I'm here.

MEL: I thought I lost you.

GI JOE and THE TOOTH FAIRY sing a lullaby.

Very quiet. As if they are singing the world to sleep.

GI JOE and TOOTH FAIRY:

> *(Singing.)*
> *I like a room where the blinds all close.*
> *Dark in the morning.*
> *Dark in the evening.*
>
> *I like the lawn underneath my toes.*
> *Cover the garden.*
> *Cover it gently.*
>
> *Tell me a story.*
> *Tell me a story.*
> *Tell me then fly away.*
>
> *I like a child who never grows.*
> *Sleep through the morning.*
> *Sleep through the evening.*
> *Sleep through the morning.*
> *Sleep through the evening.*

End of song.

The TOOTH FAIRY puts money under LANIE's pillow.

TOOTH FAIRY: I should get going.
I'm going to be late.
Next stop Beirut.
They have teeth there too.
But not as many.
No fluoride in the water.

GI JOE: Mind if I join you?

TOOTH FAIRY: Not if I join you first?

The TOOTH FAIRY and GI JOE exit.

As the lights fade…

TED: Are you sleeping?

MEL: Not yet.
Are you warm enough?

TED: I'm fine.

MEL: I'm thirsty.
             I'm thirsty, but I'm lazy.

TED laughs.

             What's so funny?

TED: I'll get you some water.

MEL: I can get it.

TED: I don't mind.
             I'm thirsty too.

             Do you want ice?
             Mel?
             Do you want ice?
             Mel?

             Are you sleeping?
             You're sleeping.
             That was quick.

End of play.

from Mark Subias

THANK YOU

Todd Almond

Lily Tomlin

Tina Howe

Pam MacKinnon Ken Rus Schmoll Sam Gold Anne Kauffman

Kent Robertshaw

Linda Attoe

Paige Evans

Kathryn Willingham

Luis Monteagudo

Jay Lipman

Merideth Finn

Lili Taylor

Dan Burson Corinne Hayoun Natasha Sinha Liz Fox

Rachel Viola

Matt Rice

Diane Morrison

Paula Vogel

John Guare

Mary Colquhoun

Jeremy Zimmer

Joni Evans

George Lane

Peggy Ramsay

WWW.OBERONBOOKS.COM

 Follow us on www.twitter.com/@oberonbooks
& www.facebook.com/oberonbook